The
Green Management
Revolution:

◆

Lessons in environmental excellence

The Green Management Revolution:

Lessons in environmental excellence

❖

Waldemar Hopfenbeck

Prentice Hall

New York London Toronto Sydney Tokyo Singapore

First published in 1990 in German as Umweltorientiertes Management und Marketing:
Konzepte, Instrumente, Praxisbeispiele
Verlag Moderne Industrie
AG & Co., Landsberg

English-language edition published 1993 by
Prentice Hall International (UK) Ltd
Campus 400, Maylands Avenue
Hemel Hempstead
Hertfordshire, HP2 7EZ
A division of
Simon & Schuster International Group

First published 1992
© Verlag Moderne Industrie AG & Co.

Typeset in 10/12 pt Palacio
by
Mathematical Composition Setters Ltd, Salisbury, Wiltshire

Printed and bound in Great Britain

Library of Congress Cataloging-in-Publication Data

Hopfenbeck, Waldemar.
    [Umweltorientiertes Management und Marketing. English]
    The green management revolution : lessons in environmental
excellence / Waldemar Hopfenbeck.
      p.   cm.
    Includes bibliographical references and index.
    ISBN 0-13-276452-0
    1. Europe—Industries—Environmental aspects. 2. Management—
Environmental aspects—Europe. 3. Product management—
Environmental aspects. 4. Environmental protection—Europe.
5. Social responsiblity of business—Europe. 6. Green marketing—
Europe. I. Title.
HC240.9.E5H6613 1993
363.7—dc20   92-41436
                                                               CIP

British Library Cataloguing in Publication Data

A catalogue record for this book is available from
the British Library

ISBN 0-13-276452-0 (hbk)

1 2 3 4 5   97 96 95 94 93

Contents

Foreword

A new book amid the flood of publications on environmental protection needs some words of justification. As I see it there is a great lack of widely accessible information on the environmentally friendly management strategies already being practised by some branches of industry. The overriding aim of this book is to portray the state of the art in 'eco-management', with copious examples of successful strategies for facing the challenges of ecology at every level. Managers tend to be on the defensive about environmental issues; and, indeed, blame for the polarization of public opinion cannot be entirely removed from industry. The atmosphere is characterized by tactics of delay and disguise, being 'economical' with the truth and playing down the importance of the situation. The conflict between ecology and economy has been 'rationalized' and underpinned with facts and figures: the emotional side has been neglected and the anxieties of the public have been divorced from economic significance or written off as a kind of 'eco-trip'. In the long term, however, an anxious public cannot be placated by passivity, public relations exercises or voluntary declarations of intent. Business cannot succeed without social consensus.

The currently predominant 'curative environmental protection' makes technologists largely responsible for the preservation of the environment; it is vital, however, that the role of sales and commercial personnel is not discounted. Environmentalism must be an integral part of every level of the business enterprise. Neither should there be a discrepancy between the professional actions and personal beliefs of business executives. The new, younger generation of managers must be given room to apply their more critical awareness. In this context, the concept of business ethics stands for harmony between work and life. One unmistakable trend in the economy is a steady but constant increase in the number of businesses with a coherent policy on ecology. For many, the process of change may be too slow. Others are still unaware of the need for an environmentally informed reassessment of our products and methods of production. The research behind this book has shown repeatedly that, although it is perhaps too soon to speak of a new philosophy, radically new ways of thinking are necessary if we are to find innovative solutions to the crisis of our environment. Time and again ideologically blinkered views and party prejudices stand in the way of fruitful dialogue on eco-management.

This book aims not only to help raise the awareness of responsible business managers towards the challenge of ecology, but to demonstrate, with practical examples, that an environmental approach to management can be cost effective even for the most profit-minded manager. Furthermore, the need to increase the survival chances of a business leave no alternative. If you do not establish an ecologically sound long-term plan in good time, your future as a business is doomed.

Some 73 per cent of businesses questioned in a survey undertaken by the Confederation for German Industry (BDI) early in 1989 regarded environmentalism as an established feature of their business policies. According to the German Institute for Economic Research (IFO), over 90 per cent of companies wish to be considered environmentally aware. There is food for thought in the fact that survey findings attribute little or no problem-solving competence to business enterprises, and that in attitude studies among young people environmental organizations such as Greenpeace are looked up to as exceptional paragons of virtue. The depth of commitment of many firms is judged sceptically even by the young generation of managers. In a sample inquiry in Germany, young people rated management awareness of ecology in the chemical, pharmaceutical and steel industries as 'average to inadequate', while 80 per cent of the new executives regarded themselves as 'more environmentally aware' or even 'much more environmentally aware' than the population as a whole. In general, caring for the environment is viewed positively. Consequently, the study recommends the adoption of an environmentally informed attitude as a universal dimension of business philosophy and practice. 'It will not be long before we see trend-setting business directors wearing Greenpeace or WWF badges in the lapels of their pin-stripes' (Apitz, market research, 1990).

There can be no real doubt about the need to restructure the economy along environment-conscious lines, although the degree of involvement will clearly vary from one branch of industry to another. Hitherto, the business response to this challenge has been one of passive adaptation to basic policy as regulations are laid down or amended. A better alternative, in my opinion, is an active response which sees the preservation of the environment as an opportunity to strengthen the future of business; action instead of reaction. Since the problems posed by ecology are so vitally important to the survival of future generations, we must find our own solutions, here and now.

Forward-looking eco-management is one of the most important tasks facing us all. If we do not act today, it will cost us far too dearly tomorrow. However, our actions must not be allowed to stimulate 'alibi' behaviour. Public relations exercises and glossy brochures are not enough to create the level of commitment which is so vital. We must learn to perceive product and production together with the burden on the environment as two sides of the same coin. In every form of economic activity we should strive to minimize such burdens on the ecosystem as natural resource depletion and the build-up of waste.

Environmental protection can no longer be dismissed as a trendy posture. Consumer behaviour and attitudes are increasingly guided by an awareness of the environment, and a corresponding commitment from the business world is ineluctably called for. The business response must be more than merely a package of market strategies aimed at a target group of 'green' consumers. A holistic philosophy is required which permeates all areas and functions of business enterprise.

In this book I present numerous examples of successful pioneers, serving to show that many companies have already succeeded in adapting to the demands at operational, strategic and normative management levels. I have deliberately not selected businesses which operate in the eco-technology market, but have shown how an environmental approach can be implemented at all functional levels of a business regardless of its particular line of specialization.

The passivity inherent in most present-day environmental policies is surely one cause of confusion among consumers, who tend to overlook the part played by the end product in environmental problems, and who see themselves as somehow less responsible for damage to the environment than manufacturers. It needs to be made quite clear that the threat to the environment is not confined to spectacular catastrophes or particular branches of industry – the chemical industry currently taking the brunt of criticism – and that routine consumer behaviour by every member of the population has a decisive impact.

The only way to avoid the slings and arrows of public criticism is for managers themselves to work towards coherent ecological management philosophies. I have drawn together here the concepts, means and practical examples required for implementing such a style of management.

I owe particular thanks to those members of the business community who have given me their support and co-operation in amassing the material for this book.

Waldemar Hopfenbeck
Munich

Foreword to the English edition

The 'greening of European industry' and 'Eco goes mainstream' are slogans indicating dramatic changes in management attitudes over recent years. Although managers in the western industrial countries are adapting to ecology at very different rates, the fact of growing ecological awareness among both consumers and the business community is quite undeniable. Countries such as Greece, Spain and Italy are in the early stages of a development process which is being led by the German-speaking countries and by Holland and Scandinavia, with Britain, France and the USA taking up an intermediate position.

Environmental influences will be felt at all stages of business activity, from product design to new forms of packaging, from marketing to disposal. Individual company responses to these new issues will be an important factor governing competitiveness in the single European market in the 1990s. The sooner businesses can assimilate these developments, the sooner they will gain the competitive edge in the open market. 'Going green' is not just a passing phase; it is an absolute necessity for the survival of many companies. 'To green or not to green' is no longer the question but the answer to the changing demands of the free market.

The Green Management Revolution contains examples of many European and American companies which lead the field in environment-friendly production methods and products. The original German edition has been expanded with numerous international examples, while specifically German legal and financial detail has been adapted for English readers or omitted.

Waldemar Hopfenbeck

1

The environmental challenge to management

◆

We do live in an effective economic system, but natural resources are underpriced or zero-rated. This renders incorrect all economic calculations because it places too little emphasis on the preservation of resources and the environment in general.

   The individual experiences this system through:

- the inescapable need to be competitive at international, national, trade and product specific levels.
- aggressive marketing without which few companies can survive. In this system no one is guilty. Or we all are, as consumers, sales personnel, technologists, teachers, politicians. (Krupp, 1989)

◆   ◆   ◆

Ecology: passing phase or long-term problem?

'One thing is certain. We are behaving like unwelcome guests on the earth. Our profit-making activities inflict losses of which we may not be immediately aware. We use the profits for ourselves, but the losses we pass on to generations to come.'

These penetrating, admonitory words from Queen Beatrix, in her Christmas message in 1988, outline a problem of our time which has become a challenge like no other, for politicians, for managers and indeed for every individual. In terms of media coverage over the last few years, there is hardly a single issue which can compare with the environment.

There are those who view the ecological crisis as a question of survival in our industrialized world, even as a 'matter of life or death', and who speak of the 'destruction of the life-sustaining ecosystem'. But there are others whose attention span for this issue is as short as for a passing fashion.

Somehow we have to come to terms with the daily catalogue of catastrophes – algal blooms today, oil slicks tomorrow. No one can remain on red alert all the time without becoming paranoid. Each individual develops a system for coping with unwanted problems: euphemism, flat denial or some other method. A particularly popular approach is procrastination: building ever higher chimneys, moving rubbish dumps out of town, merely shunting the problem further away. Even environmental technology in, for example, filtration plants just transfers waste from one medium to another. These measures may be necessary and meaningful for winning time. But we must use the time we have gained – the big problem is still out there!

If the ecology crisis is really a crisis of perception then we must find a new position for it in our set of values. We must begin by addressing what we actually perceive. Moreover, we must be cautious not to let short-term, repressive 'solutions' blind us to the irreversible long-term processes underlying the growing list of problems: deforestation, the hole in the ozone layer, the greenhouse effect, North Sea algae, the death of seals. We never know where the crisis will flare up next.

Recent surveys record a significant trend in public opinion. The high priority accorded to 'green issues' has now remained stable for six years, clearly indicating that this is no mere passing phase. A sharp rise in environmental awareness has been felt in all European countries, with the exception of France and Ireland. According to a study by Emnid in 1989, 72 per cent of the approximately 350 million Euro-citizens feel that the struggle against environmental destruction 'requires urgent, immediate action'.

The sense of a global threat has been strengthened by growing concern about climatic change, the political consequences of which are quite unpredictable. In the context of the North–South dialogue, for example, will the developing countries have to forgo the fruits of *their* industrialization programmes because of *our* environmentalism? Politicians will have to tackle some of the controversial topics which affect not only our short-term welfare but our long-term survival. And if company managers continue to treat green issues merely as a way of improving their image, they will fail to do justice to the complexity of the problem, even if there are short-term benefits.

Economic and social expansion have created record high living standards in parts of the industrialized world, but it is increasingly difficult to identify this material success with an improved quality of life. The more you travel, the more likely you are to suffer tiresome delays at airports, motorways or railway stations. The rise in consumer welfare has brought with it a mountain of waste and the prospect of an incineration plant on the doorstep. Progress in material welfare is coupled with destructive consequences in the environment. There are even social and cultural side-effects which must be evaluated as a matter of urgency. Human beings as well as nature are beginning to show the strain.

The growing threat of environmental disaster will be of dominant importance politically in the 1990s. For too long now business activity has been evaluated without accounting for the toll on our surroundings. Nature now presents its bill, with an ever-increasing interest rate. 'The size of the task before civilized societies and their managers has to be reckoned not in hundreds but in thousands of years' (Seidel, 1989).

It is no longer possible for public or private sectors of economy to push the consequences of their actions into the background. Forces which threaten our very existence cannot be dismissed. The ecological challenge is not the preserve of minorities, 'eco-freaks', Greens, 'good-lifers' or whatever you choose to call them. Our very future depends on it. Since industry has brought about many of the problems we face, industry must seek the solutions. Governments cannot meet the challenge alone and so the central sociopolitical role must be performed by the business community.

After many years of passive, defensive, avoidance strategies, people are at last beginning to think again. Starting with a few pioneer companies, the development of ecological responsibility in industry has continued to grow in response to the undeniable need for integration of 'green' concerns into the economy. The big, unanswered question is how problem-solving strategies are to be designed and implemented.

In spite of the growing concern shown by businesses, especially in contentious branches of industry, there is still a short-fall of reliable information. We are still only at the beginning of the search for an assertive, integrated theory and practice of environmental management. We have taken only the first steps on a long road. The accumulation of practical knowledge, however, is already considerable, and we should use this to create a manufacturing process which is really in tune with the environment, and to make real changes to the current 'throw-away' consumer philosophy.

Responsible human activity is always goal orientated. Therefore we need environmentally orientated management and marketing to be a major goal in corporate policy. This opening up of management awareness will not be achieved overnight, but someone has to make the first move. We cannot afford to leave it to others; we must all take part in shaping the future. The individual manager may be able to do very little, but this book gives many examples of alliances whose experiences can be built upon. It is to be hoped that the efforts of these pioneers bear fruit.

Taking stock: more trouble than it's worth?

The current state of the environment

Consider the relationship between the economy and the environment in Germany. A very cautious estimate of the annual cost of damage to the German environment is around 6–10 per cent of GNP: that is, more than DM200 billion (about £67 billion). In addition, Germany's limited natural resources are being consumed too quickly. 'This process brings profit for our generation but our children will inherit the losses. We are borrowing environmental capital from future generations with no intention or prospect of paying it back' (Bruntland Report of the UN Environment Commission, 1987).

Business expenditure on curative ecological measures is steadily increasing. Technology designed to limit future burdens on the environment, or to remove existing ones, currently brings returns in excess of DM90 billion to the European Community. The *Financial Times* estimates the world market at £100–150 billion. In Germany the growth potential of this market over the next few years is estimated at DM200–250 billion from the public sector alone. One-third of German-produced eco-technology is already exported at a yearly growth rate of 10 per cent.

This branch of industry has been described as having a 'gold-digger' mentality. It has also been maintained that interest in improving the environment is not rewarded within companies or even at a local community level. This means that little is done without government grants or national legislation. Figures from the Federal German Statistical Department confirm that waves of investment in 'green issues' only ever follow in the wake of new legislation. The only way to boost the growth of green-consciousness is to spread the message: 'Ecology today means economic success tomorrow.'

According to an investigation by the Institute for Economic Research (IFO):

- It is predominantly 'mixed' businesses which are taking up environmental technology as a form of diversification, where this technology plays merely a supporting role in their total programme.

- Market opportunities exist mainly for middle-sized manufacturers responding to a demand for tailor-made technology.

- Almost 75 per cent of suppliers are from capital goods industries (with increasing importance attached to electro-technology).

- Larger concerns – for example, the chemical or energy industries – are beginning to take an interest in this market, as they could have an advantage where integrated solutions are needed.

- The market depends heavily on the public sector (as law maker, investor and provider of grants) and on the current public budget.

- There is a trend towards package deals with service industries or producers of plant.

In a study by the business consultant Helmut Kaiser, above average growth rates are anticipated in the coming years in the areas of waste disposal, reclamation of raw materials and energy saving. Water purification and treatment will also be of great economic importance at the turn of the century. The largest national markets in 1987 were Germany with a share of 40.6 per cent, France with 14.7 per cent, Britain with 11.2 per cent and Italy with 8.5 per cent. The study identified 2,600 active suppliers in the eco-market in western Europe, with 300 enterprises taking over 50 per cent of the returns. This market will increase by two-thirds, to around DM140 billion by the year 2000.

Present expenditure on the environment is estimated at approximately 0.2–1 per cent of GNP depending on the country, with only Canada, the Netherlands and Germany spending more than 1 per cent. There will be a sharp increase in this figure in the future. According to a comparative study by the German Business Institute (IW), environmental expenditure of the ten most important industrial countries represented 0.7 per cent of the 1988 GNP for each country. While this expenditure rose by 1 per cent per year on average, the growth rate of the nominal GNP was 7.8 per cent. The total expenditure on the environment for these countries in 1988:

USA	40.6%
Japan	19.2%
West Germany	13.1%
Great Britain	6.9%
France	6.2%
Canada	5.1%
Italy	3.9%
Netherlands	3.0%
Sweden	1.1%
Denmark	0.9%

find figures for 2006.

Analysis of outgoings between state and manufacturing industries shows a heavy predominance of state expenditure. Germany is one of the few countries in which the private sector increased its eco-expenditure in the 1980s. The state spends more on water control (and, increasingly, on waste disposal), while businesses concentrate more on the atmosphere. Investment consultants such as Prudential-Bache see environmental preservation as the biggest growth industry since the Second World War. UBS Philips and Drew investigated six sectors of the economy in the study *Investing in a Green Europe* and sifted out the companies who increased their turnover.

Significant successes have been achieved in specific areas, without which the situation today would be much worse. For example, there has been a considerable reduction in sulphur dioxide pollution and improvements in water purity. In spite of this progress, however, an astronomical degree of damage is still caused by atmospheric pollutants, according to official figures. Why, then, does it still seem that the general situation is deteriorating from one year to the next, and that the costs of environmental protection to the economy are constantly on the increase? The causes are many:

- Efforts tend to be applied retrospectively, rather than industrial processes being designed which minimize pollution. Environmental management is not undertaken in a holistic manner. A holistic approach would include checking the raw materials at the planning stage, using and manufacturing environmentally friendly products, applying eco-friendly production methods, raising staff awareness and checking methods of final disposal.

- New pollutants have taken the place of those which have have been reduced.

- The problems have been transferred technologically to a different environmental medium and sometimes have even been concentrated. For example, sewage works produce millions of tonnes of sludge per year and the processes used in purifying waste gases from power stations leave a new problem of disposing of millions of tonnes of filtering plaster.

- Retrospective environmental technology only selects certain pollutants and leaves others untreated.

- Successful reduction of pollutants is often followed by an increase in output, which builds up the levels once again. A massive increase in the total number of items sold annihilates any benefit from the reductions made.

Annual growth rates of 2–3 per cent may sound modest, but they are calculated on annually increasing base numbers and therefore represent constantly increasing absolute numbers. Kurbjuweit (1989) cites one example:

> Constant economic growth is one of the greatest enemies of the environment. For instance, the paper manufacturer 'Zweckform' proudly announced that the proportion of certain types of paper recycled over ten years had increased to 40%. But total production has risen so steeply that today more normal paper is produced than ten years ago. The environment has lost out rather than gained.

The only way to reduce the net burden on the environment while increasing the total output of products is to take a radical step away from curative–retrospective eco-technology to preventive–integrative, clean technologies, and to rethink some of our consumer habits.

Some thoughts on a favourite consumer product might be appropriate here. The number of cars in Germany has doubled since 1969. Worldwide, the number has risen to 400 million cars, producing 547 million tonnes of carbon waste. Meanwhile, the traffic density in some places restricts the car driver to the same average speed as the pedestrian. Is there room for any more cars?

The latest Shell prognosis on 'motorizing' the Federal Republic of Germany sets the maximum number of cars at between 31 and 34.7 million. The density of private car ownership (per 1,000 people) will increase from over 590 to nearly

700 according to this scenario. However, lower petrol consumption and more economical cars could compensate for this increase.

1988 28.8 million tonnes petrol; 92.0 million tonnes carbon dioxide.
First scenario: 'structural change' 2000: 86.8 million tonnes CO_2;
2010: 74.4 million tonnes CO_2.
Second scenario: 'disharmonies': 2000: 58.9 million tonnes CO_2;
2010: 46.5 million tonnes CO_2.

Sociological, physical, ecological, political and technical risks become terrifying. Levy, for example, is horrified by the 60,000 traffic deaths in Europe in 1987 (400,000 p.a. worldwide) and the 1.9 million traffic injuries. The figures for Germany are just as shocking. In 1988, 8,200 people were killed and 448,000 injured, including 40,000 children. Krupp, the former director of the Fraunhofer Institute in Karlsruhe, estimates the cost of environmental damage caused by cars in Germany at around DM77 billion. Yet, in spite of the knowledge that, worldwide, almost 1,500 people die in traffic accidents every day, we continue to break new records for the number of licences issued!

Another balancing effect can be seen between the industrial use of water and general economic development. Industry exhibits an enormous thirst for water: for example, 3,000 litres per kilo of paper, 500 litres for plastic and 120 litres for sugar production. However, the total reckonable output of water in Germany has continued to decline. Energy consumption has also broken free from economic growth patterns. But that is only half the story, because the deterioration of the environment has thereby not been halted at all. There is no evidence of a real *reduction* in energy consumption, which is necessary if we are looking for actual environmental benefits. The current discussion about energy tariff incentives is an eloquent testimony to these difficulties. If the output of carbon dioxide really were to be drastically cut, it should not be by avoiding an increase in the rate of energy consumption. We should simply consume less energy.

A growth of 4–6 per cent is prognosticated in the Cecchini Report for the new single European market (Morgan Stanley Investments reckons on 7.5–9 per cent). A 1989 study by 14 economists from all EC countries, *Environment and the European Unified Market*, fears a considerable build-up of negative consequences for the environment and quality of life resulting from increased economic growth. In particular, an increase in airborne toxins is anticipated.

Increased consumer demand in eastern Europe together with the industrialization of heavily populated developing countries will doubtless lead to greatly enhanced returns for the eco-technology industries. At the same time the environmental crisis will be intensified to such an extent that ecological rethinking will be even more urgently required.

Two aspects are particularly worrying: our continued reliance on fossil fuels; and the continued global population explosion. If only one billion of the five billion people on earth were to raise their energy consumption to one-third of our current energy consumption, because of improved living standards, this would cause more than a 20 per cent increase in carbon dioxide pollution. Meanwhile, developing countries wonder why they are not being allowed to progress, and do not welcome patronizing or neo-colonial interference.

The situation is further complicated by the dual need to preserve nature while boosting exports to pay off foreign debts. At the World Economic Conference in Toronto in 1988 the concept of 'debt-for-nature swaps' was developed as a possible new way forward. The global dimension makes action more difficult. One can hardly keep count of the international conferences on the threat of climatic change, but political action is only just beginning to emerge. Are we 'talking' the environment away? Must we see these conferences as a mere expression of our impotence?

A growth of political intent can be perceived in all parties, but everyone is hesitant about taking action. The process of European unity, with the latest example being the compromise on mergers (or environmental impact assessment), paves the way for a levelling of standards to the lowest common denominator. This will be below the relatively high German standards and well below the standards in Japan and California. Further *détente* between East and West seems to promise hope. Reductions in relative defence budgets could release funds for basic changes in environmental management to be undertaken.

The administrative framework laid down in the 1970s and 1980s needs rethinking. Legislative policy is coming up against conceptual barriers, and progressive environmentalism is not served by overreliance on regulations. Retrospective eco-technology can only repair the damage which has already been done. Moreover, progress is frustrated by the fact that the industries involved have a vested interest in the status quo and not in getting to the roots of the problem. I shall need to stress again and again the need to adopt preventive rather than curative principles. Transition from a sectoral approach ('eco-tech') to integral management concepts is the only acceptable strategy.

The long-term preservation of the environment urgently requires a flow of innovative solutions. To exploit the dynamics of the market economy, the originators of pollution should be urged to initiate technological progress themselves. Instead of the traditional approach of administrative regulations ('command and control') there should also be market-based incentives for eco-technical innovation (tradable quotas, charges, etc.).

To implement these 'clean technologies' will take some time. There will still be a considerable role for maintenance; additive 'end-of-pipe' technology will be in the foreground for some time to come and will require enormous investment for many years to service the environmental damage of the past. We can only agree with Schütze in his 1984 prediction: 'Green issues will be of overwhelming importance in world politics over the next decade, just as the last decades have been dominated by the arms race and peace issues.'

The change in awareness

At last, clear signs of a change in awareness can be seen alongside increasingly restrictive environmental laws and regulations. The need to preserve the environment is becoming more and more widely understood; opinion polls confirm the absolute priority of this issue together with that of unemployment. There is, however, a widespread scepticism about the long-term future of environmental politics. If there really is a social value in preserving nature then the onus is on industry to bring about an improvement in human behaviour.

The following list gives examples of initiatives taken over recent years:

- There are unmistakable signs of a green wave in the shops – products described as 'bio', eco-friendly, etc. It is estimated that twice as many organic products are marketed in Germany as are actually produced. There must be some invisible goods on the shelves!

- Following the German Blue Angel award, many other countries such as Japan and Canada are adopting green labelling schemes. Green consumer guides are also being published.

- The EC Commission proclaimed 1987/8 'European Year of the Environment', having only just taken up environmental policies as part of the EC agreement.

- In Britain there are 'green' shopping days or weeks.

- There are a growing number of eco-prizes. 'Better Environment Awards for Industry' are awarded in Britain 'to identify, encourage and promote technical design, manufacturing and management initiatives which improve the environment and conserve resources'. The awards are given in four areas:

  1. The Pollution Abatement Technology Award.
  2. The Green Product Award.
  3. The Environmental Management Award.
  4. The Appropriate Technology Award.

  In 1990 the winners were:

  1. ICI Chemicals and Polymers.
  2. Vaisala UK.
  3. Sainsbury/Stocksbridge Engineering Steel.
  4. Robens Institute of Health and Safety/IT Transport.

In Germany the Association of Independent Business (ASU) founded the ASU Award of Excellence in Environmental Management. In 1988, the first year, 173 businesses entered; in 1989/90 the number rose to 497. A total of 49 participants were able to fulfil nine or all ten of the criteria and received the award. In the eco-contest of the Confederation of German Industry (BDI), there were 250 participating firms in 1989/90.

- The UN Economic Commission (ECE) has proposed that management of the environment is one of the most important governmental responsibilities.

- The 1985 EC regulation on environmental impact assessments has been adopted as national law in the member states.

- In Frankfurt the first eco-bank has been opened.

- Trade associations (e.g. in the chemical industry) and the International Chamber of Commerce have published revised environmental guidelines.

- Political parties in Europe are mounting a wave of green policies. The British government has recently published (1990) a White Paper with 350 steps towards a better environment. More and more countries have a minister of the environment.

- In 'new age' seminars, soft management, new philosophies, post-modern business policies, new ethics and ecological holistic thinking are presented as expressions of a changing society.

- The chairman of Daimler-Benz has spoken of an environmentally orientated industrial society, in which the goals of commerce and ecology are given equal importance.

- In Vienna the Phoenix news agency for 'eco-news' has been founded.

- The Environmental Media Association was founded in Hollywood in 1989 to raise public awareness of threats to the environment. Each year the best films and TV programmes will be given the Environmental Media Award.

- The Earth Communications Office helps environmental groups by providing famous personalities for fund-raising events.

- An estimated 136 countries and 200 million people participated in 'Earth Day', on 22 April 1990. The idea of worldwide action to raise the profile of environmental protection was first conceived in the USA in 1970. ABC broadcast a special two-hour programme.

- English and American universities are integrating ethics and green management courses into their curricula.

- The Australian prime minister has appointed the world's first environment ambassador.

- Prince Charles has spoken out in favour of environmental management and taken part in a consciousness-raising video.

- An executive guide, *Business in the Environment*, was published in Britain in 1990. It gives managers hints on how to assess and improve the environmental performance of their companies.

Although many companies and unions are slow to respond, there are already signs of a style of environmental management which is not just a passive adherence to legal restrictions, but a positive, assertive, self-motivated management philosophy.

Market-based or command and control approach to environmental protection?

Wicke (1982) has developed a programme which he considers indispensable to improved environmental policy. It consists of ten market-orientated steps in four stages.

Stage 1 enhances voluntary action for participants in the market.

- Increased consumer awareness of green issues.
- Environmentally aware business management.
- Eco-friendly government procurement policy.
- Creation of user incentives for environment-friendly products.

Stage 2 affects environmental agreements.

- Agreements between business and local victims of pollution.
- Agreements between branches of industry and the state, binding industry to defined environmentally sound behaviour.

Stage 3 introduces the profit motive of business as an incentive towards ecologically minded behaviour.

- Environmental charges dependent on output of pollution.
- Eco-licences limiting total output of pollution to a fixed level, providing incentives to reduce pollution even more and sell unused licences.
- Flexible retrospective directives whereby those who reduce pollution more than is legally required gain from this extra reduction.

Stage 4 increases the economic risk factor of eco-unfriendly production.

- Intensifying liabilities.

Uhlig (1978) identified five possible strategies for state intervention within the framework of free enterprise:

- Direct state intervention should influence individual commercial behaviour by means of injunctions.
- Free market conditions should be maintained under socially designed frames of reference for market strategy (e.g. eco-certificates, ecological accountancy).
- Individual decisions should be influenced by incentives such as taxes on waste.
- Market substitution should prevent the build-up of activity-induced surpluses or cases of real damage.
- Strategies of compensation should aim to remedy already existing cases of damage, by reforestation and oxygenation of badly polluted rivers and lakes, for example.

There are differing views on the best way of achieving environmental preservation. Some see political leadership as indispensable because of lack of guidance in the realm of business economics. Others wish to incorporate their solution into the free market, using incentives and private interest instead of legislative pressure.

Regulatory restrictions

Improving the environment by way of indicators is a yardstick for environmental policy making. The desired standard is fixed with reference to economic interests and power structures. It depends upon political decisions and social conventions.

Strebel (1980) considers that defining the quality of the environment with the help of indicators is workable but still unsatisfactory in content for the following reasons:

- There is a possibility that not all forms of pollution will be included.
- Conventionally accepted concentrations might be higher than ecologically determined values.
- Synergic effects are overlooked.
- Apart from actual toxicity, other environmental effects are ignored.

'Social means of environmental control seek either to remove, limit or avoid environmental damage caused by production or consumption and/or to cause the perpetrators of previous damage to compensate those who suffer the consequences' (Strebel, 1980).

'Green' policies in Germany are conducted on the basis of three principles. According to the 'polluter pays' principle, those who are responsible for pollution should pay the price of removing the effects. The 'co-operation' principle seeks to tie in the technical know-how of polluters with a coherent environmental policy. Finally, the 'preventive' principle seeks to instil integrated approaches for solving long-term problems.

There are a wide range of eco-regulations affecting the business world. For example, Siemens consider that 400 federal and regional laws and regulations are directly relevant to their work. The classical concept of direct intervention stands alongside regulatory measures and changes in the factors which influence decision making.

Regulations in the form of mandates or prohibitions prescribe certain forms of behaviour. The disadvantage of this indispensable mechanism is its economic inefficiency. For instance, in defining standards for waste emission everyone is treated the same, regardless of differential costs for different industries. This is not the cheapest way of bringing about improvement and it is inflexible to changing conditions. Basing eco-policies on existing technology restricts innovation.

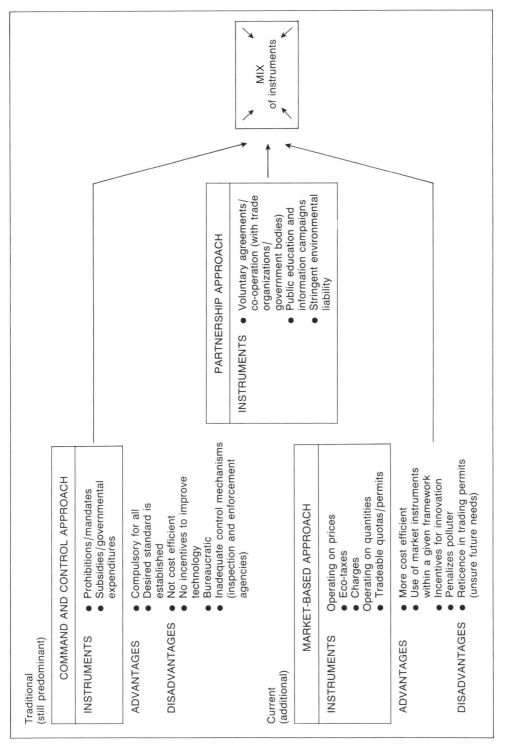

Traditional
(still predominant)

COMMAND AND CONTROL APPROACH

INSTRUMENTS
- Prohibitions/mandates
- Subsidies/governmental expenditures

ADVANTAGES
- Compulsory for all
- Desired standard is established

DISADVANTAGES
- Not cost efficient
- No incentives to improve technology
- Bureaucratic
- Inadequate control mechanisms (inspection and enforcement agencies)

Current
(additional)

MARKET-BASED APPROACH

INSTRUMENTS
- Operating on prices
- Eco-taxes
- Charges
- Operating on quantities
- Tradeable quotas/permits

ADVANTAGES
- More cost efficient
- Use of market instruments within a given framework
- Incentives for innovation
- Penalizes polluter

DISADVANTAGES
- Reticence in trading permits (unsure future needs)

PARTNERSHIP APPROACH

INSTRUMENTS
- Voluntary agreements/ co-operation (with trade organizations/ government bodies)
- Public education and information campaigns
- Stringent environmental liability

MIX
of instruments

Figure 1 Approaches to environmental regulation

Wicke (1987) sees the rationality of this defensive management approach:

> As a rule the contribution to environmental improvement and the actual benefit to victims of pollution are very slight. However, reduction in profit caused by increases in overheads can be considerable. On the principle of maximizing profits alone there is no reason for submission to environmental precepts so long as there is no threat from costly government sanctions, claims for compensation, high insurance premiums or danger to the company image, or unless environmental protection can be made to pay for itself in some way. Prohibitions are necessary with products known to be damaging to health (e.g. asbestos, DDT). They are also useful in cases where unfriendly products can easily be replaced, such as CFCs in aerosol cans. In 1989, leading Democrats in the American Congress called for the prohibition of disposable diapers.
>
> It is very important to introduce a variety of free market mechanisms to enable assertive eco-management. Taxes offer a financial incentive by putting a price on environmental resources. They encourage organizations to be eco-friendly out of self-interest. Innovative market processes should be allowed to play a part in regulating the 'synthetic' prices attached to environmental resources. The profit motive should encourage businesses to be environment friendly by creating positive or negative incentives, such as by selling off the unused surplus of waste quotas or raising environmental taxes.

Possible examples might be taxes on toxic exhaust fumes and noise pollution, or taxes on individual products such as non-returnable bottles.

Recent economic mechanisms under discussion include:

- Trade agreements or voluntary co-operation agreements. These presuppose that rival companies abide by the terms. Since 1971 German industry has witnessed over 30 such voluntary obligations, often with gentle pressure from the government.

- Calls to consumers to abstain voluntarily from purchasing unfriendly products. These fail to reach most consumers; the lack of effort can be seen in the continued proliferation of non-returnable packaging in spite of media coverage of waste disposal.

- Liability for all damage by products, to be extended to independent producer liability and protection for consumers and victims of industrial accidents. Self-interest in industry can be stimulated by adjusting insurance premiums on the basis of environmental risk.

- The right to withhold labour in cases of breach of environmental regulations.

- Appointment of a board member responsible for safety at work and green matters.

- Tax incentives for eco-friendly products and methods.

- Replacement of individual rights of appeal with the possibility of a corporate complaints procedure for ecological matters.

- Waste tax on permitted but undesirable waste emission.

- Publication of permitted waste levels.

- Policy of adjustment: permission for plant producing excess to be offset against reductions in another plant.

- Flexible licences for waste production: eco-certification.

- Prohibition of certain forms of packaging.

A price system will be developed, with the help of emission certificates, to transfer environmental resources from public to private ownership, with market prices attached. This corresponds to the concept of controlled trading developed in the USA.

The cost of avoiding environmental damage depends upon production processes. Individual responsibility for waste emission would reduce the cost while preserving the outcome. In the USA transferable licences are already being tested as a mechanism within the market economy. Emission reduction credits (ERCs) are taken to eco-banks which must be recognized by environmental authorities, such as the Environmental Protection Agency in the United States.

The decisive advantage of this kind of duty is that businesses can respond individually as 'users' of the environment. In this case it is rational for a business to reduce its toxic waste output up to the point where it becomes more expensive than paying the duty. Environmental goals will be reached more economically as users respond to the relative cost of pollution prevention duties. A disposal supplement on the purchase price of the product could be introduced as an incentive to plan ahead. Another alternative is to encourage producers to have certain products returned at the end of their life-cycle.

There is wide consensus over the need for additional regulatory mechanisms. Politicians are working on suggested forms of eco-tax as a means of controlling the burden on the environment within the framework of the market economy. Internalizing social costs should have a positive effect on consumers because, as environmentally 'unfriendly' products become more expensive, consumers will buy fewer of them. The possibility of higher pricing should encourage businesses to turn to technology to keep production costs down. This in turn will help the environment by bringing improvements in eco-technology.

The countless possibilities include taxes on raw materials, energy, packaging (especially for drinks) and advertising material. A prototype for this kind of market mechanism is the effluent charge in Germany. It was fixed at DM40 (£13) per unit per year in 1990, rising to DM50 in 1991 and DM60 (£20) in 1993. From January 1991 additional units have been calculated per 3 kg of phosphorus and 25 kg of nitrogen.

The aim of all of these eco-taxes is to reduce the sale of damaging products and induce consumers to choose the relatively cheaper eco-friendly product. This is achieved by incorporating the previously neglected external environmental costs into the overall price, with the effect of deliberately raising the price of eco-unfriendly products. Difficulties which may arise include gauging the influence on consumers and the effect on low-income families.

The German Business Institute (Institut der Deutschen Wirtschaft, 1989) envisaged a division of labour between political measures and market forces:

- Legislation taking precedence where citizens' rights or the demands of the biosphere require a definite standard of protection.

- Intensified market incentives where the search for integrated preventive technology is called for.

- The UPI Institute in Heidelberg sees a third factor not usually taken into account: voluntary abstention.

Ahrends sees a 'schizophrenic desire' to have the ecological imperative forced upon us as we would not otherwise be prepared to abstain from familiar comforts. He possibly has in mind the cases, in Zurich or Bologna, of politicians travelling on foot or using public transport; they are despised for it but still gain parliamentary seats.

> Has not this yearning after punishment for our sins against the environment been with us for a long time, to help us live with our guilty conscience? ... Clearly environmental politics is concerned with this schizophrenia. Everyone clamouring for a goal which no one really wants. Everyone desiring sacrifices which no one is prepared to make; at least not voluntarily!

Without wishing to weaken the impact of this useful sentiment, I find it falls short in failing to acknowledge man's ability to learn. Why should it not be possible to educate our children towards ecologically sound behaviour? Even politicians sometimes learn through pressure 'from below' to make their behaviour ecologically desirable.

The road to an environmental market economy

Discussion of the 'green challenge' has developed into a sociopolitical minefield over recent years. The environmental consequences of industrial growth and their impact on the quality of life have been taken up by all German political parties.

There is consensus across the political spectrum about the course of economic development in Germany. After moving from a free to a 'social market' economy, in which over one-third of GNP is redistributed for social purposes, there is now a need to expand and adapt to an environmental market economy. The social element has, in fact, strengthened competitiveness in the German economy, and added the flexibility needed for integrating the ecological dimension.

Industrial output has grown fivefold since 1900. Four-fifths of this growth has taken place since 1950 (Steger, 1990). Worldwide GNP has risen in real terms from DM2 billion to DM12 billion, which corresponds to a 5.2 per cent increase per annum. Energy consumption has risen by a factor of five and the quantity of waste by a factor of fifteen.

The quantitative overburdening of the eco-system becomes apparent if one considers that, with constant population, a rise in the standard of living in developing countries would imply an increase in economic activity by a factor of five in the coming decades. With the predicted doubling of the population this would increase to a factor of ten. For this reason, the Bruntland Report is not alone in recommending a policy of 'sustainable development' to replace quantitative growth (see Chapter 17).

From the marketing angle it will be necessary to dissociate the production of welfare goods from burdening the environment: a concept of 'qualitative growth'. 'A market economy will not attain lasting stability unless it can incorporate ecological awareness into its innermost functioning. The obstacles on this road are great, but we have no alternative' (Richard von Weizsäcker, German President, 1990).

Biedenkopf, the current minister president of the state of Saxony, was one of the first to suggest that, just as the social problem had to be addressed in the nineteenth century, so we must take on the 'green challenge' in the twentieth. He sees our present quantitative philosophy as the primary obstacle in the way of ecological progress. Within the framework of our belief in economic growth it is crucial that we 'learn to construe the limitations on consumption, without which our society cannot survive, as a political obligation to abstain'.

Dyllick (1989b) sees the basic conflict as one of production rather than distribution: 'The cutting up of the economic cake is not under criticism. It is the way it is made, indeed the whole form of industrial life which needs scrutiny.'

There is certainly a need for development towards an environmental market economy, but the social problem has not yet been solved. Conflicts over industrial rights, distribution of public money and the length of the working day still continue. Apart from the fact that the social safety net is drawn less tightly in Britain and the USA than in Germany, the old distribution conflict is still relevant. Economic interests are caught in the cross-fire between environmental and labour issues. Sometimes it appears that the two production factors, labour and capital, have sworn a pact against nature.

There need be no change of historical direction, only expansion within the framework of an open-minded market economy. However successful the market economy seems at the present time, we should recognize the need to instal social and ecological 'safety valves' within this system. The market economy needs social and environmental fine-tuning in order to survive. Our struggle for political solutions must create answers to social as well as environmental questions.

2

The environmental manager operating holistically

Nobody can be a great economist who is only an economist. I am tempted to add that a pure economist is a worry if not a real danger.   (von Hayek)

The guiding principles of integral thinking

Economic systems as open systems

Environmental problems have made it evident that economic processes take place in open systems. Traditional resource-intensive business management is too narrow to be part of a wider political, ecological and social system. Individual phenomena need to be seen in the context of the whole system.

The technology required to overcome present and future problems must be devoted to multi-disciplinary solutions to a complex system of interrelated tasks. It should simultaneously embrace ecology, economy, resource limitations and human aims. Historically, the tasks of obtaining raw materials, manufacture, maintenance and waste disposal have been

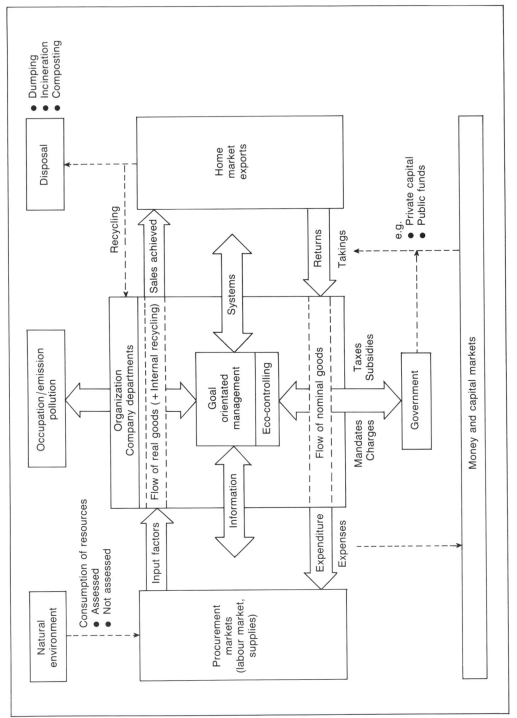

Figure 2 Ecologically enhanced business system

kept apart. They were dealt with in isolation thus maximizing efficiency. Today they have to be seen as integrated parts and the quality as well as the efficiency of the system has to be optimized. (Syrbe, 1989)

The limitations of our traditional criteria of efficiency, cost effectiveness and economic rationality become manifest as soon as we start to look at the interaction between open social economic systems with specific ecologies. Kapp, who made this point back in the 1950s, called for a new kind of thought process related to the context of systems.

- This style of systems thinking is multi-dimensional, multi-disciplinary, open and integrative.
- It requires a much wider time-scale.
- It sees economic activity as a constant interplay between economic, natural and social systems.

Human activity can appear quite rational and yet have a destructive outcome because its effects on the environment have been ignored. The economic system depends on its interaction with the ecosystem, and the natural surroundings of a business are an important variable in integrated planning and policy making. Business should be seen as an ecological model woven into the environment, the strands forming a very complex system (see Figure 2).

Holistic thinking and action

We are becoming aware that our limited, linear way of thinking and decision making, which fails to take account of this web of contexts, can bring about unintended and undesirable effects. We need to rethink our approach to management if business is to operate in an integrated world where mankind and the environment compete and complement each other. We need a holistic way of thinking and acting.

Management cannot be studied in isolation since it forms part of a much larger network. The economy can no longer be looked at in terms of directors, managers, supervisors and financiers. 'Decisions are possibly based on many isolated facts but each of them is woven into various systems. The only way to develop meaningful strategies for the future is to think in terms of contexts' (Vester, 1988).

In looking for new decision-making strategies, economists such as Vester and Ulrich have turned increasingly towards biology, evolution and the laws of energy conservation in nature. Vester (1988) has worked out bio-cybernetic principles for the survival potential of systems (see Figure 3).

Structures and processes in business are strongly governed by their natural environment. The best way to study decision making in business is therefore to analyze the mechanisms and dynamics of natural systems, asking questions

- **The principle of negative feedback**
This means developing autonomy through sets of rules for survival rather than building up individual strength to the point of collapse. Negative feedback must therefore win out over positive feedback.
- **The principle of independence from growth**
The function of a system must be kept in a state of equilibrium. It must be independent from quantitative growth because constant growth is an illusion for any system.
- **The principle of independence from product**
Systems capable of survival must be function orientated rather than product orientated. Products come and go; functions are here to stay.
- **The ju-jitsu principle**
This is a question of using available, sometimes disruptive forces according to the Asiatic system of self-defence rather than boxing with all your might.
- **The principle of multiple use**
This applies to products, functions and organizational structures. It leads through linked solutions to multi-stability and represents a renunciation of perfect solutions.
- **The principle of recycling**
This means adopting cyclic processes for waste and heat. It avoids shortfalls as well as gluts.
- **The principle of symbiosis**
This means mutual use of different forms of organization by means of coupling and exchange. It requires close contact, so mono-structures cannot benefit from it.
- **The principle of biological design**
This rule can also be applied to products, procedures and organization. It means feedback planning with the environment; unity and resonance with biological structures, particularly human ones.

Source: Vester (1988).

Figure 3 Eight principles of nature which guarantee survival

such as: what do natural entities have in common? how do they behave? how do they survive? This holistic way of thinking is a departure from previous linear, practical, analytical thought processes which are clearly not adequate for the complex situations of our time.

Central to the concept of holistic thinking are adaptability, flexibility, learning, evolution, self-regulation and self-organization.

- Outside intervention in complex systems always leads to problems with the system as a whole. We should think in terms of networks of effects and look at problems from many angles. We need to replace sectional, linear thinking with complex thinking.

- Positive and negative feedback which ensure the stability of systems show that systems are not rigid but dynamic and living.

- Instead of linear, causal thinking we should aim at an effect–cause–effect model.

- A cybernetic strategy consists in the creation of constellations not interventions. Use of existing forces allows for self-regulation (cf. the ju-jitsu principle).

- Self-regulation can be enabled through the mediation of meaning within a system, leading to motivation.

- We should strive for maximum survival as subsystems within society.

- A new aim of systematic management theory is the optimization of adaptability.

- We should think in terms of a much longer time-scale, and should not find ourselves struggling to find solutions after a problem has arisen. Gomez speaks of a new generation of holistic early warning systems.

Fallacies in dealing with complex management problems	The stages of holistic problem solving	
First fallacy Problems are objectively given and must merely be formulated clearly.	**Defining the problem** The situation can be defined from different viewpoints, in order to arrive at holistic integration.	
Second fallacy Every problem is a direct consequence of a cause.	**Investigating the web** The relationships between the elements of a problem can be apprehended and their effects analyzed.	
Third fallacy To understand a problem it is enough to freeze the variables.	**Understanding the dynamics** Temporal aspects of individual relationships and of the whole system can be investigated, and their meaning grasped in context.	
Fourth fallacy Behaviour can be prognosticated with sufficient information.	**Interpreting possible behaviour** Future developments can be worked out and simulated.	
Fifth fallacy Problems can be mastered; it is just a question of effort.	**Determining the control possibilities** Controllable, non-controllable and unpredictable aspects of a situation can be shown in a control system diagram.	
Sixth fallacy A little wire pulling is usually enough to solve most problems in practice.	**Designing control input** Control input should correspond to systemic rules to optimize their effect.	
Seventh fallacy The problem can be dismissed after the implementation of one solution.	**Evolving solutions** Intelligent, evolutionary solutions can anticipate changes in the situation.	

Source: Gomez and Probst (1987).

Figure 4 Problem-solving stages versus fallacies

The complexity of the present system of management highlights the limitations of traditional business planning and control mechanisms. Gomez and Probst (1987) and Ulrich and Probst (1988) identify a typical example of wrong thinking in the management approach to problem solving in complex situations (see Figure 4). These false processes can be avoided by holistic methods. 'The answer is to be found in integral thinking for management.' They go on to specify the components of this method as steps, which do not have to be taken sequentially:

Step 1 Defining the problem. To recognize the real problem, the situation should be viewed from a variety of different angles. Models can be set up, but one must not jump to conclusions too quickly.

Step 2 Investigating the network. An image of the network of effects should be built up using the meta-plan technique. This involves drawing a network with arrows showing the direction of the various influences, and plus and minus signs to show an intensified circulation or a stabilizing influence, respectively.

Step 3 Apprehending the dynamics. Each effect relationship is marked as to the nature of the influence, the direction of effect and the time-span. For example, different thicknesses of arrow are used to signal short- or long-term effects. The intensity of present influences can be investigated with the help of a paper computer (see Figure 5). All the elements of a problem situation are listed in a two-dimensional matrix in order to see the interconnections. The strength of

Effect on, of	Circulation	Readership	Volume of advertising	Editorial offering	Sale price	Active sum (AS)	Quotient Q (AS/PS times 100)
Circulation		3	3	1	2	9	128
Readership	0		3	2	0	5	56
Volume of advertising	1	1		2	2	6	75
Editorial offering	3	3	1		2	9	150
Sale price	3	2	1	1		7	116
Passive sum (PS)	7	9	8	6	6		
Product P (AS times PS)	63	45	48	54	42		

Source: Gomez and Probst (1987).

Figure 5 Simple paper computer from a magazine publisher

these connections is expressed on a scale of 0 to 3. The effects (of the left-hand element on the others) are shown along the rows and the intensity of influence from the other elements is shown in the columns. The example shows that sales price has a strong influence on the number of copies and a weak influence on the editorial offering. By adding horizontally and vertically respectively, the active sum (AS) and the passive sum (PS) are calculated and a quotient (Q) and a product (P) can be derived from the two sums. This enables the following evaluation of the role of each individual element.

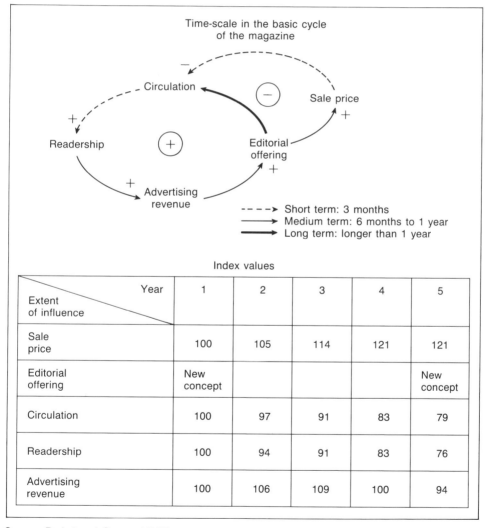

Extent of influence \ Year	1	2	3	4	5
Sale price	100	105	114	121	121
Editorial offering	New concept				New concept
Circulation	100	97	91	83	79
Readership	100	94	91	83	76
Advertising revenue	100	106	109	100	94

Source: Probst and Gomez (1989).

Figure 6 Time-scale in the basic cycle of the magazine

- Active effect (highest Q): influences the others most strongly; is least influenced by the others.

- Passive effect (lowest Q): influences the others least; is most strongly influenced.

- Critical effect (highest P): influences strongly but is also strongly influenced.

- Inert effect (lowest P): influences weakly and is influenced weakly.

The interpretation of this example shows the editorial offering as the active influence. Since it influences all the other effects strongly, it has the greatest leverage. Readership is the passive effect and is merely an indicator of the success of the newspaper publisher. The circulation is the critical effect and it will cause a chain reaction. The inert effect is the sale price. These effect-indicators are very important in the search for successful intervention strategies. It is equally important to investigate the time-span of effects (see Figure 6).

Step 4 Interpretation of behaviour. Scenarios can be set up to indicate the future development of each effect, as in the example. The probable scenario is used as the actual basis for problem solving, while a pessimistic scenario provides a trigger for contingency planning and an optimistic scenario can also be set up (see Figure 7).

Influencing factors	Probable scenario	Pessimistic scenario
Circulation	This type of publication has prospects for further growth but only 1–2% p.a. Further growth of market share is possible.	The market for this kind of paper is saturated. Regressions are likely. There is danger of a new rival causing loss of market share.
Readership	Each copy is read by an average of 3.5 readers.	Readership is declining because of smaller households.
Advertising revenue	The magazine is still a must for advertisers and has potential for further adverts.	The magazine loses status because advertisers are looking elsewhere. As a result, the volume of advertising drops.
Editorial offering	The editorial department still has development potential. New concepts are promising.	Editorial zenith has been reached.
Sale price	Price can keep pace with general price rises.	It is no longer possible to fix prices.

Source: Gomez and Probst (1987).

Figure 7 Possible scenarios for a magazine publisher

Step 5 Determination of control possibilities. The possible interventions are drawn up in a control model consisting of five components:

● Indicators.

● Controllable variables.

● Non-controllable variables.

● Positive feedback.

● Negative feedback.

A catalogue of measures can be derived from the control model (see Figures 8 and 9).

Step 6 Design of control interventions. Having determined where there are possibilities for intervention, the effect of each measure can be evaluated. These useful effect analyses based on the results from the paper computer can be set up very quickly with the help of appropriate computer software.

The rules for the functioning of complex, living systems which have to be 'translated' can be interpreted as follows (Probst and Gomez):

● Adapt your interventions to the complexity of the problem situation.

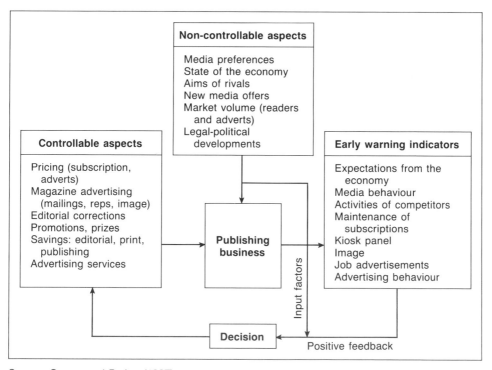

Source: Gomez and Probst (1987).

Figure 8 Control model for a magazine publisher

Early warning indicators	Decision regulator	Measures (controllable aspects)	Preventive action (non-controllable aspects)
Expectation based on the economy (collective indicators)	Change of trend (up or down)	• Pricing • Adaptation of advertising • Costs management	• More intensive monitoring of economic developments
Media behaviour (consumer data per medium)	Significant shifts between the media	• Editorial improvements • Publicity drives, prizes • Intensification of advertising	• Empirical investigation of the social background behind the shifts
Competitor activity (strategy alterations, new magazines)	Threats to market position	• Editorial improvements • Pricing • Magazine advertising • Launching a new magazine	• Advertising campaigns • Collecting strategically significant information
Subscription loyalty (long-term subscribers)	Increase in cancellations	• Editorial improvements • Publicity drives (maintaining readership) • Pricing	• Image promotion • Sounding out readers' wishes

Source: Probst and Gomez (1987).

Figure 9 Catalogue of measures for a magazine publisher derived from the control model

• Direct your interventions at the active and critical effects.

• Avoid uncontrolled development through the stabilizing effect of positive feedback.

• Use internal dynamics and the synergies of the problem situation.

• Find a harmonious balance between conservation and change.

• Encourage the autonomy of the smallest unit.

• Increase learning and developmental skills with each problem-solving activity.

Step 7 Realization and further development. Practical application of solutions should be adaptive and capable of repair and development. They should provide early warning.

In the case of the newspaper publisher, this process led to increased readership through weekly 'kiosk panels'. Development potential was relatively straightforward since editorial or conceptual changes can be made in the short term. Early warning indicators were more problematic.

The threat to the ecosystem
(or, The inescapable conflict between ecology and economy)

The global ecosystem is characterized by natural equilibrium. More or less complex life forms develop within the various habitats depending on such factors as soil structure, water balance and incidence of light. Since this equilibrium is subject to interference (e.g. from climatic variation), which leads via feedback processes to adaptation, it is referred to as a dynamic or fluid equilibrium. The important point here is that variations in single components of this ecosystem can lead to chain reactions which entirely disrupt the balance. The food chain shows possible pathways by which non-degradable substances can enter human beings (Figure 10).

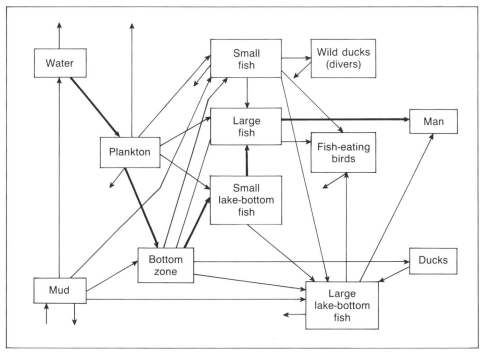

Source: *Ciba-Geigy Magazine*, 3 and 4/1975.

Figure 10 Relationships in the ecosystem of a freshwater lake

If man, as part of nature, destroys the ecosystem, he destroys himself. The artificial environment made by man is intimately connected with burdens on the ecosystem which threaten the balance of ecological cycles. Economic activity consumes scarce resources and alters or destroys the natural equilibrium. The interdependence of these two systems and their implications for planning are not yet fully recognized.

The man-made environment is both a cause and a victim of strain. It can suffer from physical or chemical effects such as the 'furring up' of a washing machine, mistakes in manufacture or the effects of pollution on the artificial world. On the other hand, artificial systems cause strain through the creation of by-products from the manufacturing process, which take the form of solid waste, toxins or wasted energy. The creation of the man-made world uses up space in the natural environment by building, clearing ground or storage. Production processes can lead to direct strain on human beings. Health and safety regulations at work are intended to control this effect.

> The effects of human occupation and emission are evident in countless ways. They are mixed together by weather factors and varied means of transportation and combine as an enormous strain on the environment. Chain reactions arise in the natural world, in the food chain for example, and between the animate and the inanimate world. The damaging effects are felt far away from the original causes, and, depending on the length of the chains, finally reach man. Sometimes they are easily identifiable, sometimes hidden, occult. Then, as a result, hectic activity and dull anxiety about the environment are combined often in quite irrational ways. (Siemens, 1986)

Alongside these barely comprehensible mechanisms and feedback systems comes the problem that strain on the environment can be traced back to a multiplicity of perpetrators.

Schütze sees the conflict between ecology and economics as insoluble for two main reasons:

- Economic activity is connected with human intervention in the natural ecosystem, with the aim of gaining benefits for man.

- Economic growth contributes more to the burden on the atmosphere because refinement processes cause an increase in entropy.

> The saying 'ecology and economy must present no contradiction, they can be reconciled' may express ignorance or the need for harmony. It may also have been invented to disguise the politics of self-interest. It is false but has tradition behind it. The economy is supposed to include a clean environment as one of its production goals. (Schütze, 1988)

Other commentators, such as Seidel (1989), seem to find economy and ecology irreconcilable:

> Contrary to everything that is said about post-industrial, post-material 'service' society, most products cannot be 'dematerialized' or 'idealized' without incurring a horrendous cost for adequate environmental control. In general, it has to be admitted that the motto 'more profit through ecology' is a lie. (Seidel, 1989)

Since production is always connected with a strain on the environment industrial ecology can only ever be relative. However, every possible opportunity should be seized to reduce the environmental burden through industrial measures.

Environment as a production factor

Economic internalization

In the industrial system of production factors, the natural environment is regarded exclusively as a source of raw materials. It is logical that the environment is left out of business accounting as it has a market value of zero. Market value is given only to scarce materials; the rest of the environment is free. Even when demand increases there is no price rise because there is no scarcity indicator connected with free goods. There is therefore no incentive to use the environment sparingly. However, the natural environment should be seen as a receptacle not just a resource (Strebel, 1981).

The phenomenon of 'social costs' has long been the subject of penetrating discussion in economics. The central thesis in *The Social Costs of Private Enterprise* (Kapp, 1979) is that 'the maximization of net income in micro-economic units leads to reductions in income elsewhere and that traditional attempts to measure the performance of an economy are unsatisfactory'.

Social costs are disadvantages and injuries suffered by the economy because of private production activities. They can take the form of a variety of diseconomies, increased risks and uncertainties, which often reach far into the future. They are 'external' because they are borne by third parties or by society. Social costs connected with the process of production are increasingly internalized: that is, damage caused by business activity is paid for by polluters.

Strebel (1980) distinguishes two forms of internalization.

- Ecological internalization. The polluter takes responsibility for cutting down pollution.
- Economic internalization. The polluter pays the cost and continues to cause the damage.

Industry has to pay a part of these external effects already as a result of state-imposed restrictions on environmental damage. The more these restrictions increase and the connection between environmental damage and industrial costs is established, the sooner the environment will become a production factor.

It is necessary here to redefine 'economic interest'. The insight that the environment is a scarce production factor underlying the principle of economy is indispensable to an ecological revaluation of business and management studies. If modern industry has to 'pay off' nature, there will be distribution conflicts because parts of income, labour and capital will have to be sacrificed to this new production factor. As a result:

- The price of traditional products will rise to meet the cost of repairing the damage.

- Business will be given an incentive to design environmentally friendly products, procedures and uses of resources.

- Consumers will have to be prepared to pay the extra cost for eco-friendly products as a price for improved environmental conditions. (They will also face loss of spending power and standard of consumption.)

- The burden on nature will be reduced but never completely removed.

- Business managers will recognize that ecologically responsible activities represent a potential competitive advantage.

For Kapp, a normative economy consists in trying to express social aims quantitatively, in the form of social and ecological indicators. Determining these desirable macroeconomic norms involves a number of conflicting factors. Examples of norms might be tolerance levels for atmospheric and water pollution, minimum levels of health care or nutritional norms. Politically formulated norms would need to be introduced into the socioeconomic system and interdisciplinary research would be required.

The following mutually contradictory factors would need to be reconciled in determining a normative economy:

- Fairer distribution.

- Economic stability.

- Full employment.

- Efficient use of scarce resources.

- Participation in decision making.

- Maintenance of dynamic ecological and economic equilibria (Kapp, 1987).

    If one wishes to change these relationships one must ally one's
    ecological position with economic insight, which testifies that excess
    consumption of the environment is based on an error in the economic
    system. Environment is used as if it were an unlimited resource with no

danger of prices rising due to scarcity. In this state of affairs, government is required in its classical role. It must prevent manufacturers from ruining the environment and thereby removing the very basis of production. The situation is comparable to the emergence of the welfare state with child labour and deforestation, the workers' movement and the ecology movement. Who could fail to see the parallel? Eco-politics is part of the struggle for power and distribution in society. People must fight for the preservation of the bases of life, just as workers fought for the seven-hour day. (Vahrenholt, 1987)

The onus is on the state. The idea of autonomous environmental policy directed by business is seen by Stoll (1984) as a contradiction in terms: 'Environmental protection is above all a question of setting up ecological restrictions on individual industrial decisions.' He perceives a fundamental disparity between ecological production and the 'polluter pays' principle or the internalization of costs. He urges the replacement of reactive environmental policy with long-term preventive measures, 'which would necessitate a co-ordination of all decentralized decisions from the start. There would have to be a systematic dovetailing of political and private decision making.' Since the process of unburdening the ecosystem through actual economic activity would be a question of external costs for the business economist, the following measures would have to be implemented:

- Making the environment into a costly commodity: that is, internalizing the costs of pollution.
- Reducing energy consumption through taxation.
- Setting up targeted government procurement offices.
- Providing extensive ecological information.

Ecological internalization

National and company-level environmental protection has only been 'bolted on' as a kind of 'end-of-pipe' solution, years after the occurrence of ecological damage. As already mentioned, retrospective reduction and disposal measures (curative) should be replaced by preventive measures. Manufacturers ought to test the environmental effects of a new product from the development stage right through its life-cycle: procurement, production, consumption or use and ultimate disposal. Management responsibility is said to last 'from the cradle to the grave'.

Consistent application of these preventive principles, integrating ecological demands into the economic process, should involve the following:

- Recyclable materials and energies used whenever possible.

- Eco-friendly resource extraction.
- Sparing use of all the non-renewable raw materials.
- Recyclable materials manufactured.
- Internal recycling increased.
- Stronger controls on emission during production.
- Increased consumer reuse of raw materials.
- Reduction of emissions caused by transportation and the energy used.
- Dismantling problems considered at the early planning stages.

The corporate view of environmental problems

From a manufacturing perspective, the natural environment has two technical functions:

- Providing raw materials.
- Acting as a receptacle for waste.

The problem of scarcity resulting from these uses of the environment primarily affects the use of resources for raw materials and energy. The depletion of many raw materials is widely acknowledged and is not necessarily connected to price fluctuations. The drop in crude oil prices stands in stark contrast to the long-term scarcity of this raw material. In the last 100 years the consumption of raw materials has risen by a factor of eight. This unparalleled exploitation has one often forgotten consequence. What is removed today is lost for the future. As against this, there are three ways of preserving resources: avoiding, substituting and saving.

A rough outline of the complex problem of eco-strain is as follows. Alongside atmospheric pollution (increasing concentrations of carbon dioxide and CFCs, and the effects on health and forestation), there is both water pollution and noise pollution, as well as the problem of dealing with various other forms of waste. The cost of space for disposal has risen, and there is widespread opposition to the siting of new incineration plants. The ecosphere is threatened by the removal of resources and by the creation of dangerous substances during production processes. The environment is becoming too overloaded to be able to regenerate. Whole ecological systems are on the brink of destruction.

3

The need for proactive environmental management

◆

Two years ago I was given the latest economic report by one of our largest economics research institutes. I opened it and read: 'Till the end the basic trend in economic development in Germany has been upwards.' This 'Till the end' meant that up to the publication deadline for this report there had been no indication that economic growth would end. I thought this sentence might be used in the not too distant future as an obituary for industrial society and its economy. I keep it in my memory as a future obituary.   (Meyer-Abich, 1985)

◆   ◆   ◆

First steps to an environmental management theory

The widespread public awareness of green issues identified in surveys will, in the long term, lead to changed behaviour among consumers and manufacturers. New demands are being made on businesses in particular. Taking on social, cultural, political or ecological responsibilities can seriously detract from the realization of commercial goals, so these new areas have to be merged into the field of eco-management.

The following six important reasons should inspire every responsible manager or entrepreneur to adopt eco-management methods, even out of self-interest (Winter, 1987):

● There can be no green economy without green business – and without a green economy there can be no dignified survival for mankind.

- Without green business there can be no consensus among the business community – and without public consensus there can be no free enterprise.

- Without eco-management competitiveness will be lost and there will be a risk of environmental liabilities amounting to millions, endangering business and jobs.

- Without eco-management there will be a risk of job losses and bad prospects at all levels of employment.

- Without eco-management companies will miss chances to cut costs.

- Without eco-management there will be difficulties of conscience – and without a clear conscience there cannot be full identification with one's work.

Only the preliminary stages of 'environmental management theory' are discernible. Its main goals are to improve industrial relations with the environment, to monitor the economic consequences and to respond to government policies. The social and ecological interests of society should be catered for alongside those of business itself. Eco-management and marketing should be applied with the goal of improving competitiveness.

A much better understanding of the problems of 'green management' is required than exists at present. Strategic responses to environmental changes are among the most important management duties for the future; without them government intervention will become more and more restrictive.

Adaptation to the new terms of reference should be brought about by means of competition: that is, by means of self-determined activities which improve business. Eco-management should be proactive rather than passive and reactive, and it should aim to integrate environmental demands. It should seek green solutions which go beyond legal requirements along the following lines:

- Reduce energy and raw materials used in production.

- Register and settle the cost of green measures.

- Adopt eco-friendly products.

- Increase the volume of recycling.

- Design eco-orientated marketing.

- Improve your environmental image.

- Appoint environmental officers.

- Register and record the effects of industrial activity on an ecological data base.

- Settle disposal costs.

- Finance green measures taking account of government grants.

Long-term profit can be assured only when agreement between green demands and business requirements has been reached by creating a green image and displaying environmental competence. It is not sufficient simply to jump on to the green bandwagon. Technical solutions and superficial marketing strategies often merely provide an alibi. We need the systematic incorporation of ecology into every aspect of business and industrial life within the framework of eco-management.

In many cases there are actual financial gains to be derived from 'corporate ecology':

● Savings on raw materials and energy.

● Additional possibilities for recycling.

● Stronger staff identification with the company.

● Reduced costs in provision and disposal of resources (e.g. purification of waste water).

● Avoidance of the cost of future waste disposal.

● Additional sales, since in the long term only eco-friendly products will have a chance.

> The existence of the economy is at stake because of the imbalance in the ecosystem. Environmental protection is not a barrier to growth, it is a prerequisite. (Necker, President of the Confederation of German Industry)

The principles of reducing environmental damage

All technological production leads to environmental stress in some form or other. Although it is impossible to put an end to this, we can make systematic moves towards a reduction of these strains. This is not simply a technological problem, and the important social dimension will be explored in Chapter 7.

There are four basic principles applicable to input, production process and output.

First, the causes of eco-stress should be avoided using preventive strategies. This involves abstention through:

● Prohibitions on certain materials.

● Partial solutions (e.g. reduce packaging to a minimum).

● Voluntary self-control of consumer needs.

Preventive strategies can be applied effectively only to specific areas. Measures are often described by the media as 'preventive' when they are really forms of reduction.

Second, reduction strategies should be adopted to minimize eco-stress.

● Conservation: economizing on the quantities of raw materials, energy or space used in production.

● Substitution: replacing harmful procedures with less eco-stressful solutions.

- Reduction of emissions: lowering the output of toxic, noise or solid pollutants.

Third, output can be fed back into the system as input so long as it makes technical, economical and ecological sense.

- Recycling: reusing emission or waste products as material or energy.

Fourth, strategies for the removal of unavoidable waste should ensure appropriate, harmless disposal.

- Landfill: conversion/diffusion.
- Incineration: 'energy recycling'.

Since individual businesses are only part of a larger network of input–output relationships, environmental measures should not be limited to manufacturing processes. Other forms of input, such as systems, labour and materials input, must also be produced and they too create emissions.

The problem of input emission helps one to realize the complexity of the pollution chain. A vast amount of information would be needed to trace back through the network of technical production to find the originator of each form of pollution. One thing is certain: 'Every producer has a certain responsibility for the emissions caused by his supplier' (Schober, 1987).

Systematic, proactive eco-management must consider the originator of input and the recipient of output as well as the actual manufacturing process of any enterprise.

4

Design and implementation of an environment information system

◆

There is no progress against nature. (Meyer-Abich, 1985)

◆   ◆   ◆

Elements of an environment information system

Information is the life-blood of management. Efficient information and communications systems, in conjunction with creative consultancy, form the basis for action. A model for the future might look something like this.

- Use of information and communications technology.
- Use of consultancy services.
- Collaboration with a range of institutions (see Chapter 11).
- Eco-assessment (see Chapter 17).

The need is mainly in medium-sized companies which feel overstretched by the requirements of environmental regulations. They are under pressure to find a balance between business and ecological targets. While large companies can draw on in-house specialists, medium-sized firms are often forced to turn to external consultants. There are numerous possibilities:

- Private consultants.

- Local chambers of industry and commerce.

- Local trade associations.

- Self-help organizations like BAUM in Germany, OBU in Switzerland or TREE in Britain, which aim to bring eco-management to a wider public.

- Industrial associations like the International Chamber of Commerce, the BDI in Germany or the CBI in Britain. The CBI has a central environment committee with eleven regional committees; it is carrying out programmes to improve waste disposal, energy efficiency, etc.

- International consultancy agencies. These include the International Environmental Bureau (IEB), founded in 1986 as a special department of the International Chamber of Commerce (ICC) in Geneva, and the environment departments of the World Bank.

Use of information technology

Controlled environmental protection relies on effective information and communications technology. These systems should facilitate:

- The acquisition of knowledge about natural–technical interrelations. This new science is called 'eco-systems research'.

- Provision of regular feedback to management, embracing comparison of the real with the desired situation, analysis of anomalies and the introduction of correctives.

- Better description of the current state of affairs, enabling better preventive measures.

Databanks and expert systems help to deal with the vast amount of accumulated information. In some subsections of environmental protection the use of computer technology represents the 'state of the art'. But it has only recently become possible to draw together isolated solutions into an integrated system, with eco-planning, control and protection. Information technology plays a key role in collecting and interpreting data as well as in decision making. There is an increasing use of simulation programmes to analyze the consequences of encroaching on the environment.

Syrbe, the president of the Fraunhofer Institute, believes that the qualitative leap to holistic solutions will require special working methods:

- Modelling based on deeper theoretical and practical knowledge, linked with the use of information banks.

- Computer simulation of problem and solution.

- Use of expert systems and forms of artificial intelligence.

- Man–machine interfaces for complex problems.

An integrated, holistic eco-information system consists of a core system and the components to support specialist systems and/or their subdivisions. Data are stored, prepared and administered in the core system according to given criteria, having been loaded manually or via an automatic network. The system checks all the data and acts as an early warning against exceeding the limits. As a user interface it provides accessible specialist and management information and is closely linked to the data preparation system.

The core system operates via interfaces with support systems. Data relevant to the task are drawn from the memory, condensed, selected and combined. This intelligent system with independent components and databanks (single source principle) is located at individual workplaces and consists of the following:

- 'Tools' for processing eco-data, such as word-processors, desk-top publishing, E-mail, mathematical and statistical support, graphics and expert systems.

- 'Pools' for knowledge-orientated data support, such as information on locations, specialist databanks on substances and eco-laws, literature, research projects, etc. (see Figure 11).

◇ Siemens

A wide range of data is indispensable for dealing safely with dangerous substances and transporting them in accordance with the law. The information system SIGEDA provides direct access to data on research and development, construction and production, industrial safety and medicine, environmental protection, fire prevention, purchasing and sales, storage and transport. SIGEDA is of inestimable value in emergencies when quick decisions have to be made about damage control and safeguard of persons and valuables. The SIGEDA system was introduced for internal use after pilot tests in 1989. It is now available for external sale in a mainframe version on BS2000 and in a PC version.

For Siemens Ltd the information system covers the following:

- A central information system for 800 positions from all sections of Siemens.

- 350–400 dangerous substances and preparations typically for each factory.

- A total of around 5,000 dangerous substances (many connected with semiconductor production).

- Up to 200 data fields per dangerous substance or preparation.

- All data on dangerous substances are checked for consistent quality.

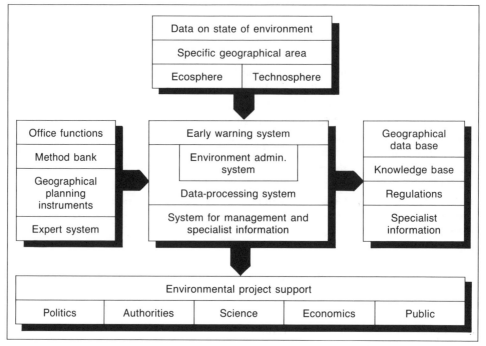

Source: Siemens (1989).

Figure 11   Model of an environment information system

■ All information from SIGEDA Central is attestable in cases of conflict.

SIGEDA consists of eleven blocks with space for expansion:

1. Basic data.
2. Physical and chemical data.
3. Danger classifications.
4. National control limits.
5. International control limits.
6. Public health.
7. Preventive measures.
8. Transportation of hazardous materials.
9. Environmental protection.
10. Emergencies and injury procedures.
11. Analysis of hazardous substances.

The main source of data is expert knowledge, technical literature, publications of transport companies, etc. SIGEDA was conceived for practical use in industry and operates with a largely self-explanatory menu system. Block compilation of data enables ready access, for example, to the following:

- Quick information for the company doctor.
- Quick information for safety staff.
- Lists of hazardous substances.
- Operating instructions.
- First aid for emergencies.

◇ IBM/Du Pont

As a combined project by IBM and Du Pont, the European Chemical Data System (ECDS) represents the first European online system of its kind. Data sheets on safety used to be manually drafted for the 5,000 chemicals used by IBM. They were used as a kind of worldwide identity card for each substance.

Du Pont, one of largest chemical manufacturers, made available its eleven-language library which contains appropriate expressions for writing data sheets on safety. IBM developed the software and logistics for the online system which provides access to information in every European country in its relevant language.

Expert systems are taking over support for this kind of task. They store, administer and evaluate specialist knowledge. Within a narrowly defined area, expert systems have an inferential component which is modelled on how an expert would solve this kind of problem. There are applications in many areas. Siemens gives the following examples:

- Testing environmental tolerances. Which eco-factors should be considered in planning large-scale plant?
- Reciprocities within the ecological system. How does changing one variable affect the other variables in the whole system?
- Treatment of waste materials. How can we make more use of waste materials?
- Transportation of hazardous materials. What steps need to be taken to prevent and deal with accidents?
- Treatment of existing waste. What is to be done if an unknown substance seeps out from a dumping site?

◇ IBM

Together with the German Society for Works and Safety and the Berlin Department of Technical Supervision (TU), IBM has developed an expert information system

(ALEXIS) which helps companies fulfil the regulations on clean air, water and land, and on waste disposal. In Germany, the estimated 50,000 existing waste dumps are recognized increasingly as potential sources of danger and chemical time bombs. With the new expert system presented by IBM at the CeBIT 89, it is possible, for the first time, to compare the potential danger of various refuse dumps and industrial sites.

The knowledge of water pollution experts was transferred to an Expert System Environment (ESE) and an expert system was developed on the prototype of ground water. There are plans for expanding this to land, surface water and air.

The expert system assesses and identifies the dangers from waste disposal sites. The data are evaluated and compared with other sites and the results are displayed graphically with explanations. Great experience is not necessary because of simple menu selection.

IBM is also involved in one of the most ambitious environmental projects, the Global Environmental Monitoring System (GEMS), which collects and evaluates information on environmental damage. Part of this work entails the establishment of a Global Resource Information Databank (GRID) which will enable comparison of data. Furthermore, link-ups with other databanks are envisaged.

The Research Institute for Applied Information Processing at the University of Ulm is currently investigating the introduction of expert systems as early warning devices. WANDA, the Water Analysis Data Adviser, is preparing suggestions based on expert water analysis. Expert systems are also used to help find one's way through the maze of environmental regulations.

◇ IUCN-Bonn

The International Union for the Conservation of Nature and Natural Resources, whose aim is to collect, document and evaluate information on environmental law, has built up an Environmental Law Information System (ELIS). It opens up the enormous wealth of legal and contractual texts to consultants.

ROMULUS (Retrieval Orientated Multilingual Online Updating System), a privately developed software package, solves the problem of multilingual document retrieval. ELIS is competent in English, German and French. The user is given not only explanations and instructions in the chosen language but also related concepts from the Thesaurus.

ELIS also includes ENLEX, the environmental databank on the twelve EC member countries. The documents are stored not in the full text system but by means of formated data which are supplemented by abstracts and descriptors. The machine document search can locate these references. Some 36,600 national legal documents, 440 EC documents, 960 inter-state agreements and 40,150 bibliographical references are stored in the IBM/38 Databank computer.

◇ Hewlett Packard

Hewlett Packard and Philips Systeme und Sondertechnik have jointly developed ULIS, Umweltleit- und Informationssysteme (Environment Control and Information Systems), to provide a holistic solution to all areas of modern environmental information technology. It provides effective decision-making tools for those responsible for the environment. The complexity of the system shows how important it is to draw together the flood of available information. This kind of condensation of data is the only way to facilitate decision making, and although all the models required for environmental problem solving are included, this is not enough for Hewlett Packard. 'Conservation of space, financial feasibility, the existing or planned infrastructure and peripherals must be taken into account, as well as integrating the emergency services or the fire brigade into the system.' (See Figure 12.)

It is important to develop the whole system on the basis of standard drive systems if mutual communication is to be possible via networks. At least, this will be the only way to integrate partial solutions and guarantee openness. In fact, there are plans to include modern relational databank systems.

Demands on systems software are more important than hardware aspects. Information management and databank facilities should be mentioned in this context (e.g. for office communications, reports, licensing procedures, etc.). Measuring data, from geographical information to thematic cartography, represents another applications area.

At present, Hewlett Packard sees the realization of a multiplicity of partial solutions which cannot be linked together in integrated information systems. 'It is therefore necessary to think holistically, in large- and small-scale operations.'

Corporate environmental consultancy

Private consultants

It is sometimes necessary for intermediate companies to resort to external consultants to help them form a clearer view of the market for environmental technology. The solution must be tailor-made for each company. This creates a need for comprehensive eco-consultancy in operational, strategic and normative sections of management, dealing with questions of organization, personnel, production technology and economics. (For risk analysis, see Chapter 15.)

The remit of consultants embraces advice on ecological matters such as how and where a company might be causing environmental stress, eco-laws, improvement programmes, problem solving, etc. They also help inexperienced companies to deal with the authorities and aspects of the environment.

Bringing in experts with broad industrial experience can be combined with knowledge specific to one industrial branch. Consultants' experience might range from an overview of industry, academic research or in-house experience of eco-analysis to fully fledged marketing strategies.

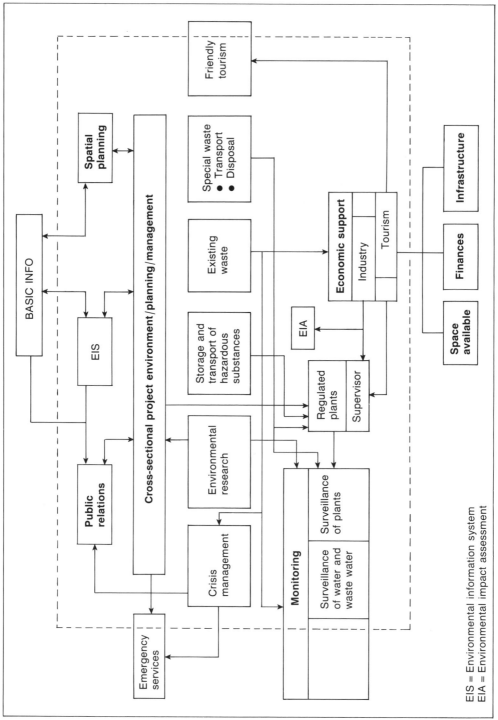

Figure 12 Environment protection information system

EIS = Environmental information system
EIA = Environmental impact assessment

Source: Hewlett Packard.

According to the German eco-consultant Kaiser, around DM3.5 billion (£1.2 billion) was spent in 1988 on engineering, consulting and environmental assessment. The UK market researcher Ecotec estimates the value of the green consultancy market in Britain at around £420 million p.a., rising to £1 billion by 1995. Other sources find these figures on the optimistic side. The cost of green consultancy is relatively high. The German weekly *Wirtschaftswoche* sets the range of prices between DM10,000 (£3,300) for a general market analysis and DM0.5 million (£170,000) for a detailed analysis and evaluation of, say, a programme for disposing of existing pollution.

Choosing the right consultant is no easy matter. While some deal with specific problems, others offer eco-consultancy as part of their wider services. There are more and more heavy plant and machine manufacturers offering ready-made solutions, with subsidiary companies in the service sector.

National publications give useful guidance. For example, in Germany there is the *Addressbook of Eco-consultants* published by the German Environmental Foundation (Deutsche Umweltstiftung), and in Britain, the *Directory of Environmental Consultants*, published by Environmental Data Services Ltd. (ENDS).

In consultancy, several factors need to be borne in mind because of the complexity of environmental protection. Eco-measures such as the installation of a waste water purification plant have to satisfy the legal regulations and be technically and commercially feasible. The interdisciplinary nature of eco-consultancy presupposes a comprehensive knowledge of all the relevant subsections.

Even banks are now offering service packages including consultancy as well as finance. The Deutsche Bank, the biggest banking institute in Germany, has set up appropriate packages for environmental protection over the last two years. At CeBIT 89 the services db-data and db-select were exhibited using ecological materials. A system was presented at CeBIT 90 whose nucleus consisted of a single databank of hazardous substances, environmental procedures and traders in eco-technology (see Chapter 14).

Businesses of all sizes should be able to obtain tailor-made, state-of-the-art, financially optimal solutions. The Deutsche Bank has published a brochure for intermediate companies entitled *Environment, Facts, Prognoses and Strategies*, which contains comprehensive checklists to facilitate self-diagnosis (Deutsche Bank, 1989).

The number of UK-based environmental consultancies has dramatically increased. The ENDS directory of Environmental Consultants, which listed 125 consultancies in 1988, has increased its entries to 225 in the 1990 edition. To assure quality in the environmental services sector an Association of Environmental Consultants is needed.

◇ SustainAbility

One of Europe's leading consultancies on corporate environmental excellence and sustainable development is SustainAbility, 'The Green Growth Company'. Founded in 1987, SustainAbility offers a wide range of services, with the focus on such areas as policy and strategy formulation, environmental auditing, mediation, consumer and market research, issue briefings, communication and training. Members of the company have published various best-sellers on the greening of business, technologies of sustainable development and green consumerism.

◇ Dragon International

Dragon International is an international consultancy, specializing in brand development, product innovation and the management of corporate reputation. The company was founded with the support of Dragon Rouge, one of the leading French marketing services groups. The Dragon Group offers consultancy services across Europe from bases in Paris, London and Germany. The emergence of the 'green consumer', encouraged by campaigning groups, the media and governments, demonstrated that purchasing criteria can widen far beyond functional product delivery or even traditional brand values, to embrace details of manufacturing, supply and disposal. Interest is now broadening to include other aspects of company behaviour. This move towards the inclusion of corporate behaviour into the marketing mix will cause many companies to rethink their branding and communication strategies.

The company's aim is to help clients develop and manage their products, brands and corporate reputation positively and responsibly, to create new opportunities, improve business performance and ensure long-term success. The issues of environment performance, corporate standards of behaviour and community involvement are crucial aspects of business and marketing strategy. They approach areas such as branding strategy, communications and product development which must change in response.

Dragon International was formed to meet the need for marketing, communications and design advice, sensitive to the age of 'conscious consumerism' but still within the mainstream.

Environmental management associations

Although early attempts at ecological management were often ridiculed, and were mostly confined to medium-sized companies, commitment to environmental management is becoming increasingly evident over a much wider area. A vital contribution to this development has been made by two self-help organizations of environmental entrepreneurs: BAUM, the German Environmental Management Association, in Hamburg; and the 'Future' association in Osnabrück.

There is no trace of green eccentricity in these organizations, which are run on the basis of sound management experience, aimed at reconciling harsh

NOW WHEN YOU BUY ARIEL ULTRA, OR LIQUID YOU'LL BE DOING SO MUCH MORE THAN LAUNDRY.

PROTECTING THREATENED SPECIES

PRESERVING THE DIVERSITY OF LIFE

SAFEGUARDING COASTLINES AND WETLANDS

LIMITING THE LOSS OF RAINFORESTS

We're trying to raise over £400,000 for World Wide Fund For Nature and you can help. Buy specially marked boxes of Ariel Ultra or use the special coupons on Ariel Liquid and we'll donate cash directly to

WWF, for these, and other environmentally important projects. The bigger the pack, the bigger the donation. Look for the special Ariel Ultra and Liquid packs today. Together we'll do a lot more than laundry.

WORKING WITH WWF TOWARDS A BETTER ENVIRONMENT.

Pampers

Helping to care for your baby … and the Environment

1. Pampers pulp production makes effective use of wood.
Cellulose fibres purified from the wood become the finished pulp. The separated non-cellulose material and other wood residues are burned to generate energy to run the process. The trees used to make the pulp are re-planted in a systematic way according to local environmental require-ments of the pulp producing countries. More trees are re-planted every year than are harvested.

2. Preserving Water Quality.
Pampers pulp is purified with a new oxidation purification process, in partnership with our suppliers. This new process generates less waste and helps maintain the quality of the natural waters.

3. Less Packaging.
Ultra Pampers use 30% less pulp compared to previous Pampers, but give outstanding Pampers dryness. This saves packaging, volume and weight, meaning less waste in your dustbin.

Ultra
– 30%

4. Pampers pulp consists of purified cellulose fibres.
The pulp manufacturing process purifies the pulp by removing wood residues from the cellulose fibres, this results in a naturally white pulp that is strong and absorbent.

Pampers

7. Composting.
Pampers is running pilot projects both in Europe and the USA to produce compost from used nappies and other household waste. This compost has uses for landscaping, gardening and agriculture.

5. Recycling.
Pampers has started projects on how nappy components might be reclaimed and recycled in much the same way as glass or paper. Soiled nappies will be cleaned and the components separated for poten-tial re-use in other products like wallboard, flower pots or rubbish bags.

6. Incineration.
The materials used to make Pampers have high fuel value and are acceptable for incineration in modern facilities. Such facilities can use the heat to generate electricity.

Photo: Alcan Germany

Photo: Johnson Wax

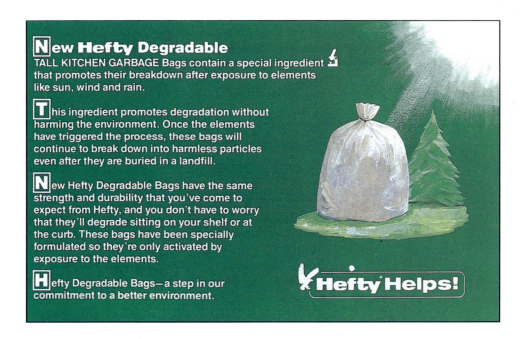

New **Hefty Degradable**

TALL KITCHEN GARBAGE Bags contain a special ingredient that promotes their breakdown after exposure to elements like sun, wind and rain.

This ingredient promotes degradation without harming the environment. Once the elements have triggered the process, these bags will continue to break down into harmless particles even after they are buried in a landfill.

New Hefty Degradable Bags have the same strength and durability that you've come to expect from Hefty, and you don't have to worry that they'll degrade sitting on your shelf or at the curb. These bags have been specially formulated so they're only activated by exposure to the elements.

Hefty Degradable Bags—a step in our commitment to a better environment.

Hefty Helps!

Hefty **NEW!**
*DEGRADABLE**
Tall Kitchen Garbage Bags
30 LEAKPROOF BAGS & TIES
2 FT. X 2 FT. 5⅜ IN. / 1.01 MIL
*ACTIVATED BY EXPOSURE TO THE ELEMENTS

FITS **13** GALLON CONTAINER

The front of Hefty bag packages played up the degradability claim, while the back gave an explanation of the process.

Green roofscape of a banking complex in Frankfurt   *Photo: H. Grub*

economic realities with the exigencies of ecology. Their role is important in that it symbolizes corporate responsibility towards society. Initiatives are taken to research, develop and disseminate new methods of environmental management. Environmental protection is not construed as a mere technical repair job, but permeates management thinking at operative, strategic and normative levels. The work of the associations is an expression of changing awareness, and in no sense represents an attempt to hide environmental sins under a cloak of deception.

BAUM is based on the model described by Winter, one of its founder members. It is a type of corporate management which includes environmental preservation as an integral component from procurement to production and processing technology through to ultimate disposal. One of the key factors is that environmental protection is seen as an equally valid strategic goal at policy and organizational levels. (See Winter, 1987.) This model is developed and expanded by drawing on combined experience. An additional goal is to intensify the motive of self-interest in environmental management.

Both of these self-help organizations aim to promote the exchange and pooling of experience and knowledge, especially in the provision of urgently needed know-how for medium-sized companies. The following measures are anticipated as a means of providing ecological knowledge particularly at management level:

- Setting up lectures, seminars or symposia.

- Staging forums and workshops.

- Promoting the exchange of information.

- Building up information services and pools.

- Co-ordinating and promoting research projects.

- Promoting models for the training and environmental education of staff.

- Consultancy for newcomers (members or outsiders), analyses of weak points, integrated management concepts.

- Providing information to the public.

There has been a recent wave of interest in forging international links between environmental associations. In 1989, for example, ÖBU, the Swiss association for environmental management, and the British 'Business and Environment' were formed. The success of BAUM (*Baum* means 'tree' in German) has led to the creation of similar organizations in Austria (1988), Sweden (1990) and the United Kingdom (1990). Associations are also currently being founded in Canada, Denmark, France, Holland, Indonesia, Norway, Israel and South Africa. TREE UK (Technology, Research, Enterprise and Environment) and the other national members joined the International Network for Environmental Management (INEM), founded in 1991, which regroups all national organizations on the BAUM model worldwide. The synergic effects from this international network hold great promise for national associations. The members of INEM continue to work closely with existing national and international organizations such as the United Nations Environment Programme (UNEP) and the International Chamber of Commerce (ICC).

5

Building 'green'

◆

In a devastated environment there can be no justification for industry.
(Rodenstock)

Environmentally orientated site location

Economic factors have always had a considerable influence on industrial building and workplace design. In recent years ecological considerations have taken on more importance. Progressive solutions are needed in the triangle of forces, product–man–environment.

Decisions about siting business premises are usually very long term, since they cannot be changed easily. Careful deliberation over factors influencing price or profitability is required.

In the single European market there will be much more choice about industrial siting, but decisions will be complicated because the question of siting is embedded in a mass of influences which have to be looked at holistically. Social and technological surroundings, infrastructure, workforce, national and international political factors, economic frames of reference, population growth, competition and target market must be viewed together. Singling out individual factors produces an unreliable picture. The ecological surroundings and the legal restrictions protecting them are only elements within a wider framework.

In a speech at the 125th anniversary of Bayer Chemicals, Strenger, the chairman, said that his company had never had to make site location decisions on the basis of ecological considerations because the laws in Germany are more stringent than in other countries: 'There has never been such a thing as ecological dumping at any time.' He continued that a responsible company must apply the same standards at home and abroad. The choice of a site is always influenced by existing environmental factors. Because of the sociopolitical importance of environmental protection, sites with high pollution potential should not even be considered.

> People are not nearly as ready as they used to be to accept interference with the environment through atmospheric pollution, noise or vibration. Industry is urgently compelled to reflect on how to secure its sites for the long term. The environmental restrictions on industrial sites are of critical importance, especially since locations are so carefully scrutinized by the authorities. The more carefully a site is chosen, the more 'secure' it will be in the future. Companies should also be aware of changes in the surroundings in order to respond in good time. (Dreyhaupt, 1987)

Within the siting factors discussed, the surrounding community and ecological infrastructure will doubtless gain in significance.

The Economics and Employment offices in Wiesbaden have renewed their support for qualifications in ecology and described eco-consultancy as an important community task. Businesses undertaking eco-management are given support. Since companies with any kind of plans for the future are frightened off by heavily polluted sites, local authorities will have to scrutinize applications for new industrial developments. Interference with nature and the landscape will have to be kept to a minimum, and extensive greening and good design will be looked on as signs of preventive environment protection.

Frequently businesses are put in jeopardy not just because of the existence of strict environmental laws but through inadequate measures to ensure environmental preservation. In the conflict between residential land use and industrial siting there are sometimes factories which have to be 'sanitized' for the safety of the neighbourhood. In addition to financial support they clearly need environmental consultation.

Since the size and quality of plots for sale is becoming more crucial, old sites will have to be recultivated or decontaminated before they are reused. Purchasers of old sites will try to avert the danger of finding that they own someone else's pollution by making test drillings in the plot. One form of reprieve for old industrial sites is that the increasingly eco-conscious population is reluctant to let new buildings be sited on potential green areas.

One of the main worries in the quest for building plots is inadequate provision for the removal of waste. Harsh laws alone are not enough to improve this situation, especially if politicians and businesses continue to see the solution only in terms of new dumps or incineration plants. Public anxiety obstructs any further development of traditional disposal methods, and new concepts such as consistent waste avoidance strategies are introduced too late or too half-heartedly.

Green industrial architecture

Every industrial building necessarily represents an 'occupation' of the environment and is inevitably a cause of environmental stress. It is therefore useful to understand natural habitats and the factors they all have in common, as a basis for eco-building. In this respect Krusche (1982) has listed the following:

- Adaptation to factors inherent in the habitat.

- Use of natural energy and materials.

- Formation of cyclic processes with internal balance and reciprocity leading to system stability.

- Self-sufficiency.

- Appropriate size and density.

- Succession as a development process towards the optimum.

Krusche sees the introduction of these principles into eco-architecture as follows:

- Environmental and energy factors determine choice of site, conception, form, position of building, building materials, use of space and organization and use of local vegetation.

- Minimal demand on energy and natural resources for building and future use.

- Intelligent use of natural systems and self-regenerating resources such as passive solar energy, natural ventilation and green areas.

- Minimization of quantity and concentration of pollution, heat loss, waste products and covered areas.

- Enrichment of the plant and animal life around the site.

- Integration of buildings into the landscape to ensure healthy living and working in the future.

The aim of eco-construction is to produce buildings with a spiritual and material dimension responsive to the needs of people and the environment. It integrates biological, psychological, physical, chemical and artistic disciplines. Discussion of eco-architecture has taken on something of the nature of a holy war – the for and against of traditional building methods. As many practical examples show, ecologically better solutions do not always mean the abandonment of technical progress. However, where economic considerations are the only design criteria, green building tends to be rare.

We should be aiming to optimize the various components of function, construction, interior design, civic architecture, working environment and so on. Once again a holistic approach is called for. The German *Industriemagazin* (2/89) highlights five interconnected ideas for 'building green':

- Reconciliation with nature and with social desire for an aesthetic environment.

- Creation of humane and motivating working conditions.

- A new harmony between form and content: the wish to display the quality of one's product and business style.

- Openness towards unconventional artistic or academic ideas, with the goal of reconciliation with the next generation.

- Incorporation of industrial buildings into their urban background: reurbanization.

The Hamburg company Ernst Winter & Son was one of the pioneers in green industrial architecture, and there have been many followers in this new tradition. Landscaping, frontage, colour, building materials and energy sources all contribute to the new design approach.

The new interdependence of functionality and environment is now seen as one of the features of personal marketing. Highly qualified staff do not find job satisfaction and motivation through money alone. An attractive workplace and surroundings are just as important. A green working environment offers:

- Increased identification of staff with their eco-friendly company.

- A better working atmosphere.

- More suggestions for improvement.

- Better health among staff and therefore a reduction in costs.

- Stronger commitment from satisfied staff leading to less wastage and better product quality.

The Federation of German Architects reduces these arguments to a short slogan: 'A pleasing workplace means productive workers.' However, there is a danger that this type of motivation strategy remains shallow and short-sighted. It will not really be effective unless it is linked with a qualitatively deeper, enriched conception of work.

Over the last 15 years the design of administrative buildings has turned volte-face from open-plan offices with their hygiene problems ('sick building syndrome'), to individually designed rooms paired with modern communications technology ('intelligent buildings'). Of particular interest are the reborn importance of daylight, ventilation and integration with the landscape.

◇ Ernst Winter & Son

Ernst Winter & Son tried to incorporate eco-architectural principles into their factory in Hamburg in 1985/6. As part of an integrated concept of eco-management, this was a unique project in Germany at the time.

The plans were made in close collaboration with an industrial architect and an eco-architect. A checklist of point-for-point bio-architectural alternatives was placed alongside the traditional plan, and prices were compared. Planning and design,

Photo: Ernst Winter & Son

construction, lighting and illumination, technical installation and choice of materials were all taken into account. The following measures are worthy of note:

- Brick-built exterior.
- Extensive daylight through windows and skylights.
- Use of wooden window frames.
- 'Greening' of frontage (although no roof greening).
- Windows can be opened (no need for air conditioning).
- Use of quartz glass transparent to ultra-violet light.
- Carpeted with high percentage natural fibre or linoleum.
- Carpet and paints low in solvents.
- Paints with eco-friendly label.
- Partial use of recycled water.
- Extensive waste water disposal facilities.

◇ Busak + Luyden

After winning the Stuttgart environment prize in 1986 for outstanding use of green areas, including a pond and many local trees and shrubs, in 1988 Busak + Luyden incorporated extensive roof greening into the plans for a new 1,600-square-metre warehouse block. The roof consists of various levels which were first coated with bitumen. The largest area of the roof was landscaped to allow for the inclusion of ponds and taller plants. An inner courtyard was planted out with climbing ivy and vines, and asphalt was replaced with grass. Judicious planting has made it possible to have green throughout the year.

◇ Schweizer & Sons

This award-winning firm has also excelled in greening a new 7,000-square-metre factory roof. In a unique design, roof gardens are used as insulation and as a filter and rainwater collector. Surplus water collected from the roof is reserved in case of fire.

◇ Public spa at Brückenau

The management of the public spa at Brückenau based the construction of its new building on a comprehensive integrated environmental concept using ecological building methods in an exemplary way.

- The motto for the interior design is 'wood not plastic'.
- The wood treatment is boric salt instead of a chromium compound.
- Skylights to maximize the use of daylight.
- Many indoor plants to improve the interior atmosphere.
- Mineral wool soundproofing in the walls and ceilings of the bottle-filling room.
- Wall coverings made from recycled materials.
- Environment-friendly paint.
- Natural materials in flooring of public areas and offices.
- Parquet floor treated with natural resin not sealed with varnish.
- Flooring maintained with natural resins, beeswax, cork and sandstone.
- Thermal power station for producing electricity and heat. The heat from waste gas and cooling water is recaptured and serves to heat water and ventilation systems. The efficiency of the system is 90 per cent. Gas turbines are cleaned by a three-way catalytic converter and exhaust condenser.
- Energy-saving lamps and appliances (50 per cent saving of energy).
- Rainwater collection system on site with oil separator.
- Everything is recycled apart from a minute residue.
- Chemical store fitted with acid/alkali resistant flooring, pump-sump and catch basins; transport of chemicals via closed system.
- Plants in the locality tended according to eco-gardening methods.
- Greening of frontage for aesthetic and climatic reasons.

The new building, public spa, Brückenau   *Photo: r + s, Karlstadt*

◇ Sainsbury

Over half of Sainsbury's new supermarkets built in the past four years have used derelict or run-down urban sites; others make use of land unsuited for other development because of its proximity to motorways or railways. The company supports green belt policy and does not seek planning consent on green belt land.

Sympathetic architecture and considerate landscaping are other factors to which Sainsbury attaches great importance. In more rural sites, land has been given for nature conservancy, and care taken to retain local wildlife and its habitat. Sainsbury believes in a comprehensive approach to landscape design, which not only caters for the functional needs of retailing but also recognizes the obligation of a new development to its local environment. This comprehensive approach is achieved only by ensuring that landscape design is part of the initial planning of a new development.

To ensure a landscape setting of quality, compatible with its surroundings, Sainsbury employs the expertise of the country's leading landscape architects and supports each scheme with a long-term aftercare programme of regular and continued maintenance by approved contractors. Wherever possible, existing vegetation is seen as a valuable asset and is used within a design to provide scale and shelter. In some developments existing trees on site have been moved, using the most modern methods, and successfully retained.

As well as the mass planting of young trees and shrubs, semi-mature trees and shrubs are used to provide an instant effect. Trees as mature as 25 years old have been included in landscape schemes, and the use of five–ten-year-old trees is frequent. As well as using building materials which blend visually with the environment, Sainsbury has banned all building insulation materials containing CFCs. No building insulation materials covering walls, roofs, pipework, ductwork, etc. contain CFCs or utilize them in the manufacturing process. The specification for new stores also states that tropical hardwoods will not be used in the construction.

In the past five years, Sainsbury stores have won twelve awards for various aspects of design. Sainsbury is jointly sponsoring a new assessment system which has been developed by the government's Building Research Establishment with the aim of applying a 'green label' to new commercial buildings which are judged to be environmentally friendly. The label is available to developers who have their buildings assessed at the design stage. Points are awarded for improvements in design, measured against current practice.

In 1974 Sainsbury began a deliberate programme of energy saving and energy efficiency, and since then its success has been marked by numerous accolades. By recycling heat from refrigeration plants, no new supermarket requires a boiler; and radical changes in lighting, environmental control and refrigeration have resulted in today's supermarkets using only 60 per cent of the energy consumed by similar stores built ten years ago.

Sainsbury is active in both its retail and distribution operations in complying with the requirements of the Montreal Protocol in relation to the CFC refrigerants used in its plant. All the cold stores in distribution depots already use HCFC22, and all new supermarkets and those due for refurbishment use HCFC22 as the sole refrigerant. HCFC22 exhibits only 5 per cent of the ozone depletion potential of commonly used refrigerants such as CFC12.

Electronic leak detection is now a permanent feature of the planned maintenance regime at all Sainsbury stores. The Streatham Common supermarket, which opened in November 1989, was the first to employ a unique prototype CFC leak detection system. An alarm is sounded if a leak occurs in the plant room, and the condition is communicated to a computer which relays the alarm automatically by telephone to the maintenance contractor.

Sainsbury is already holding technical discussions with chemical manufacturers on the development of a new, totally ozone-benign refrigerant and its significance for the design of the company's refrigeration plant. The company is watching the development of totally CFC-free, blown-foam insulation materials for use in cold stores and display cabinets. Suppliers are encouraged to conduct tests on new materials.

All CFC refrigerants are decanted when equipment is being disposed of, and are returned to storage depots for subsequent reuse. This nationwide recycling service, established by Sainsbury in conjunction with seven major refrigeration contractors, is believed to be the first of its kind.

6

Necessary framework for an environmental corporate policy

Society will only grant business its freedom if business can demonstrate that
its goals serve the good of the community.   (Schmidheim, 1987)

◆   ◆   ◆

First steps towards environmental management

It is only since public opinion has been moved to recognize the commercial
significance of environmental problems that the ecological challenge is being met
with practical market-orientated corporate policies. Since a return to the age of the
bicycle or coach-and-four would be utopian, it is incumbent upon industrialists
to solve problems in the environment before their livelihoods are destroyed.

Meffert *et al*. (1987) identify four possible strategies for corporate adaptation:

- Passivity.
- Reactive behaviour.
- Confrontation.
- Creative transformation.

They call for a proactive response to the new strategies of eco-friendliness in the
business world. A corporate policy strengthened by the awareness of ecology
transcends mere considerations of profitability and can also lead to competitive
advantage.

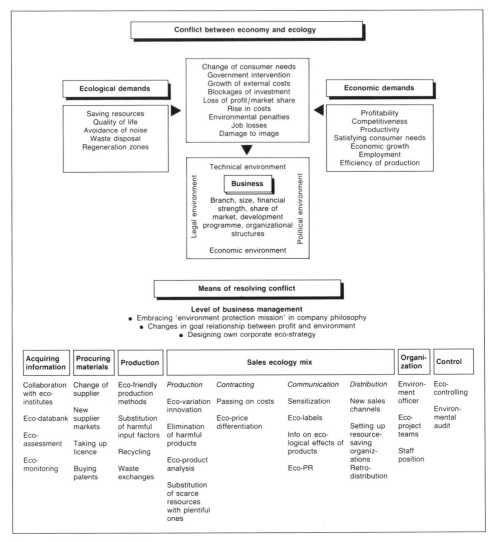

Source: Meffert *et al*. (1987).

Figure 13 Environmental policy of an organization

Companies should give up the practice of hesitating, ignoring the demands of environmental protection or giving them absolutely minimal attention. Besides, it is often quite wrong to approach eco-marketing in a defensive way. Concealing environmentally harmful aspects of a product, playing down environmental problems, often leads to missed opportunities for protecting the environment and to a loss of image. (Wicke, 1987)

The demands of ecological production and consumption do sometimes present economic threats but they also provide new opportunities. Dyllick (1989) sees both both winners and losers in this situation. The winners are not the suppliers of rapidly growing environmental technology, but the manufacturers devoted to competitive green production methods and products. This is for the following reasons:

- Disposal problems are solved in the favour of producer or consumer.

- Integrated concepts reduce the risk of liabilities.

- New product design improves sales in eco-friendly segments of the market.

- The environmentally conscientious image of the employer has a positive effect on the acquisition of new staff.

The losers are manufacturers:

- Whose production methods, under social and legislative pressure, cause large costs in avoiding pollution.

- Whose products themselves are subject to growing criticism; this can range from pressures for substitution to a total prohibition (e.g. asbestos, PVC, CFCs, PET [polyethylene teraphthalate] non-returnable bottles, etc.).

- Whose capital is the 'damaged' environment (e.g. the tourist industry, fishing industry, etc.).

The following procedure, based on the holistic concepts suggested by Winter, can be used to set up and run environmentally orientated business management:

- Identify the key ecological problems in the business.

- Instigate ecological concepts in the values of management and staff, thus encouraging a transformation of business culture.

- Use the results of the current-status analysis to check and, where necessary, expand corporate policies.

- Draw up an integrated system of objectives.

- Decide on adequate strategies.

- Ensure that ecology pervades every aspect of the business.

- Ensure that ecological thinking is embedded in institutional forms by nominating supervisors, an environment committee, etc.

- Instal an eco-controlling-system for planning and control of environmental measures.

Guaranteed success for the introduction of environmental measures depends on corresponding motivation. Not only top management but also staff at all levels must be persuaded that the new eco-policies make sense. Otherwise the

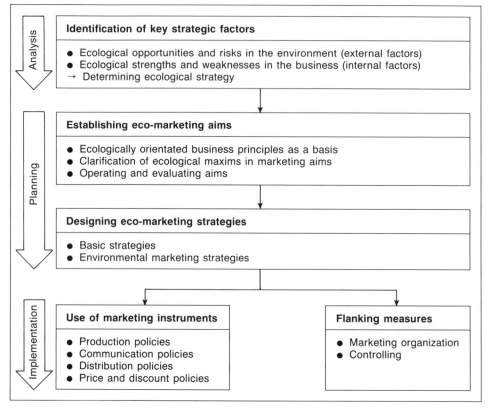

Source: Meffert *et al.* (1988).

Figure 14 Design process for an eco-marketing concept

whole plan will collapse ineffectually. The following priorities should be adhered to:

- Development of *preventive concepts*, i.e. using integrated technologies to stop ecological damage happening in the first place.

- Development of *reduction strategies*, i.e. using technology to minimize unavoidable damage.

- Development of *exploitation strategies*, i.e. feeding waste materials into a system of recycling.

- Development of *disposal concepts*, i.e. disposing safely of any waste left after running through the above procedure.

Current-status analysis

Ecological questions must be subsumed into business planning and decision-making processes. But before an operational, strategic and normative eco-corporate policy can be established, an analysis of the internal and external strategic factors at the inception of the programme must be undertaken.

The findings from this current-status analysis will be used to identify key issues in the various fields of the business. The essence of this procedure is to determine to what extent the business, with its profile of strengths and weaknesses, is ready to meet the opportunities and threats of the new ecological dimension.

To start with it is a good idea to request individual and common profiles of business values from the board of directors, in order to establish whether or not there is a unity of doctrine on social goals among board members.

Resource analysis: strengths/weaknesses

At this stage, ecological key issues in each field of the business are identified using individually drafted checklists, and solutions are proposed (strategic key issue analysis). The information is collected for relevant zones of observation, evaluated relative to the strongest rival, and its particular character noted.

The purposes of the information obtained from this analysis are as follows:

- Recognition of own strengths on which new strategies can be built.
- Recognition of own weaknesses, to be avoided in new strategies.
- Recognition of synergic potential to be gained from new strategies.
- Recognition of available means.
- Evaluation of present situation with regard to profitability factors.
- Recognition of strategic success potential (Pümpin, 1980).

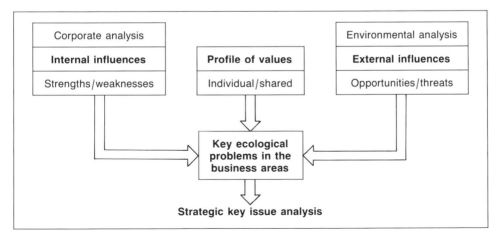

Figure 15 Eco-situational evaluation

By comparison with environmental analysis this information is relatively easy to gain from company data bases and control systems.

An analysis of internal strengths and weaknesses in the area of ecology relates to the following factors:

- In purchasing, do contacts exist with manufacturers of eco-friendly products? How secure is supply?

- Is sufficient finance available to fulfil legal regulations in the future? And to invest in eco-friendly solutions?

- Does the whole management have a positive attitude to ecological problems?

- Are the staff in agreement?

- To what extent do existing products and services conform to ecological changes: range, quality, price, packaging, distribution, etc.?

- To what extent are research activities and technical expertise already geared to the environment?

The answers to these questions will help to confirm whether the internal potential of the company is equal to the challenge.

The results of the resource analysis can be effectively presented in the form of a profile of strengths and weaknesses.

Environmental analysis: opportunities/threats

Any company stands in a relationship of open exchange with the environment and with other subjects of the economy, such as business rivals, suppliers, customers, investors, government and employees. It is therefore essential to have up-to-date knowledge of developments in the surrounding environment and to be prepared to respond to them. Change has to be built into the systems of planning and control. Although the means are already available in the form of environmental analysis, this is often treated like an unwanted child, particularly by small and intermediate companies.

> Business should not live in spite of environmental change but because of it. (Duch, 1985)

Investigating environmental factors relevant to business implies a prognosis about their future development. 'Environmental analysis is not about foreseeing the unforeseeable. It is about creating time before the problems become insoluble' (Grünewald, 1983).

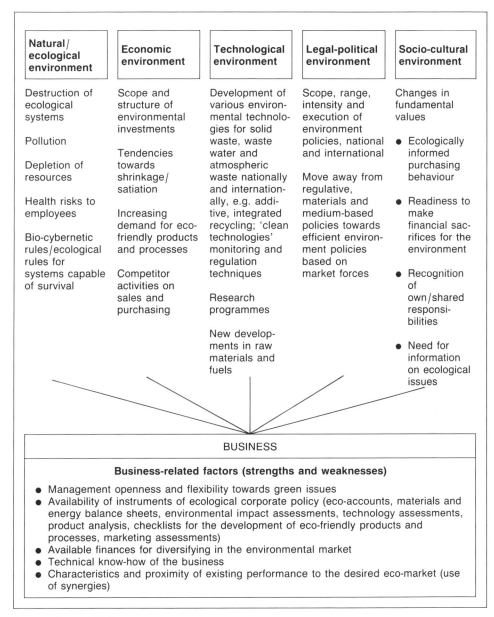

Natural/ ecological environment	Economic environment	Technological environment	Legal-political environment	Socio-cultural environment
Destruction of ecological systems	Scope and structure of environmental investments	Development of various environmental technologies for solid waste, waste water and atmospheric waste nationally and internationally, e.g. additive, integrated recycling; 'clean technologies' monitoring and regulation techniques	Scope, range, intensity and execution of environment policies, national and international	Changes in fundamental values
Pollution	Tendencies towards shrinkage/ satiation		Move away from regulative, materials and medium-based policies towards efficient environment policies based on market forces	• Ecologically informed purchasing behaviour
Depletion of resources				
Health risks to employees	Increasing demand for eco-friendly products and processes			• Readiness to make financial sacrifices for the environment
Bio-cybernetic rules/ecological rules for systems capable of survival	Competitor activities on sales and purchasing	Research programmes		• Recognition of own/shared responsibilities
		New developments in raw materials and fuels		• Need for information on ecological issues

BUSINESS

Business-related factors (strengths and weaknesses)

• Management openness and flexibility towards green issues
• Availability of instruments of ecological corporate policy (eco-accounts, materials and energy balance sheets, environmental impact assessments, technology assessments, product analysis, checklists for the development of eco-friendly products and processes, marketing assessments)
• Available finances for diversifying in the environmental market
• Technical know-how of the business
• Characteristics and proximity of existing performance to the desired eco-market (use of synergies)

Source: Antes (1988).

Figure 16 Environment-related factors (external opportunities and threats)

Possible areas of investigation and their associated data are unlimited, so it is necessary to be selective. There are various useful checklists available. External factors can be divided into the following fields of analysis:

- Social developments: changes in public opinion, value dynamics, priority given to environmental preservation, etc.

- Economic developments: trade and market analysis for eco-friendly products, purchasing power, activities of rivals as action/reaction, etc.

- Technical developments: technology for environmental protection, environmental clean-up, etc.

- Legal developments: national and international law making on environmental protection, the introduction or tightening of limits, changes in risks through the planned environmental liability law, etc.

In addition to general analysis, evaluation and analysis of the specific trade, or subsections of it, should be carried out. This can be further enhanced through competitor analysis, since a business has to build up and maintain its own competitive edge against rivals in the field. The following questions on rival ecological efficiency should be investigated:

- Which strategies are competitors following, and with how much success?

- What ecological values and goals can be discerned?

- Which strategies can be expected of competitors in the future? What are the possibilities, and the dangers?

- On which principles will rival strategies be based?

- What are their strengths?

- What are their weaknesses?

Internal factors \ External factors	OPPORTUNITIES	THREATS
STRENGTHS	New environmental protection laws offer new sales opportunities. Flexible management facilitates early entry into new areas.	New scientific knowledge about harmful effects from the production process. Technical know-how facilitates conversion to eco-friendly production methods.
WEAKNESSES	Potential demand, created by increased green awareness, cannot be responded to because of insufficient finance.	Rivals are offering eco-friendly alternatives. Lack of know-how slows down reactions to this.

Source: Meffert (1988).

Figure 17 Possible relationships between internal and external factors

The analysis should provide data on the probability and scale of reactions to the company's marketing conception, as well as the company's ability to protect itself from the forces of competition and to counter the reactions of rivals.

The effects of environmental developments on the company can be prognosticated in an analysis of opportunities and threats (see Figure 16).

Comparing the strengths and weaknesses profile with the results of resource analysis gives an enhanced evaluation. For example, if a development affects a business strength it could lead to an opportunity; if not, the danger signals can be seen. Meffert (1988) suggests a matrix to give an overview (see Figure 17).

Both analyses help to determine the corporate philosophy on ecology and to shape consistent strategies for solving key problems. They also facilitate an evaluation of the strategic eco-balance.

7

The environmental dimension in normative and strategic management

Ecology is the best form of economics. (Bosste/Nestle)

Influences in the normative field

Changes in corporate culture

Corporate culture is generally defined as the internally developed immutable 'hallmark' of a business. Management theory, however, has taken a long time to recognize that a company as a whole can generate powerful shared values which control the behaviour of its members. The close connection between corporate culture and corporate mission/guidelines is nowadays becoming more apparent. If values are taken as a yardstick, then every activity in a company contributes to the expression of these 'shared values'.

Organizational culture finds expression in the most varied forms, and to a certain extent it is also governed by external influences.

Key factors in ecological organizational culture

1. *Ecologically sensitive senior management*. This is most important as an example to the company, particularly since environmental protection is largely seen as something for the 'bosses'. In this leadership role managers must be prepared to encounter learning processes at every level of the hierarchy; these experiences should be accompanied by personal successes, providing the opportunity to gather experience. Active participation in company associations, attendance at lectures and conferences, writing articles in the company newsletter and formulating personal values as part of management image can all act as a trigger.

There should be no discrepancy between words and deeds. A manager's behaviour ought to reflect the ecological values he or she stands for.

2. *Setting the tone through symbols*. This can be achieved with cultural artefacts such as 'green' architecture, or through human actions. Such symbols can be developed ecologically in the following ways:

(a) How suggestions are made.

(b) The range of topics in discussion groups (e.g. eco-quality circles).

(c) Publication of an environmental bulletin.

(d) An eco-notice board.

(e) A new form of public relations.

(f) Dialogue with environmental organizations.

(g) Recycling containers for staff use.

(h) A post with environmental responsibility.

(i) Plants in the forecourt.

(j) Eco-friendly company cars.

3. *Changing behaviour via experiences of success.*

(a) Prize giving for suggestions.

(b) Special staff visits.

(c) Setting up courses and seminars.

(d) Changing training programmes.

(e) Staff pride in company image.

(f) Targeted bulletins about management activities.

(g) Press reports, etc.

Extension of corporate mission and guidelines

In every company there is a conscious or unconscious philosophy in which the values of the company or its directors are expressed. The company mission helps to give a business its identity in the minds of staff and the public. A growing number of companies have formulated the values they hold in the form of written guidelines or management profiles.

To conduct 'green business' with minimum harm to the environment and careful use of natural resources, ecological views should be incorporated into the guidelines. This gives company policies a new direction. Objectives, strategies and instruments are imbued with an ecological dimension. If company behaviour does not change in response to increased concern about the environment then conflict could easily arise and market opportunities could be missed.

The current intensification of economic, legal and ethical conditions makes it imperative to change from defensive environmental protection policies to a more proactive approach which is firmly fixed in institutional forms. In other words, environmental management must be used as an instrument for building up competitive advantage. Increasing public criticism of the relentless accretion of material welfare and technological advancement alongside a worsening of lifestyle makes it clear that 'quality of life' is not simply a function of economic living standards.

The new call to base strategic management on socially orientated marketing should be looked at in the cold light of day. Very few businesses attribute high enough status to ecological or social aspects in their company guidelines. The success of this strategy depends on a high investment of confidence in the public and the ability to develop socially relevant solutions.

> How is the time-honoured discrepancy between Sunday-talk (ethics) and workday-action (politics, economics) to be narrowed? How are ethical maxims ever to be realized adequately, concretely, operationally? Formulating maxims sometimes amounts to saying goodbye to reality. Insignificant improvements are boosted up out of all proportion to create a diversion. Words are no substitute for action. (Seidel, 1989)

This type of business plan has been treated with caution at various symposia. These 'paper principles', it has been claimed, will 'wait in the archives until their resurrection'. The need for real-life ethics has been stressed (Nahrendorf, 1989).

Managers planning social guidelines should not forget that organizational change has to be introduced carefully and that planning instruments, strategies and management concepts are required. Otherwise one cannot expect staff who are labouring under short-sighted, profit-based systems to take up socially orientated attitudes.

Some criteria for social responsibility are as follows:

• Company recognition of social and therefore environmental responsibilities.

• Responsible use of resources.

• Active quest for eco-friendly products, production and disposal procedures.

• Positive moves towards integrated concepts of environmental protection.

- Co-operative exchange of information between various groups in society and company staff.

- Equal value given to economic, social and ecological goals.

With a company eco-philosophy formulated in this way, environmental protection can be drawn under the umbrella of company policy as an integral component. The guidelines contain evaluation criteria on which successive levels of the hierarchy can base decision making. The content of these regulations is binding on all staff.

◇ Ciba-Geigy

In its management profile Ciba-Geigy sets 'Environmental protection and safety in line with the latest technology' as an equal goal along with production innovation and profitability. The following paragraphs appeared as early as 1973 in company principles published by Ciba-Geigy:

> We are aware that business is not an end in itself but that it must serve man and society. Economic success depends upon fulfilling the following tasks.
> In the pursuit of its economic goals the company must not only follow its own advantage but take account of its impact on staff and the environment. To do justice to these claims, norms have been formulated which will guide future behaviour ... We recognize that supplies of natural raw materials, earth, air and water, are limited ... We make an active contribution to environmental protection, particularly making use of the most recent scientific knowledge to ensure that our products do not have deleterious effects on the environment, either in production or in their intended use.

In 1984 a directive on production was issued to company subsidiaries worldwide:

1. The protection of the environment is an important determining factor in the manufacture of our products.

2. We aim to solve potential environmental problems at source. For this reason we employ environmentally just processes in the manufacture of our products. Reusable materials are reintroduced into the manufacturing process whenever possible.

3. We dispose of by-products and waste using technologies which keep environmental damage to a minimum.

4. Each member of staff is co-responsible for the protection of the environment. We cater for training and instruction.

5. We inform our staff, customers and the public about our environmental protection methods.

6. We seek to nurture open collaboration with the authorities.

◇ Hoechst

The guidelines on environmental protection and safety formulated by Hoechst are very similar:

> We strive to improve our international competitiveness. Alongside the goal of profitability stand, equally, responsibility for our staff and social acceptance of our business, sparing use of our resources and care of the environment. Our company goals are at one with the ethical values of our culture and society ... Economic viability and security of our operations are of equal importance. Production and productivity must never be at the cost of safety ...
> Environmental protection is a component of our company policy. At Hoechst the demands of environmental protection on our initiative and responsibility lead to the following principles:

- The environment should be polluted as little as possible by our activities.

- We adopt preventive measures; research, development and production departments give due consideration to the environment in the early stages of product development.

- Raw materials and energy are used economically and by-products are fed back into the production process.

- Pollution is reduced through the choice of suitable methods and through transfer to more suitable methods where possible.

- We use advanced technology for cleansing waste gases and water, for waste disposal and noise reduction. We are also developing methods which can help others to solve environmental problems.

- We constantly monitor our emissions with modern instrumentation. By checking our own waste we form a good basis for wider environmental protection.

- We wish to improve staff knowledge by means of specialized information, regular training and instruction, and to make full use of knowledge gained in our laboratories and production plants.

- We encourage suggestions from staff for improvements in the field of environmental protection.

- We provide customers and consumers with details on the properties of our products and their safe transportation and disposal. Our products are intended to be safe and harmless to the environment.

- Hoechst collaborates with experts and with the authorities in the area of environmental protection.

- At Hoechst we seek good relationships with our neighbours. Alongside our own measures for protecting the environment we have growing confidence in public information on environmental issues.

◇ IBM

At IBM, management documents are viewed as a kind of internal constitution, the highest being the 'corporate principles'. The document covers respect for the individual, service to the customer, the achievement of excellence, effective management, responsibility to shareholders, fair treatment of transporters and finally 'responsibility towards society'.

Management principles derive from corporate principles. Within 'Personal Responsibility' the topic of environmental protection is treated in more detail:

- All laws, regulations and duties imposed by the legislature as well as the even stricter internal standards are to be followed.

- Environment-friendly production processes are to be developed using environment friendly materials.

- A minimum of raw materials are to be used, and resources are to be reused if possible.

- Energy-saving processes and technologies are to be used.

- All technically possible measures are to be taken for the protection of the environment.

◇ Elida Gibbs Germany

Under the heading 'Environmental and Health Issues Policy', Elida Gibbs makes the following pledges:

1. Elida Gibbs wishes to ensure and to preserve for the future, the freedom to use new and existing raw materials and production methods which
   - conform to legal and environmental restrictions
   - are seen by ourselves and society as safe for staff, consumers and the environment.
2. Elida Gibbs assures that its policy will not be put out of force by other operating policies.
3. Elida Gibbs is collaborating with leading experts on the environmental scene to maintain an up-to-date view.
4. Elida Gibbs will research all products and manufacturing processes and alter anything potentially hazardous.
5. New products will be developed on the basis of observation of trends in the field of environmental health.
6. Elida Gibbs will have a positive attitude towards the environment even when this is not perceived by the consumer (packaging, disposal, production).
7. Elida Gibbs ensures that all staff understand their responsibility for the environment. Elida Gibbs will create information, training and motivation to fulfil the requirements of the policy.
8. The policy will be implemented by the chairman.
9. Company strategy will expressly embrace environmental and health issues.

◇ **BP**

The following environmental principles apply to BP Germany:

■ Basic regulations and duties represent the minimum standard.

■ Audits will be carried out at appropriate intervals to ensure that our plants meet environmental requirements.

■ The company takes an active part in the further development of environmental protection and will collaborate closely with the authorities, research institutes and both scientific and technical bodies to fulfil this purpose.

■ The effects of new products on the environment, their manufacture and their use, will be carefully evaluated and acted upon.

■ Management and staff must be adequately informed about their duties and the duties of the company towards environmental protection. Suppliers must also be fully informed and abide by the detailed regulations.

Codes of behaviour

In recent years, various institutions at national and international level have developed guidelines for members. The Davos Manifesto, one of the first of these, states under point 4: 'Businesses must serve society. Management must preserve a worthwhile environment for future generations and use the knowledge and means at its disposal for the good of society.'

The International Chamber of Commerce (ICC), the only worldwide economic organization, with 7,000 members in 100 countries, is also a pioneer in the promulgation of rules to which the economic community should respond voluntarily. In 1974 it published environmental guidelines which were revised in 1981.

The chemical industry is one of the areas most directly affected by environmental issues. The European Chemical Industry Federation (CEFIC) has published guidelines for the protection of the environment. A range of work has been carried out by other organizations: for example, the Valdez Principles (1989) of the Social Investment Forum (Boston) in the project 'Coalition for Environmentally Responsible Economics'.

In April 1991, with the collaboration of the International Chamber of Commerce and the UN Environmental Protection Agency (UNEP), the second World Industry Conference of Environmental Management took place. Decisions were made on a plan already drawn up by the ICC in Bergen (The Industry Agenda for Action). The plan outlines a Business Charter for Sustainable Development, which, by the end of May 1991, had already been signed by over 250 companies and business organizations. (The author was one of the members of the German Commission which prepared a draft for

THE BUSINESS CHARTER FOR SUSTAINABLE DEVELOPMENT:
Principles for Environmental Management

1. Corporate priority
To recognize environmental management as among the highest corporate priorities and as a key determinant to sustainable development; to establish policies, programmes and practices for conducting operations in an environmentally sound manner.

2. Integrated management
To integrate these policies, programmes and practices, fully into each business as an essential element of management in all its functions.

3. Process of improvement
To continue to improve corporate policies, programmes and environmental performance, taking into account technical developments, scientific understanding, consumer needs and community expectations, with legal regulations as a starting point; and to apply the same environmental criteria internationally.

4. Employee education
To educate, train and motivate employees to conduct their activities in an environmentally responsible manner.

5. Prior assessment
To assess environmental impacts before starting a new activity or project and before decommissioning a facility or leaving a site.

6. Products and services
To develop and provide products or services that have no undue environmental impact and are safe in their intended use, that are efficient in their consumption of energy and natural resources, and that can be recycled, reused or disposed of safely.

7. Customer advice
To advise, and where relevant educate, customers, distributors and the public in the safe use, transportation, storage and disposal of products provided; and to apply similar considerations to the provision of services.

8. Facilities and operations
To develop, design and operate facilities and conduct activities taking into consideration the efficient use of energy and materials, the sustainable use of renewable resources, the minimization of adverse environmental impact and waste generation, and the safe and responsible disposal of residual waste.

9. Research

To conduct or support research on the environmental impacts of raw materials, products, processes, emissions and wastes associated with the enterprise and on the means of minimizing such adverse impacts.

10. Precautionary approach

To modify the manufacture, marketing or use of products or services or the conduct of activities, consistent with scientific and technical understanding, to prevent serious or irreversible environmental degradation.

11. Contractors and suppliers

To promote the adoption of these principles by contractors acting on behalf of the enterprise, encouraging and, where appropriate, requiring improvements in their practices to make them consistent with those of the enterprise; and to encourage the wider adoption of these principles by suppliers.

12. Emergency preparedness

To develop and maintain, where significant hazards exist, emergency preparedness plans in conjunction with the emergency services, relevant authorities and the local community, recognizing potential transboundary impacts.

13. Transfer of technology

To contribute to the transfer of environmentally sound technology and management methods throughout the industrial and public sectors.

14. Contributing to the common effort

To contribute to the development of public policy and to business, governmental and intergovernmental programmes and educational initiatives that will enhance environmental awareness and protection.

15. Openness to concerns

To foster openness and dialogue with employees and the public, anticipating and responding to their concerns about the potential hazards and impacts of operations, products, wastes or services, including those of transboundary or global significance.

16. Compliance and reporting

To measure environmental performance; to conduct regular environmental audits and assessments of compliance with company requirements, legal requirements and these principles; and periodically to provide appropriate information to the board of directors, shareholders, employees, the authorities and the public.

this code.) This charter is a key element in industry's commitment to voluntary action.

The main thrust of these declarations is rhetorical, since voluntary obligation to the environment is purely a moral question. Also, the goals are formulated in very broad and general terms.

There is a need for a universally accepted and precisely worded code of behaviour for environmental management. With this framework standards could be assessed in the context of real industrial activities. Common goals and guidelines with a moral or ethical dimension are to be welcomed, but they have to be made into legally binding obligations to have a real effect on the disparity between norms and facts.

Influences in the strategic field

Changes in goals and objectives

Those affected by the relationship between economic interests and ecological demands may have divergent views, for the following reasons:

● The fundamental contradiction between ecology and economy.

● The tension between ecology and economy requiring compromise.

● The precedence of ecological demands over economic interests, or vice versa.

There is wide agreement about integrating environmental protection with overall goals, but the status of environmental protection is disputed. Some say it is a government concern; others a basic right. Environmental protection can be construed as a problem of choosing the optimum way forward for everyone.

Individual evaluations of environmental stress expose the essential conflict between the man-made and the natural environment. On the one hand, man wants to preserve the natural world; on the other hand, he wants to avoid any restrictions on the satisfaction of his consumer needs. In the first stage of seeking the best solution, political decisions lead to a consensus on how far each goal could be fulfilled. According to Steger (1989): 'The question of how much pollution we accept as the result of economy and the processes of living, how much damage to nature we are ready to accept, is normative. In a democracy, it must surely be decided upon by the relevant parliamentary committee.'

At the Conference of German Engineers in 1989, Poppel, the president of the Association of German Engineers (VDI), stressed the need for social consensus on what 'standard of consumption' we can 'afford' in terms of ecology and economy.

The resulting balance thus reflects social priorities. Linke (1988) sees the following requirements:

- The system of regulations must be based on what is currently feasible.

- Once priorities are established they must be fulfilled within a time-scale which agrees with the timing of economic planning and realization.

- Laws and regulations must be agreed on a worldwide basis in accordance with the network of international political and economic relations.

- Regulations should specify effects, not the means of achieving them. The character of each company is expressed by how it interprets the details of the social context set out by the legislature.

In the second stage of seeking the best solution, the technology of the business has to be set up with minimal negative effect on the environment. 'For an individual company this means not merely directing technology against pollution but basing the actual company policy on environmental goals' (Siemens, 1986). It is possible to assume that:

- Profitability is the primary goal of business.

- Environmental measures involve financial costs or loss of revenue.

and that therefore there is a conflict between economic and ecological goals.

This view of environmental protection as a competing factor in the fulfilment of market aims leads to a tendency to do only the minimum required, or to try to gain time or leniency in dealings with the authorities. Not enough recognition is given to the fact that our efforts to achieve profitability and environmental protection can, in some specific areas, complement each other well against the backdrop of changing consumer attitudes. For example, there might be the following benefits:

- Competitive advantage through innovation in environmental protection.

- Active anticipation of legal developments and, later, of consumer demands.

- The possibility of diversification.

- Opportunities for image improvement; innovation potential.

- Savings on energy and materials.

The overlap between ecological and individual economic goals is greater than one might think. In cases where environmental protection is seen not as a burden, but as a market opportunity, it seems necessary to plan a corporate concept:

- In which company goals are to be expanded with the new components of tolerance and care for the environment.

- On the basis of an appropriate long-term policy document, in order to ensure that ecological values will influence company decisions in the future.

If there is no modification of corporate goals and objectives, the short-sighted profit orientation will begin to reduce the strategic competitive potential offered by the development of eco-friendly products and procedures.

It is not difficult to introduce profitable or at least neutral environmental measures and the following pragmatic series of priorities is suggested:

- Legally prescribed measures.
- Measures useful to the company.
- Measures with neutral effect on costs.
- Finally, measures which the company has to pay for.

Strebel (1980) emphasizes the point that a flow of information is vitally important in helping to anchor the environment into the bed-rock of company goals:

> Technological possibilities must be known in advance and it is useful to be apprised of alternative eco-friendly materials, procedures, processes and products. Input and output stages of production can be assisted by chemical analyses and calculations of energy consumption. Even with these measures it is not always possible to determine which processes or substances will constitute 'pollution'. Often the ecological effects of new synthetic materials are quite unknown.
>
> In addition, cumulative effects from different emissions, synergic effects and interactions cannot easily be anticipated. There are so many gaps in technical knowledge of toxins, combinations of pollutants and concentrations that it is generally rather foolish to describe any substance as environmentally friendly.

During this process of evaluation a company also has to take into account the system of values held by society.

Traditionally, organizational objectives have been directed towards achieving economic and financial success, which is then supplemented by social objectives. According to Dyllick (1989b), an environmental objective must apply to protecting resources, limiting emissions and cutting risks (see Figure 18). This has the effect of expanding the economic profit principle by the addition of a 'human principle' and the principle of 'least possible harm to the environment' (Figure 19).

Development of environmental strategies

It is the responsibility of strategic management to ensure the future competitiveness of a company by developing or initiating success potentials such as image, competence or share of the market. Successful management will have to expand its sphere of influence to embrace a considerably wider concept

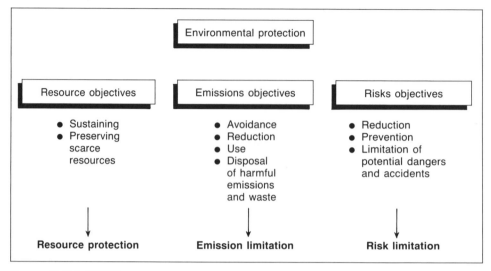

Source: Dyllick (1989b).

Figure 18 Environmental objectives

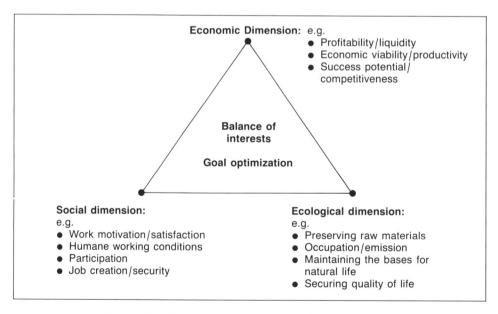

Figure 19 The enlarged context of management

of the environment including ecological and social as well as economic and technical factors.

The need for these strategies is imposed by constantly changing conditions. To respond to this state of flux a company should undertake the following:

- Identify long-term tendencies as soon as possible to reduce risks (early warning system).

- Try to control threats and opportunities by active influence on the market.

- Create time for rebuilding and reorganizing potential.

- Replace short-term views with strategies for increasing potential as the basis for long-term survival and profit.

- Build up long-term advantages based on meeting customer needs, but not by transplanting the values of the past into the future.

Companies respond to the influence of the environment in two basically different ways:

- Passive strategies of environmental protection, i.e. responding to governmental pressure, operating just within the limits, reactive communications policy.

- Active strategies of environmental protection, i.e. a priori integration into all phases of planning in order to gain competitiveness, active communications policy.

For Wicke (1987) proactive environmental protection is preferable to a defensive position for a number of reasons:

- Defensive behaviour means that chances of lowering costs and increasing turnover are missed in the long term.

- Defensive behaviour provokes growing pressure from environmentalism.

- Eco-friendly product creation can be cheaper.

- Many companies lose kudos through clumsy, defensive handling of information.

On the basis of this, Meffert et al. (1986) set out four types of adaptation:

1. The innovation type: pursues active, customer-orientated marketing.

2. The social responsibility type: characterized by lack of customer orientation in marketing.

3. The adaptation type: does have an ecologically based marketing strategy, but only as much as legally necessary.

4. The ignorant type: has neither an ecological marketing strategy nor an active environmental strategy.

Ecological strategies demonstrate innovation, co-operation and communication (Dyllick, 1989b). Innovation applies to all three environmental protection objectives: use of resources, limitation of emissions and limitation of risks. Co-operation is particularly relevant to other agents in the production chain (consumer, trade, neighbouring community, etc.). Finally, the role of communication is principally to widen the range of company strategies, to develop dialogue and so on.

Different marketing activities need to be planned for the various strategic units of a company. Established planning instruments such as portfolio analysis and scenarios are available for evolving basic ecological strategies.

Meffert proposes an ecology portfolio for the derivation of sound strategies with the following dimensions:

- Threat to the environment; extent of the negative effects produced by the business.

- Advantages to the company from ecologically orientated behaviour; quantitative advantages such as share of the market and qualitative advantages such as improved image. (See Figure 20.)

In its matrix the portfolio uses data from the current-state analysis (strengths/weaknesses–opportunities/threats). Both dimensions can be described with a set of given indicators. For example, pollution could be the atmospheric, water, ground or noise pollution caused by production, use or disposal. Increasing the share of the market, profit, productivity, loyalty to brand and co-operation with

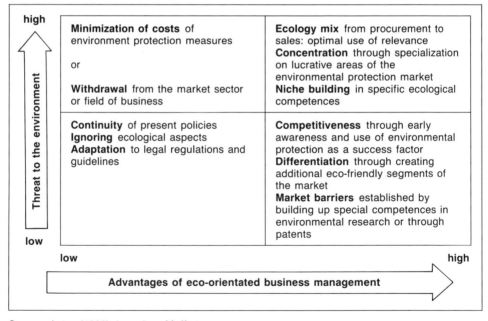

Source: Antes (1988), based on Meffert.

Figure 20 Ecology portfolio

the authorities, and lowering costs, are all possible determinants of commercial advantage which can be gained from green behaviour.

Individual combinations of products and market (strategic business units) are located in the four matrix fields according to the characteristics of the dimension (low/high). From the resulting position in the matrix, norms of behaviour associated with this quadrant are derived. Individual interpretation is required to define appropriate market strategies:

Quadrant 1

● Low in both dimensions.

● Increasing marketing activities brings no advantages; better to wait for further developments.

Quadrant 2

● Low burden on the environment, high advantages.

● Targeted introduction of instruments to increase image as an environmentally conscious business; possibilities for checking modifications or diversification.

Quadrant 3

● High burden on the environment, no advantages.

● Withdraw or improve environmental performance, although no advantage to be gained in this sector.

Quadrant 4

● High in both dimensions.

● Intensify the concentration of ecological measures; eco-concept has been recognized; develop innovations in communications policy.

After this rough positioning, the next step is to 'check the effects of additional environmental activities, analyzing compatibility with present strategy and effect on the market, in order to clarify the relationship between environmental goals and profitability' (Steger, 1988). (See Figure 21.)

Since the same environmental protection measures can have different consequences according to the type of business strategy, four possible outcomes are projected on to three market structures in a market–environment–reaction matrix (Figure 22).

> The analysis of goals and decision criteria gained from this exercise puts us in the position to discuss the opportunities and threats of individual strategies. It is already clear, though, that they are most successful when they induce innovations or provide added value. (Steger, 1988)

Competitive strategies Environmental effects	Rise in costs	Reduction in performance	Additional value	Innovation
Price dominance	–	0	0	+
Differentiation	0	–	+	+
Niche policy:				
a) Cost orientated	–	0	0	+
b) Differentiated	0	–	+	+
	– Negative relation			
	0 Neutral relation			
	+ Positive relation			

Source: Steger (1989).

Figure 21 Environmental protection–competition matrix

Market sensitivity to environment protection Environmental effects	Rise in costs	Reduction in performance	Additional value	Innovation
Sensitive	+ / 0	+	+	+
Potentially sensitive	?	?	+	+
Insensitive	–	–	0	0/ +
	+ Positive market reaction			
	0 Neutral market reaction			
	– Negative market reaction			
	? Uncertain market reaction			

Source: Steger (1989).

Figure 22 Market–environment reaction matrix

The following measures are needed for environmental strategy planning based on ecological market choice decisions:

1. Determine the extent of market cover and diversification of marketing programme.
2. Establish one's essential behaviour in relation to other participants in the market.
3. Refine product and programme strategy.
4. Establish the introduction of marketing instruments (Meffert *et al.*, 1986).

8

The materials management approach to a 'closed loop' economy

Financial gain can also be acquired through environmental forms of business, provided that we shift from an open-ended input/output economy to a circulatory economy. Classical, one-way economy is characterized by short-lived products which use large amounts of raw materials and energy for production and which cannot easily be reused and therefore quickly become waste. Circulation economy aims at maximum use of products which are made from reusable resources. It is quite likely that we can switch from curative to preventive strategies much more quickly than is currently imagined.

(Atteslander, 1989)

Away from cowboy economics

An ecological materials economy is absolutely indispensable to any attempt at environmental business management. Blom (1988) identifies two forms of change which are required in this context: changes within the triangle of the traditional materials economy; and the change from a one-way economy to a circulation economy.

This involves giving new priority to the following environmental objectives:

- Conservation of resources.
- Full use of input materials.
- Product and production low in pollution.

Instead of a wasteful one-way 'cowboy' economy characterized by waste of energy and raw materials, assuming endless supplies and unlimited consumer needs, manufacture of 'high-entropy', throw-away products and mindless use of the sea, air and ground as dustbins, Blom recommends a circulation economy. Its main features are as follows:

- Reusable resources.
- Low drain on energy.
- Low-entropy economy.
- Consciousness of the limits of material growth.
- Manufacture of long-life, eco-friendly goods.
- Extensive recycling.
- Ecological company planning.

The ecological yardstick extends to:

- Choice of supplier and product quality.
- Choice of materials.
- Description of performance (construction and function in terms of environmental impact).
- Sparing use of materials.
- Reuse, recycling, transport, disposal.

Stahlmann (1988a) sees materials management as the natural forerunner of ecological business management. Thinking in terms of materials is self-evident at this level. Ecologically integrated materials management has to address the following problems:

- Investigation of material needs: co-operation in developing environmental primary needs, co-ordination of sales prognoses and materials objectives, the investigation of secondary needs via parts lists, etc.
- Procurement of materials considering ecological criteria.
- Control of materials: investigation of process parameters, work plans, batch sizes, running times, timing, draft planning, fine tuning, workshop management.
- Storage of materials: access, types of store, organization, avoidance of accidental damage to the environment.
- Distribution of materials and logistics: principles of material flow, internal transportation, haulage, physical distribution.
- Stock planning, analysis and control: according to various net product levels, groups of materials, locations, measures for keeping stock to a minimum in order not to tie up resources unnecessarily.

- Rationalization: through numbering, standardization, material analysis and cost minimizing; eco-friendly use of materials.

When the requirement for economical, eco-friendly production methods is intensified, materials management will play a key part because the necessary innovations depend upon the provision of adequate materials. Stahlmann (1988a) sees logistic thinking, based on careful observation of each stage of the production process, as a prerequisite for dealing with ecological questions (see Chapter 17).

Implications for purchasing

The area of materials purchasing will be looked at more closely by way of an example. Corsten and Götzelmann have drawn up a comprehensive list of input factors:

- Creation of purchasing regulations for eco-friendly raw materials, subsidiary materials and fuels, including other production factors.
- Checklists for investigating the suitability of recycled production factors at each stage.
- Summary of internal and external recycling possibilities.
- Principles for choosing suppliers (e.g. awareness of the ecological dimension of services offered or influencing suppliers in ecological terms; see Chapter 16).
- Close co-operation with other areas in the company, e.g. R & D and sales.
- Co-operative agreements horizontally and vertically.

Within the realm of materials purchasing a company can attempt to induce suppliers to substitute eco-friendly alternatives to, for example, paint, paper, plastics, cleaning materials and cars. This presupposes, of course, that detailed research has been carried out in the purchasing market, and it also relies on the co-operation of suppliers. Various manuals are available, giving details of environment-friendly products.

It is also commendable to have the environmental effects of materials specified in purchase agreements. Many companies put strong pressure on suppliers to provide data sheets on the contents of materials purchased.

◇ Students' Supply Organization, Munich

At the beginning of the winter semester 1988/9 the Students' Supply Organization in Munich transferred to the use of eco-friendly cleaning materials and disinfectants.

With its ten refectories and bars the Students' Supply Organization has a special role to play in protecting the environment, not only because of the number of facilities but also in order to set an example.

The organization's environmental protection measures do not merely diminish environmental problems, they help to motivate others to do so. Furthermore, these measures increase competitiveness in the market for eco-friendly products and methods.

For these reasons the cleaning department of the Students' Supply Organization, Munich, has developed a scheme for introducing environment-friendly cleaning materials and disinfectants. The goal is:

■ Reduction of total amounts of cleaning materials used.

■ Predominant use of eco-friendly products.

■ Withdrawal of materials dangerous to health.

■ Introduction of a dispensing system to cut down work and reduce materials.

During stocktaking all materials have been listed and a catalogue of the different substances required has been produced. It sets down the following conditions:

■ Products should, as far as possible, be free from chlorine, phosphates, formaldehyde, chlorinated hydrocarbons, strong acids, alkalis, bleaches or hydrofluoric acid.

■ Contents, recommended amount and use should should be clearly marked on packaging.

■ Empty containers should be returnable to the manufacturer.

On the basis of the catalogue of requirements the Students' Union gave out a tender and received offers from various manufacturers, which were examined with the help of a chemist. After talks with individual firms the cleaning department started a three-month trial on selected cleaning materials in summer 1989. Individual products were evaluated under the following headings:

■ Chemical composition.

■ Ease of handling.

■ Safety.

■ Returnability of empty containers.

■ Dispensing systems.

■ Cleaning results.

■ Cost.

Cleaning materials were chosen with the help of these criteria and have since been used exclusively in all areas.

The cleaning department hopes to have found a long-term solution which will lead to improved health and protection of the environment as well as the highest standards of cleanliness.

◇ Bischof and Klein

Apart from substituting eco-friendly raw materials, purchasing can have an influence on product development and production technology. This example from Bischof and Klein, a distinguished manufacturer of packaging materials, shows some of the difficulties of obtaining information from suppliers.

At Bischof and Klein:

- The first stage is to record each material used in production, with the help of a materials list.
- In the second stage, criteria of environmental compatibility are drawn up on the basis of this list and applied to purchasing policies (cf. the example of Siemens Ltd on cooling lubricants, p. 91).
- In the third stage, the environmentally friendly alternative is selected for the 100 or more materials provided by over 100 suppliers.

Lists of requirements for eco-friendly raw materials were sent to all possible suppliers. Half of them did not respond to the first mailing and only 15 per cent of the replies were useful. Today, after the sixth set of mailings, Bischof and Klein has a good overview and is in the position to give its customers details of product constituents and to work on environmental product development in its own laboratories.

◇ IBM

At IBM, the suppliers' responsibility for environmental protection is controlled by a set of company instructions. The general goal is to ensure that suppliers to IBM remain within environmental protection laws.

When complete processes are contracted out to suppliers, IBM has to ensure that pollution levels are not higher than on its own premises.

Notes on the selection and assessment of suppliers at IBM Germany

- Decision to move the process in the first place.
- Note environmental influences from the process (statement/evaluation).
- Seek suppliers.
- First assessment of a potential supplier: visit to supplier, general assessment of supplier and his business environment, gathering information on the supplier, overall evaluation.
- IBM must inform suppliers of risks to the environment.
- Suppliers must confirm annually to IBM that all environmental laws are being upheld; all necessary licences have been obtained for storage, transport and disposal of waste; appropriate waste water treatment is available and approved; appropriate treatment of waste gases is available and approved; an environmental protection insurance policy has been taken out.
- File on other environmentally relevant data.

Supplier environmental impact assessment at IBM Germany

Aim: to facilitate environmental evaluation, current overview as well as quick information in case of emergencies. Detailed information is not required as it is for in-house processes in the form of environmental impact assessments (EIAs). The contents of these supplier EIAs are as follows:

1. Description of the process.

2. Machine-list, with previous EIA as a reference.

3. Chemicals list (types and quantities).

4. Supplier chemicals balance sheet, for IBM processes (planned quantity; residue: solid, liquid, gaseous waste, recycling).

5. Blue book: basic care and disposal requirements.

6. Environmental protection statement, influences and first evaluation by supplier.

Not included:

■ Confirmation of any kind by supplier.

■ Copies of licences, reports from investigations, etc.

■ Supervisor's signature for chemicals provided.

■ Individual EIAs.

Procedure:

■ Issue of a supplier EIA before taking on a potential supplier, so that the evaluation is ready before the decision to use the supplier.

■ Up-date required in cases of alterations to chemicals or machines, at least annually.

■ Appointment of a member of staff for each supplier, responsible for dialogue on environmental protection.

◇ Siemens

This example shows the kind of problem which can be caused by large numbers. It is often no longer possible to achieve the dialogue between supplier and receiver which aims to reduce environmental strain.

Environmentally responsible behaviour at input affects three areas (Siemens, 1986):

■ Information about pollution caused by one's own input and the attempt to minimize supplier pollution.

■ Environmentally sensitive organization of the acquisition process, by using appropriate storage during transportation and minimizing energy consumption.

■ Avoidance of excessive product requirements placed as a customer on the supplier.

The number of relationships between an organization and its suppliers can be seen from a breakdown of purchasing quantities.

At Siemens Co. these figures for the business year 1983/84 gave the following picture:

Total volume of materials	DM19.2 billion
Number of suppliers worldwide	120,000 suppliers
Orders for Siemens Co.	3 million orders, about 5 million items
Classified internally as	1,000 groups of goods
Dealt with by	216 purchasing departments

Source: Siemens (1986).

Figure 23   Purchasing: a problem of numbers

There are typically five problems encountered within the critical areas of input, production process and output. Siemens provides an exemplary outline based on environmentally dangerous input behaviour:

■ One must be aware of the relationship between input and environmental burden in order to look for suitable alternative solutions.

■ Knowledge, often not available within the company, is needed to find such alternatives.

■ The question of resulting costs.

■ Environmentally relevant information is not passed on.

■ The threshold of social inhibition about passing on environmentally relevant information.

Internal data collection by Siemens on cooling lubricants
Special lubricants are used for removing metal in the construction of power stations, plants and motors, and in the mechanical preparation of electrical appliances. These lubricants are pumped on to the working surface to cool it and to minimize wear on the cutting edges. The composition of this kind of lubricant is the outcome of years of experience.

Due to technical considerations it became necessary to rationalize the unmanageable range of cooling lubricants used at Siemens. This was an opportunity to look into working conditions and environmental hygiene. The 30 or so European manufacturers included in the Siemens research named about 300 products, of which 200 were selected for closer inspection.

As a result of this stocktaking there is now an internal catalogue of information on manufacturer specifications to which the production engineer can refer.

Historical data on suitability, durability, material tolerance and residue-free cleansing are recorded, as well as data on composition, toxicity, safety, possible problems in disposal and environmental causes for concern. Only with this document is it possible to select subsidiary materials with consideration for the environment as well as on technical criteria.

The medical knowledge gained will be published after collaboration with company doctors.

Demand patterns of public procurement

Germany was one of the first countries to take account of the fact that public and commercial procurement offices order products and services. In the Federal Republic this amounts to approximately DM120 billion (£40 billion), and this size of demand potential could provide a significant boost for environment-friendly products. This potential has been activated in a responsible move by the public procurement offices to amend the regulations. This is clarified in the explanation for Section 8, Number 3, of the VOL/A (German official regulation on contractual services). 'In consideration of the principles of economy and cost effectiveness, only such requirements are to be placed as are absolutely necessary for carrying out the service applied for. In this framework the exigencies of environmental protection can be observed.'

Numerous notices at federal, state and local levels expressly draw attention to these possibilities. There is no obligation to take the cheapest offer. The eco-friendly option is accepted as the more economical if 'its price is higher by a reasonable margin than a less environment-friendly offer' (Wicke, 1989).

In almost all federal states of Germany, the 'Blue Angel' (Germany's eco-label) is shown as a useful guide to placing an order.

9

Production management as the management of residue

◆   ◆   ◆

Environmentally orientated production

Although the principle of prevention is officially given precedence, in reality environmental politics as they are currently practised consist of retrospective improvements or the removal of damage already done. It is absolutely vital to move forward from this curative position towards direct influence on production methods and products themselves. Instead of repair, avoidance or at least reuse.

The concept of prevention makes it necessary to see the complete process of procuring raw materials, production and disposal as a unified whole. Optimization must embrace ecological as well as economic and technical criteria.

However, figures for 1989 from the Federal Statistics Office in Germany show that investments in integrated environmental technology have been stagnating at 20 per cent of total investment since the middle of the 1970s. Environmental protection plant (DM63 billion, £21 billion) as a proportion of stock in hand (DM1,734 billion, £600 billion) has risen in the production industries from 2.8 per cent in 1980 to 3.6 per cent.

As mentioned earlier, industrial production is inevitably connected to some kind of residue. To reduce this residual burden, the ecological instruments (i.e. avoidance, reduction or use) must be applied at two levels:

● The residual burden induced by production.

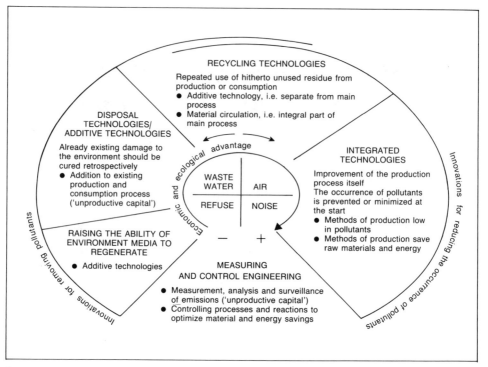

Source: Antes (1988).

Figure 24 Rules for product design

- The residual burden induced by the products themselves, at development, consumption or disposal stages.

At the production stage, planning and implementing avoidance strategies are largely technical problems. As well as thinking in terms of the circulation of usable materials, we must begin to think about the cycles of actual substances we use, paying particular attention to the protection of natural resources and limiting emissions.

Vester (1988) suggests cybernetic technologies, meaning combined technologies like symbioses, recycling, energy chains and multiple usage. Industrial use of residue in the form of recycling will be dealt with separately in Chapter 10, but it must be emphasized that, even with the best recycling management, product-induced emissions will remain with us.

Stahel (1990) calls for a 'strategy of durability' as the centre of a new kind of sustainable development. Connected with this is the move away from short-term product and sales strategies towards a policy of long-term usage, without damaging progress and comfort or changing fashions. The concept of durability is at the heart of holistic product management from design to disposal.

All these concepts have in common the call to make the quantum leap from the rapid linear progress of production–consumption–waste, to a strategy of 'usage loops'. Stahel suggests the following:

- *Modular construction*. This kind of design system facilitates standardized functional units and a means of connecting together the individual compatible components, thereby prolonging the durability of the system.

- *Long-life goods*. As complete products, these last longer than traditional competitive goods. An example is the energy-saving light bulb.

- *Prolongation of usefulness*. This can be achieved in various ways at the level of product and component: reusability (returnable bottles); repair (cars after an accident); refilling (ink cartridges); hi-tech (upgrading PC performance by making circuit boards replaceable).

- *Usage cascades*. Old goods can be used for less demanding purposes (e.g. an express train can be used for goods and then shunting).

- *Fleet managers*. Do not sell a single product or system but rather the use of it (e.g. car hire).

Prolongation of use which depends on reusing the goods themselves can be distinguished from recycling, which only reuses the raw materials.

New inventions are one way of serving the need for better design and production methods, and we will now look at some practical examples. The German Institute for Economic Research (IFO) has recorded an extraordinary increase in research in 1988/9 in the field of dynamic technology. The proportion of inventions in this field was 10.9 per cent of the total range of inventions. Only Japan has slightly more with 11.1 per cent. German companies play a leading role with eco-patents, the greatest activity being in the field of technology with ecological aims. Some 43 per cent of inventions worldwide which have registered for patent in more than one country have their origin in Germany.

Research and development

An ecologically focused research and development department offers the best prospects for improving the success rate of environmental business strategies. R & D provides the essential information for the future introduction of new, directly effective instruments of corporate environment policy.

For this reason, R & D can be described as a preparatory stage to environmental protection, providing the technical know-how needed for the direct introduction of strategic goals. It provides a basis for the use of instruments of adaptation, such as new production methods or new forms of waste disposal (Müllendorff, 1981).

Further advantages initiated by R & D are as follows:

- There will be an improvement of image.
- Additional increases in productivity and savings could result.
- Forward-looking strategies lead to better adaptation than merely reacting to environmental restrictions.
- Innovative products draw higher initial profits.
- There are more possibilities for diversification.

Companies need to appreciate that ecologically orientated R & D pays for itself in retrospect, and that it is worth pursuing out of self-interest. Only when self-interest is activated for environmental protection can we hope to clean up the environment.

In developing new products it is important that they are constructed so that they can easily be repaired, and so that they can be broken down into parts and the materials reused.

◇ Creightons

The enormous complexity of creating a product with 'real' environmental care can be seen in a project which took place at Creightons. As the largest manufacturers of natural toiletries in the UK, Creightons use exclusively natural active ingredients and do not use animal testing or permit cruelty to animals in the design and preparation of their products. With the help of several consultants they have been working on the production of a 'green' toothpaste. The product was designed according to the complete life-cycle approach, 'from the cradle to the grave'. In terms of ingredients, energy consumption and packaging, every effort has been made to produce an environmentally friendly or less damaging toothpaste.

Stage 1 Background market research – diagnostics

- A substantial part of the mass market is now defined as 'green consumers'.
- Market size and market structure of the new product is as follows:

   (a) *The toothpaste market.* Mature; brand loyalty high; four major manufacturers; opportunities for products with 'added value'; new packaging forms have been successful. Conclusion: 'Opportunity for innovation'. (In November 1988 ECM profiled the expanding European oral hygiene market, where increasing consumer health awareness has stimulated launch activities.)

   (b) *Who would buy it?* Women buy most toothpaste; women and young people show the highest level of environmental concern; people with special needs place this first. Conclusion: Primary target market is 'Mums buying for themselves and their older children'.

(c) *Is there an opportunity for environment-friendly toothpaste?* Everyday product, but small quantities used; no consumer awareness of specific problems; high interest in environment-conscious products, but concern over integrity, quality and price; supermarkets keen to stock environment-conscious products, particularly from known suppliers. Conclusion: 'Could be an opportunity, but consumers must feel it makes a difference'.

(d) *The opportunity*. A 'mass market' brand, offering the benefits of efficacy, good taste and environment consciousness.

Stage 2 Data research for the toothpaste

- Establishing the basic data from computer data research about what toothpaste is made of and where there may be potential environmental problems in the ingredients.
- Identifying new developments.
- Academic advice about tests carried out on toothpastes (stain removal, abrasive qualities, etc.).

Stage 3 Brainstorming session

- The members of the brainstorming group try to throw out, in this creative process, a great many ideas defining the product ('exploring every conceivable way of getting toothpaste on to the brush in an environment-friendly way'); all contributions are written down.
- Evaluating the concepts thrown up, refining them (through judgement and common sense) down to three or four feasible care concepts: the 'propositions'.

Stage 4 First consumer tests

- Preparation for the first consumer tests of the final four product propositions by a carefully selected group of consumers.
- The proceedings are audio-taped.
- Groups of participants produce 'mood boards', defining their view of the product's appeal (a refillable toothpaste dispenser is the system they want!).

Stage 5 Presenting a lead proposition

- Based on consumer response, the initial four propositions have been refined to a lead proposition. This and the rationale of its selection are to be presented to Creightons by the consultants.
- General discussion and agreement that this is the product concept.
- Thinking about compromise (the preferred system is very sophisticated; it is going to be quite difficult to produce; it will take a couple of years; in the first instance, how about a conventional plastic tube?).

Stage 6 Laboratory

- Preparing a formulation based on the found proposition.
- First list of ingredients is drawn up; use of natural ingredients wherever possible.
- Ingredients are tracked down to source to check there are no environmental complications in the way they are produced or disposed of.
- The appropriate suppliers are selected.
- A trial formulation is sent to an institute for testing for efficacy.
- As Creightons is a recognized cruelty-free company, it is keen to encourage the development of alternative scientific tests.

Stage 7 Checking the manufacturing process

- Checking the possibility of using 'friendlier' energy sources instead of conventional power generation (wind power or land-fill gas).

Stage 8 Product packaging

- Work starts on the product packaging; the interactions between product and packaging have to be considered.
- Packaging experts discuss, with roughs and samples, some of the packaging issues (overpacking, use of bleached, virgin board, etc.).
- The availability/cost/acceptability of alternatives.
- To manufacture the tube from truly biodegradable plastic seems not to be a good environmental option.
- Idea of marketing tube as 'recyclable' plastic tube (how is the current state of plastic recycling?; only small pilot in the UK so far; also labelling 'recyclable' would be misleading to the consumer.
- To produce the tube from recycled plastic is no good because of the danger of contamination.

Brainstorming concepts based on:

- Reducing packaging (a pack which needs no cartons; use a very large stand-up cap; but how will this effect the [highly automated] manufacturing process?; and what is the consumer to think?).
- A refillable dispenser.
- Recyclability.
- A measured dosage system.

Stage 9 To come up with a name

- A small group has to come up with a name.

- A shortlist of possible names is fed into a computer system that rejigs syllables and word-crunches the human suggestion.

Stage 10 Final consumer test

- After the formulation has come through all its scientific tests, volunteers are recruited for a final consumer test by diagnostic researchers.
- In a home test the product is used for a couple of weeks (will it clean teeth?, opinion about foam, taste, after-taste).
- Consumers didn't like any of the carefully chosen brand names; new meeting of consultants (considering the 'caring aspect' and the 'idea of friendliness'); new proposal: 'Protect'.

Stage 11 To make a production batch

Designing the production process

Wicke (1990) believes that there will be rising demands on all companies in the realm of eco-production:

- Through the use of inspection and enforcement agencies to regulate deficits in compliance with environmental laws.
- Through the use of high-technology for the treatment of air and water.
- Through additional requirements in refuse and ground protection.
- Through increased security against accidents and intensified environmental liability.

Effects on the environment can be reduced considerably by corresponding developments in production technology, and these come about largely through R & D. Such developments might include energy-saving methods, noise protection apparatus and exhaust gas cleaning plants. Preventative technologies must certainly be integrated into the structure of industrial production. However, it is not within the scope of this book to cover these aspects of technology.

Any manufacturing process is generally determined by technological considerations, and both economic and ecological parameters need to be considered. The choice of input materials is also relevant as this will have a bearing on the production method used.

Ecological process development concentrates on the reduction of resources used during production, and also on reducing pollution output through efficient curative cleaning or the use of clean technologies. The question of noise pollution should also not be overlooked. The production process has to be modified to minimize both resources used and residues formed. 'Even if no form of production is completely eco-neutral, the least we can do is to choose the most eco-friendly' (Seyfferth and Pfriem, 1985).

At the German Engineering Day in 1989, set up under the auspices of the Association of German Engineers (VDI), a call was made to integrate the guidelines of environmental protection directly into industrial production processes. The most difficult task facing engineers is to create 'closed cycles'. Residues, subsidiary materials and fuels have to be fed, through purpose-built circulatory systems, back into the production process. The finishing departments are increasingly responsible for this type of environmental technology. Not only raw materials are affected, but also issues of disposal which are best dealt with internally: that is, preventively.

Once environmentally sound production methods have been developed and are on the market, decisions on new investment should not only be based on increased productivity but should also take into account any resulting reductions in the use of resources, reduced waste, pollution and so on. Since energy is so vital to all industrial activities, developing efficient management of this scarce and costly resource will be of paramount importance in the design of new production processes.

An attitude of environmental awareness at work is equally important:

> All processes of production and all damage to and protection of our environment depend on how individual people work. No matter how advanced the environmental technology is, its efficacy in the long run depends on the measure of environmental awareness enjoyed by those who operate it. (Siemens, 1986)

A general business concept must be carried by the commitment of each and every member of staff (see Chapter 13).

◇ 3M

In 1974, 3M published its official corporate environmental policy. The policy consists of a number of absolutes aimed at solving its own environmental pollution and conservation problems. In addition, the company sets itself measurable environmental goals as and when necessary to ensure that its many diverse operations are focused on policy objectives. The current corporate goals, to be achieved by the year 2000, are to reduce emissions to air, land and water by 90 per cent from a 1987 base.

As early as 1975 3M had unveiled a programme called 'Pollution Prevention Pays' (3P), to eliminate or reduce sources of pollution in 3M products and processes. The concept of applying pollution prevention on a company-wide basis through a globally organized effort and recording the results had not been done before. In the first 14 years the programme cut 3M pollution in half. In 1988, the company initiated a new short-term phase, a five-year plan called 'Pollution Prevention Plus' (3P+).

With 3P and 3P+ both in place, 3M estimates that it can eliminate or control more than 85 per cent of 3M's US air emissions by mid-1992 (facilities outside the USA by mid-1993). As an intermediate step, the company has initiated a programme to achieve 'Best Available Control Technology' (BACT).

3M complied with the new laws and regulations of the 1970s by conventional end-of-line control. As the capital expenditures involved added to production costs, harming the company's competitive position, 3M brought innovation back into its environmental management equation by focusing not on control but on prevention. The idea was to stop pollution before it started: to seek out prevention opportunities within all its manufacturing, engineering, research and development activities. Under 3P, 3M encourages technical innovation to prevent pollution at source in the following ways:

- 'Product reformulation': the development of non-polluting or less polluting products or processes by using different raw materials or feedstocks.

- Process modifications: changing manufacturing processes to control by-product formation or to incorporate non-polluting or less polluting raw materials or feedstocks.

- 'Equipment redesign': modifying equipment to perform better under specific operating conditions or to make better use of available resources (such as by-product steam from another process).

- 'Resource recovery': recycling by-products (for sale or use in other 3M products or processes).

These concepts, of course, are not new. None the less, 3M does represent the first organized application of pollution prevention principles throughout one company, worldwide.

The 3P selection process works like this. Any technical employee, or group of employees, can nominate a project for 3P by filling out a standard evaluation sheet. Each application is reviewed by a co-ordinating committee made up of representatives from all the technical groups. The committee meets quarterly to discuss the entries from all 3M locations. In practice, the 3P programme is a composite of individual environmental audits: mini-audits performed every day by individuals looking for a better way. The projects are evaluated by the co-ordination committee for their success in reducing pollution, saving resources and money, and advancing technology and/or engineering practice. Over the years more than 3,000 projects have been recognized for doing just that.

Globally, 3P projects have ranged from improved control of process coating weight at Gorseinon, to recovery of waste ammonium sulphate from a plant in Minnesota and recovery of a cleaning solvent from mixer tanks at Hilden in Germany. To provide extra incentives for longer-term R & D efforts, 3M dramatically raised the charges for in-house incineration and waste disposal at its US plants.

3M made the decision not to use the regulatory reform option of bubbling to reduce control requirements. In the vicinity of existing plants, net improvements in air quality will be achieved because of the plan to donate emission credits to local permitting agencies. Under current environmental regulations, credits for emission reductions at 3M facilities can be sold to nearby companies, which can then increase their emissions. 3M will not sell its credits, however, and will retain only those credits needed for future plant operation. So 3M has donated back the emission reduction units granted as a result of voluntary reduction in air emissions from its plants in New Jersey (1,000 tons) and Los Angeles (more than 150 tons) to the state or local agency.

To help senior executives focus on key objectives, IBM issues corporate instruction documents, one of which is entitled, 'Responsibilities for Environmental Protection'. This directs operating units to assess and reduce environmental risks associated with production supply vendors, chemical supply and waste disposal contractors, and to carry out routine audits on their procedures for safe and responsible plant operation.

In Europe, overall responsibility for environmental affairs rests with the managing director and the operating management committee. Each manufacturing company has resident environmental engineering, toxicology and health and safety departments, and even the smaller sales and marketing companies employ specialists in product safety and packaging engineering. Two steering committees, reporting to a European manager for environment, health and safety, provide the strategic direction necessary to maintain the highest standards of performance. The Environment, Health and Safety Committee comprises specialists from the larger 3M subsidiaries in Europe. Its objectives are as follows:

- To provide objectives and implementation guidelines for environmental protection, safety and industrial hygiene.

- To identify opportunities for improvement and suggest appropriate courses of action.

- To monitor new European legislation and its impact for 3M businesses in Europe.

- To implement environment, health and safety auditing systems.

- To encourage the exchange of information and resources among 3M subsidiaries in Europe.

Similarly, the European Product Responsibility Committee stimulates resource sharing and the exchange of information between subsidiaries. Among the issues within its sphere of influence are the liability, safety, testing and certification of aspects of the thousands of products 3M sells in Europe.

◇ Dow Chemicals

Dow Chemicals in Stade, Lower Saxony, provides a good example of change in environmental awareness. After negative headlines in the 1970s a radical change of attitude led to the development of a comprehensive environmental protection plan through to the year 2000. The following is an extract from the Dow environmental protection philosophy.

Progress in environmental protection requires research, innovation and investment. In the Dow works in Stade primary environmental protection and recycling ensure that residues, subsidiary materials and emissions do not arise or are reduced as much as possible. Primary environmental protection means:

■ Optimal use of energy and raw materials through close connection with production processes.

■ Avoidance of residual materials rather than waste disposal.

■ Installation of technology which causes less pollution.

If waste products are unavoidable they are reused as far as possible by Dow or treated with the most up-to-date technology. In this way significant amounts of energy and raw materials are conserved and costly dumping space is preserved for the future. Unnecessary burdening of the environment is prevented.

At Dow Chemicals the idea of making full use of raw materials as an integrated concept has been realized. This is particularly difficult in the chemicals industry, where almost every process produces residues and by-products. The technical and economic reasons for developing 'closed-loop systems' in the chemical industry are now supplemented with an environmental dimension.

Thanks to a broad, integrated concept, the company has become independent in the sphere of disposal. The total waste produced in the works can be kept to a

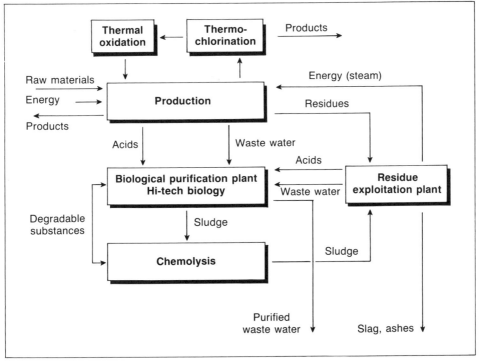

Source: Dow Stade.

Figure 25 Compound concept production/environmental protection

minimum, used in an eco-friendly way and disposed of without problems. This compound system comprises three elements:

- A chemolysis plant to minimize sludge.
- A system for improving existing biological waste water purification.
- A plant for exploiting solid residues.

In thermo-chlorination and chlorolysis the unusable fluid residues from several production plants are treated and made into valuable solvents. The remainder is channelled to thermal oxidation plants and converted into water, carbon dioxide and hydrochloric acid. The acid is extracted and fed back into the production process. There are no liquids to be disposed of, even though 90 per cent of the total production consists of fluids. It has been possible to reduce atmospheric emissions by about 80 per cent, completing the compound system in which all exhaust gases are collected centrally and fed into an incinerator.

Chemolysis at Dow Chemicals

1. By converting an oxidation process from utilization of air to pure oxygen it was possible, in another pioneering move, to dispense with the main source of pollution in the works.
2. The chemolysis process is used to reduce the sludge which forms in every biological purification plant. The sludge is converted by thermo-chemical hydrolysis into biodegradable substances which are then fed back into the purification plant. With further improvements it might be possible to reduce the annual 12,000 tonnes of sludge output by over 90 per cent.

Chemolysis   *Photo: Dow Stade*

3. Hydrochloric acid (25,000 tonnes HCl aq. 20 per cent) is fed back into the production cycle. Some 5,000 tonnes of ecologically questionable slag is suitable for road building but is used as packing for stabilizing a salt store. Sediment which accumulates during the running of the plant (capacity approximately 30,000 tonnes/year) is fed back into the incinerator where it combines with the vitrified slag.

4. DM120 million was invested in the complete compound system between 1986 and 1990. Further investment is due.

5. The positive effects of investment in the waste water plant can hardly be quantified; in the long term, savings in the order of millions are anticipated.

The water treatment is carried out on site. After pre-treatment comes the final purification stage in a hi-tech, fully biological plant, which achieves ten times the efficiency of traditional plant in terms of oxygen utilization during bacterial aeration. This closed system demonstrates a maximum performance in waste water purification and energy exploitation, and reduces the quantity of waste gases by more than 90 per cent.

The residue cycle was completed in 1989 with the construction of a plant for exploiting solid waste. High-temperature incineration brings about total oxidation of residual matter and produces hot exhaust to make steam (annually 100,000 tonnes).

Now that the project is complete the company has an almost closed material circulation system that does not depend on dumping. 'In this way we have exhausted all the presently known possibilities for minimizing environmental pollution from our works in Stade.'

Detail: Biological purification plant   *Photo: Dow Stade*

Residue exploitation plant *Photo: Dow Stade*

Dow has gained the following financial benefits:

- With the chemolysis plant, a yearly saving of about DM2.1 million because previously the sludge had to be transported to Potsdam at the cost of DM174 per tonne.

- 5,000 tonnes of hydrochloric acid and 100,000 tonnes of steam are produced per year from previously unusable residue which used to cost around DM600 per tonne to dump.

In the automobile industry, enormous efforts are being made during production to prepare low-solvent body finishes as one means of reducing pollution.

In Germany approximately 700,000 tonnes per year of liquid finishing materials and thinners are used, causing emissions, waste and strong smells. The toxic fumes are particularly unpleasant. Paints with solvents were traditionally sprayed on to body work, causing an evaporation zone. The solvent-enriched air can only be released into the atmosphere after purification processes such as burning or filtering through activated carbon.

Car body finish is applied in three coats with a preliminary coating of phosphor primer. The final coating is a complex process, and technical development in this area seems to be in full swing.

◇ BMW

Development is at a crossroads. Attempts can be made to reduce emissions via air purification plants, or new kinds of water-based bodywork finish can be introduced. Both routes require new technology and in most cases the rebuilding of the paint shop. The present interpretation sees a meaningful combination of both developments. It has to be ascertained whether the initial finishing process affects the success of 'touching up' using traditional methods.

In Munich a new air-cleaning plant has been installed for the spraying bays which use traditional, solvent-based finishing systems. The paint shop in the Regensburg factory has already been set up for the use of water-based finishes on the new series. BMW was the first German manufacturer to introduce 200 cars with water-based metallic finishes. These are being trialled in California and the results of quality tests will take several years to evaluate.

◇ Daimler-Benz

Since 1985 Daimler-Benz has been using a low-solvent process for the first coat on the 190 model from the Bremen factory. It is a two-component polyurethane finish made by Bayer in conjunction with two other paint manufacturers.

◇ Volkswagen

With an investment of almost DM1 billion, Volkswagen is transferring to water-soluble paint. The new finishing plant is due to be in action by 1993. Toxic solvents will be largely replaced by water, but totally solvent-free finishes cannot be expected until the mid-1990s.

Environmentally orientated products

Product design

The marketing term 'product life-cycle' is confusing from an ecological point of view because residue from production can take years or even decades to disperse. Strebel and Hildebrant (1989) speak of the 'superimposition' on the 'product life-cycle' of a 'residual life-cycle'. Only when the residue has broken down into harmless substances do product and residual cycles reach parity.

A much larger time-scale is needed. The harmful effects from a given product, say a car, occur in a time-scale 'which makes this type of residue seem like history to the manufacturer and the purchaser'. Industry has tended to give only partial consideration to the total output of residue. Even when it can be attributed directly to a manufacturer, responsibility is often foisted on to others. The problem of disposal is increasing because of lack of space or insufficient incinerator facilities, and those affected by waste (e.g. local communities) will be turning to the manufacturer who caused it. The producer will be required to respond by developing ecological product design and contributing to the reduction of waste.

Once established, the problem of residue cannot be solved exclusively in the disposal phase. The cause must be tackled through avoidance or at least reduction. Creation of products which cause minimal damage at all three phases (production, consumption and disposal) is a valuable long-term goal (see Figure 26).

Production phase	Sales, consumption and use phase	Disposal phase
• Use of environment-friendly, low-energy materials • Use of readily available raw materials • Minimum use of resources • Maximize product life-span • Product-related contribution to emissions and energy factors in production • As far as possible, intensification of production (and sales) not only of relatively environment-friendly products (e.g. quiet cars with catalytic converter), but also absolutely environment-friendly products (e.g. bicycles and biologically farmed produce)	• Damage to environment and health through packaging • Recyclability, reusability of packaging • Minimum production and packaging volume • Safeguard to health during consumption and use • No gaseous emissions or only environmentally compatible emissions during consumption and use • No effluents or few effluents which can be removed in an environment-friendly way • Energy-saving use and consumption phase • Low-noise use and consumption phase • Facilitation of the most environment-friendly and economical use (product instructions, customer service and consultation) • Increased ease of repair and maintenance, easy replacement of parts subject to wear • Other ways of increasing life-span (style, function and materials)	• Low volume of waste • Problem-free opportunities for dumping, incineration or composting • Minimum disposal volume, by means of re-exploitation (even of parts) • Recyclability of waste products • With dangerous (special) waste: easier re-exploitation or possibility of separate collection and disposal • Problem-free, energetic exploitation by means of waste incineration

Figure 26 Environmental criteria (after Wicke)

Environmental simulations can be used to great effect to gain an under-standing of the reciprocity between object and environment, and to adapt a product to its environment. The introduction of a pollutant into the environment and its various stages of transformation can also be simulated effectively. Environmental testing contributes to the improvement of materials and the minimization of packaging by simulation of the transportation procedure, and can investigate the properties of recycled materials in new applications.

Unprecedented demands are being made on development and construction departments. Claims for long-life, easily repairable products, regenerative raw materials, cleanliness and recyclability place completely new demands on development and construction. However, enormous ingenuity is required from the designer, who needs to:

● Undertake research into new materials, with the help of the environmental authorities or ecological research institutes.

● Gather up-to-date information on source materials and store it in accessible files.

● Acquire information on similar products and analogous parts (with the help of CAD systems) to cut down unnecessary production and save resources.

● Participate regularly in value analyses involving ecological criteria.

● Study new production and assembly methods by means of production planning and materials control.

● Agree with the marketing department on limitations in the range of products and sales strategies.

● Create products from low-entropy components which are easy to recycle.

'Construction constitutes less than 8 per cent of the overall cost of a product but it determines about 70 per cent of the final cost' (Stahlmann, 1988a).

Disposal and usage are becoming most important decision-making factors at all levels of business from product development to choice of materials and finishing methods.

Product design operates on three levels as an instrument of environmental politics:

● Economic: as a marketing instrument, influencing customers.

● Production policy: as a direct determining factor of the production process.

● Ecological: the side-effects of production, use and disposal, e.g. product design for recycling and safe disposal.

Decision-makers must be familiar with the ecological effects of alternative product designs in order to decide where the ecological advantage lies. In a sense, the whole fate of a product, from cradle to grave, has to be considered in terms of waste. 'If the analysis is limited to one phase of production, then changes made might have effects on earlier or later stages, which override the advantages gained from the phase analyzed' (Strebel, 1981).

The phase of production design must be interpreted very widely, with regard to its effect on eco-management. All of the following need to taken into account:

- Measures within the actual production phase.

- Measures already taken at the product development stage.

- Retrospective measures such as recycling and disposal following use of the product.

Collaboration and the combined knowledge of countless experts is vital to the development of an environment-friendly product. Follmann (1989) notes the need for partnership throughout the manufacture of an eco-friendly wallpaper.

- Paper suppliers: Dioxins? Furane in the cellulose? Chlorine in the bleaching process? Waste water treatment on site?

- Print-dye manufacturers: Type of pigments? Heavy metals in dyes? Type and proportion of solvents? Preservatives in water-based dyes?

- Glue manufacturers: Type and quantity of preservatives in glues? Machine builders: Energy-saving machine? Plant with minimum emissions?

- Wallpaper manufacturers themselves: Check energy, raw materials, subsidiary materials used. Are undesirable by-products made during production?

- Disposal experts: Suggestions for disposal of industrial waste and wallpaper after use.

Two types of improvement can be made during production through product design.

1. Increasing the net product per unit. This means a quantitative saving in preliminary stages or a qualitative functional increase in the value of the products.

2. Reducing the effects on the environment per unit through changes to the product at the manufacture, use or disposal stage (Müller-Wenk, 1980).

If ecological demands are to be met by means of eco-product design, the products must have the following general properties:

1. Improved environmental qualities.

2. 'Friendly' input of resources (e.g. substitution measures).

3. Long-life characteristics whenever possible.

4. Easily repairable.

5. Improved possibilities for reuse and harmless disposal.

The cost of implementation can be a problem. The need for investment often inhibits technical progress.

The market price for ecologically scarce materials is sometimes considerably lower than for abundant materials. This causes businesses to opt for the scarce raw materials out of competitiveness rather than considering their product design measures (Müller-Wenk, 1980.) An example is crude oil which, although very scarce, is often sold at rock bottom prices.

Two points deserve particular emphasis:

- Large retailers are increasingly offering environment-friendly goods in their ranges and this puts pressure on other manufacturers (see Chapter 16).
- Consumers are becoming more environment conscious in their buying habits. This change is overwhelming. The proportion of households ready to make compromises rose to 59 per cent in Germany in 1988 (core group of green consumers 32 per cent). Demand will also be intensified by the obligation on public acquisition departments to give preference to eco-friendliness in orders and tenders.

If there is already an increase in environmental awareness in a given market sector, and a corresponding reaction from competitors, a company must intensify its environmental product management. According to Wicke (1990) the following issues have to be clarified in the planning phase:

- Official environmental regulations, consumer requirements, other demand factors (e.g. trade, public involvement).
- Eco-friendliness of own and competitors' products (existing? modifications possible?).
- Alterations to research, development, production, input materials and their effect on liquidity; costs.
- Price and market preparedness.
- Competitor reactions.
- Changes in the circle of purchasers and in the sales system.
- Positive/negative side-effects of eco-friendly products on image and sales.

Since the terms 'natural', 'bio', 'eco' and 'environment friendly' are not legally protected they are often abused, and this has been extensively reported by the media. For this reason, fulfilling eco-criteria set out by independent institutes can have a beneficial influence on sales (e.g. Eco-Test or Stiftung Warentest in Germany).

There follow some case studies to demonstrate changes in business behaviour and new ethical trends.

Case studies from various branches of industry

A wide range of environment-friendly products are currently available to consumers. Most of these products will be referred to later in the text.

- Organic (bio) food.

- Batteries: without mercury (Varta, Ever Ready, Philips, Panasonic).

- Nappies: disposable, dioxin free, non-bleached (Peau Douce, Procter and Gamble).

- Cars: catalytic converter, unleaded petrol, recyclability (all German manufacturers).

- Detergents/washing powder: phosphate free, sulphate free, biodegradable, liquid detergents, refillable packets (Lever, Procter and Gamble, Henkel).

- White goods, e.g. refrigerators: water and energy efficiency, insulation foam and refrigerants, CFC free, easily recycled (AEG, Bosch-Siemens).

- Aerosols: ozone friendly (Johnson Wax, Wella).

- Lighting: energy efficient, long-life (Osram, Philips).

- Paper products: recycled paper (coffee filters, kitchen towels, toilet paper) (Scott, Melitta).

- Plastic bags: biodegradable.

- Personal hygiene/cosmetics: natural ingredients, special packing, not animal tested (Body Shop, Beauty Without Cruelty, Revlon, Elida Gibbs, Wella).

The availability of green products has greatly increased over the last few years in most European countries, notably Germany, Holland, Switzerland and Scandinavia, and also in the USA, Canada and the UK.

Food and drink

A natural and healthy way of life is intimately associated with the environment. Nature, 'naturalness', environment and health are certainly closely identified in people's minds. For years now a growing number of consumers have given preference to products made from natural raw materials.

Some idea of the chaos which reigns in the unprotected market for ecological farm produce (which is waiting for EC ruling) can be gleaned from the case cited by the German Federation of Farmers. In 1988 Bavarian supermarkets offered a quantity of alleged organic produce ten times the total output of eco-farms. The higher price for this kind of product led to 'conventional production at biological prices'. There are many cases of look-alike products and trickery with labelling. In spite of a large increase in the amount of organically farmed land, the demand for natural produce has exceeded the supply for many years now. Compared with 1,450 farms and 24,700 hectares in 1985, the Federal Ministry for Food Farming and Forestry in Germany gave figures of 2,330 farms and 42,000 hectares of organically cultivated land in 1988. A growth rate of 20–30 per cent is expected for the 1990s, and the turnover for organic products from these alternative farms is already nearly DM1 billion (£330 million approx.).

DON'T SACRIFICE TOMORROW

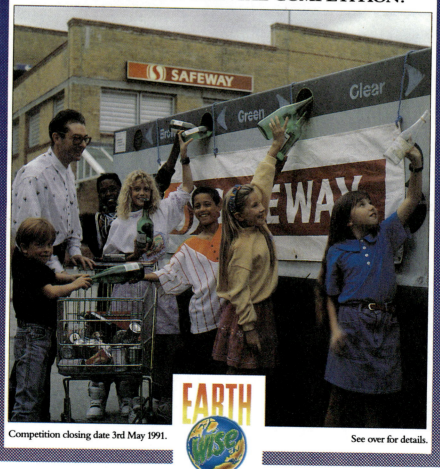

◇ The Neumarkter Lammsbräu Brewery

The Neumarkter Lammsbräu Brewery brews eco-beer and is determined to make as close an approach as possible to an integrated concept of environmental management. The company has produced guidelines for the consumer in which the management philosophy is set out. It begins with the need for purity at the crop-growing stage and continues the idea uncompromisingly through the brewing process up to and including bottling. The booklet also serves to protect the public interest since there are as yet no official conditions concerning eco-food products.

The holistic company philosophy embraces the entire life-cycle of the product from the purchase of raw materials, through energy reclamation plants and packing (exclusive use of returnable plastic crates, no metallic foil capping, minimum heavy metal in label printing dye) up to disposal (waste from production goes back to the farmer as cattle feed, waste water is passed through a local purification plant and other waste is sorted at the local refuse centre).

Raw materials are purchased from controlled biological farms which are all members of organizations recognized by AGÖL (the Association for Ecological Farming) and operate according to fixed regulations. One of the biggest problems is finding enough farmers, and the brewery is forced to purchase from all over Germany. Fortunately more farms are switching to ecological methods, and it is becoming easier to buy barley, wheat and hops locally and keep transport costs down.

An agricultural engineer is employed to supervise purchase and to advise farmers on growing methods or conversion requirements. The grain is stored without fumigation and only top-grade, untreated hop flowers are used (on no account are bitter hops, hop pellets, hop extract or sulphur treatment used). Farmers are instructed which type of hops to grow.

Consistent quality control is the only guarantee that the self-imposed guidelines are adhered to, so Lammsbräu reserve the right to carry out unannounced assessments twice a year, and the farmers' associations also impose product controls. Soil tests are conducted regularly by the agricultural engineer; grain and hops are tested for residues by registered trade chemists.

The water comes from private underground springs sheltered from contamination. It is low in sodium and extremely low in nitrates. Water treatment plants are considered inadmissible. The yeast is line bred on the premises and fed exclusively on home-produced beerwort. The brewery has its own malting for the ecologically produced grain, and the malt is dried in a low-temperature kiln causing very little pollution.

Production methods are gentle so as to preserve valuable nutrients right through to the finished beer. Traditional fermentation methods are used, but unnecessary pumping, filtration, centrifuging and pressurizing are avoided, and technical apparatus is kept to a minimum to allow the bio-enzymic properties of the ingredients to unfold. Modern methods such as rapid processing, clearing, the use of protein stabilizers or raising the alcoholic yield are not applied.

'The important thing for us is not just the biological equilibrium during the growth of the raw ingredients, but that this equilibrium is maintained throughout the production process. Beer is a colloidal system which must be kept in equilibrium to guarantee the optimum taste, enjoyment and digestibility.'

Ecologically brewed beers from Neumarkter Lammsbräu

Household cleaning products

In contrast to other European countries, discussion of the environment in Germany has had a strong influence on the development of the market and has led to a fall in the total consumption of washing and cleaning products. The largest section, universal cleaners (also fabric softener, washing-up liquid and household cleaner), was also retrograde in 1989, while there has been an upturn in liquid and concentrated detergents as well as detergent for dishwashers.

The classic example of environmental innovation in this field is the introduction of phosphate-free detergents. More recent examples are as follows:

- Concentration of washing powders.
- Concentrates which have to be mixed with water and refill packs with fabric conditioner.
- Building-block systems.
- Biodegradables.
- Refill facilities in shops.

Initial trials indicated an information gap in the marketing of environment-friendly products as consumers failed to attribute the same efficiency to the concentrates as to the 'usual amount' of earlier products. Automatic dispensing systems could be of assistance here (cf. see p. 137).

◇ Werner and Mertz

With its placing of 'the little green wonder' Frog items, Werner and Mertz has enjoyed one of the greatest success stories for new eco-friendly products in Germany. The brand was specifically designed for the eco-section of the market and the following claims are made:

- A reasonable balance between thorough cleaning and the lowest possible environmental damage has been achieved (it is important to remember that eco-friendly products must be effective as well).
- The products are particularly kind to the skin.
- Most of the substances used are biodegradable.

The Frog range, which now covers six products, will be examined in detail in Chapter 11.

◇ Procter and Gamble

Procter and Gamble is making strenuous efforts to develop environment-friendly packaging because of the large contribution its products make to the build-up of refuse. In addition to this obvious response, the company is engaged in a range of activities such as energy-saving programmes, reforestation projects and collaboration with environmental groups to protect local wildlife and habitats. The success of these measures can be seen from a nationwide Gallup survey commissioned by the magazine *Advertising Age*, in which Procter and Gamble is described as the most 'environmentally conscious' marketer in the USA. When the survey asked, 'Overall, which one company comes to mind as the most environmentally conscious?', Procter and Gamble received the most support (6 per cent), followed by McDonald's with 4 per cent. Interestingly, however, 66 per cent of those surveyed said 'none' or 'don't know' (*Advertising Age*, 29.1.91).

There are many projects under way throughout the world, and a common factor among them is 'doing more with less'. In order of importance, the key elements are as follows:

- Source reduction to limit the amount of waste to be managed and to conserve resources.

- Recycling, reuse and composting.

The proportion of plastics in many bottles has been reduced, and bottles made of 100 per cent recycled plastics have been tested. (Spic and Span Pine won a first place designation from the DuPont Packaging Awards for its 100 per cent recycled PET bottle.) Procter and Gamble has also successfully used recycled HDPE plastic in liquid detergent bottles by 'sandwiching' the recycled material between two layers of new plastics.

Several concentrated cleaning products have been trialled in 'enviro-paks'. The product is sold initially in a large plastic bottle, but it is also available for subsequent purchase as a concentrate in small refill pouches, cartons or bag-in-box packaging. The concentrate is mixed with water at home in the original bottle. Packaging can be dramatically reduced in this way, by as much as 85 per cent.

A 'compact version' of several powder detergent brands is also offered in a smaller box to reduce volume. Volume has already been halved in the case of disposable nappies.

Environmental information such as biodegradability and use of recycled material is given on packages, in addition to the usual information on the constituents of the product and their function. To promote easy separation, Procter and Gamble is among the first companies to code plastic packaging, so that recyclers will be able to recognize the plastic components. Procter and Gamble is also encouraging other end-use markets: for example in testing (in Seattle) the feasibility of recycling the paper portions of nappies into cardboard and insulation, the plastic portion into plastic lumber and garbage bags, and the absorbent gel into a moisture-retaining agricultural aid.

Environmental impact assessments are carried out on products and processes, 'from cradle to grave'. Arthur D. Little Inc. and Franklin Associates have been commissioned to study the overall environmental impact of Pampers versus traditional towelling nappies. Procter and Gamble is also co-operating with Newcastle City Council (UK) in a pilot scheme to collect plastic waste directly from households for recycling.

In 1990, 30 million households were sent brochures explaining that biodegradable nappies, offered, for example, by R Med International and American

Enviro Products, are not the solution. Pilot projects in collaboration with commercial composting firms (Recomp, Minn./Asslar, Germany) are being used to demonstrate that disposable nappies can be composted. In the Asslar composting plant nappies are mixed in the proportion 1 : 9 with organic waste. They are pulverized, stored for a week at $70^{\circ}C$ and composted. Polyethylene is extracted periodically by sieving. The final compost can be used as fertilizer for plants.

Procter and Gamble is supporting several sponsoring projects, helping to preserve history as well as wildlife, and in 1989 it signed a five-year contract with the Worldwide Fund for Nature.

◇ Lever

Over the years washing powders and cleaning materials have come to symbolize the cold war between ecology and economy. At last, compatibility with the environment has become established as a marketing criterion (see Chapter 10).

Phosphate-free detergents had cornered more than 80 per cent of the market after four years or so in the shops, so in 1989 Lever decided to introduce sulphate-free powders as the next step in their long-term programme. (In 1988 Lever had already introduced phosphate-free detergents and Domestos without chlorine.) There were 323 TV advertising spots across Germany for the new Sunil. The proportion of sulphate in normal powders is somewhere around 25 per cent, although Procter and Gamble had already produced Ariel Ultra in 1989 with a 5 per cent content. As additional environmental extras, Lever is stressing a 33 per cent reduction in weight and a 20 per cent saving on packaging materials. Unlike ionic surfactants, sodium perborate or optical brighteners, sulphates are not one of the most dangerous components and the whole concept may, as critics claim, be just a side-issue.

There can never be really eco-friendly detergents in the strictest sense, but these are steps on the way to improved compatibility with the environment.

Lever continually invests in the development of efficient and acceptable packaging. For example, it introduced a carton pack for heavy-duty liquid detergents, and launched, in 1991, a 'greener bottle' for major brands with 85 per cent less plastic, which uses just over half the packaging material. Designed to be used just like a bottle, when empty these sturdy carton packs can be crushed to take up less space in the bin and in landfill sites. The carton pack product launch was backed by a high-profile advertising and promotional programme, including national TV and radio exposure, a heavy-weight poster campaign, press advertisements in national colour supplements, national dailies and women's magazines, and 16 million leaflets (made from recycled paper) dropped door-to-door.

Cosmetics

◇ Revlon

To combat the harmful effects of the polluted atmosphere on the skin, Revlon has developed a new collection for all skin types: 'Ecologie' with EPS (Environmental

Protection System), which detoxifies, hydrates and protects to 'retard premature skin ageing caused by the world we live in'. The range consists of detoxifying cleaner, rehydrating spray, humidifying fluid, humidifying cream and a skin stress mask.

All products are irritant free, hypo-allergenic, non-pore clogging, perfume free and based on non-animal-tested formulas. Packaging for Ecologie is entirely recyclable. Purchasers are urged, through information leaflets, to sort cardboard packing and glass bottles into the appropriate recycling containers. Pump sprays and atomizers should have their springs removed after use and then be disposed of in the correct plastic recycling container, or sent direct to Revlon which will pass them on to a recycling firm.

◇ Elida Gibbs

In 1989 Elida Gibbs brought out an alternative to traditional toothpaste for the environment-conscious consumer. It is marketed under the name 'Mynta'.

- It is made from natural ingredients.
- A full list of ingredients is given for consumer information: natural chalk, glycerine, natural xanthum gum, sodium palmitate, aromatic oils, plant extracts, citric acid, chlorophyll.
- The packaging is as eco-friendly as it can be while still giving adequate protection to the product.
- The carton, which is needed for hygiene, transport and storage, consists of 60–70 per cent recycled paper.
- Preservatives are not needed because of the large proportion of glycerine.

◇ Wella

Another example from the area of personal hygiene is the development of the 'Sanara' series by Wella, which was introduced in April 1987. After initial discussions in 1984 the R & D department was set the following problem: 'In terms of ingredients, packaging and marketing claims, Sanara must be objectively credible and as unassailable as possible according to the present aims of health and environment.' Subjectively, all possible attitudes, information and associations on the topic of health and the environment had to be taken into account. The ideas of 'nature' and 'natural ingredients' took on great significance, in contrast to 'chemistry' which has strong negative connotations in consumers' minds. One limiting factor was that there was to be no impairment of quality compared with other Wella products.

Market analyses revealed the target group as all men and women who buy quality products and who are progressive and sensitive to nature and the environment. Demographically, this included women between 20 and 49 living in larger towns on a net budget of DM4000 (£1,330 per month). The total user population was defined as 30 per cent of all Germans between 14 and 49.

This hair care shampoo has the following properties:

- It cleans very gently using plant extracts.

- It is extremely kind to the skin.

- It has environmentally neutral packaging which can be incinerated without producing harmful substances.

- It is biodegradable according to legal definition.

- It contains preservatives which occur in nature.

In an interview in *Stern* magazine (40/1989) a member of the board of Wella emphasized the widespread input of natural raw materials. He said they were not always better than synthetic ingredients and not always healthier. The principle behind Wella's advertising was to create credibility and acceptance by communicating the main advantages such as plant ingredients, biodegradation, natural aromatic oils, no colouring, regulated pH value to be kind to the skin and environment-friendly packaging.

In designing the packaging, care was taken not to be drawn into the current controversy on this subject. The natural aspect of the product was represented not by a picture of any kind but by a symbol, a square with green shading through to blue.

Advertising was focused on the German magazines *Stern* and *das Beste* for the broad base of the public, and *Brigitte, Geo, Cosmopolitan, Vogue, Style, Vital, Bio, Pan* and *Ambiente* for the target group in particular. There were also TV spots and, to build up trade, sample sachets were distributed at the points of sale, where posters and shelf displays were set up. A large-format sales folder with trade information was sent out together with an insert from the magazine *das Beste* for sales staff.

Placing this good-quality product in the high price range was wholly successful. The introduction of this particular eco-product is associated with the attitude of the company as a whole, since awareness of environmental protection is an important aspect of Wella's corporate policy.

In the German hair care business the use of CFCs in sprays is declining. However, the first spray without propellant gas received a cold reception from customers. In 1986 Wella had to remove from the market the pump-sprays it had introduced in 1976. Similarly, Johnson Wax, joint leader in the anti-perspirant aerosol business, suffered a 10 per cent loss in turnover in the months following the banning of CFC gases.

◇ The Body Shop

The Body Shop formulates, manufactures and retails products that cleanse, polish and protect the skin and the hair. Since the opening of its first outlet in 1976, the Body Shop has grown to over 550 shops and operates in 38 countries. In 1984 the company went public. The latest figure for annual turnover is £55 million.

The Body Shop symbolizes business's new ecological consciousness. The company's worldwide network was founded on a number of common principles:

- To sell cosmetics with the minimum of hype and packaging (no advertising, comparatively low cost of the product). The Body Shop originally sold just 15 products, whereas today it sells over 350.

- To promote health rather than glamour; reality rather than the dubious promise of instant rejuvenation.

- To use naturally based, close-to-source ingredients wherever possible (natural materials such as honey, lavender oil, camomile extract and kaolin). The percentage of base ingredients is extremely high, for example, the Aloe Vera range has up to 98 per cent pure gel from the aloe plant.

- Not to test ingredients or final products on animals. Suppliers are asked to sign a declaration to enforce the code: 'no component of the products has been tested on animals within the past five years'; the labelling was changed from 'Not tested on animals' to 'Against animal testing'.

- To provide a refill service in all shops. Most of the empty plastic bottles can be refilled at the refill bar; there is a 20p reduction on every refilled bottle; there are over 2 million bottles refilled a year in the UK. The 'golden rule' is reuse, refill, recycle.

- Waste is recycled, and recycled paper is used wherever possible. The Body Shop uses plastic packaging for its products. Most synthetic polymers can be recycled, but they need to be sorted; by the end of 1991 the Body Shop had implemented the standard labelling scheme identifing the plastic on each of its bottles, tubes, jars, etc. by means of an abbreviated code, which makes the sorting process easier.

The Body Shop takes a holistic view of its business, one in which it is not simply a creator of profits for its shareholders, but a force for the welfare of its staff, the community and ultimately the planet itself. The company sources raw materials from all over the world and has a policy of extending sustainable trade agreements with communities in economically disadvantaged countries. It provides employment in an unpatronizing and non-exploitative manner.

A key element of the Body Shop's sense of responsibility is to educate. Body Shops all over the world are used, and will continue to be used, as arenas for raising public awareness on a wide range of crucial environmental and human rights issues. It is seen as a force for social change by introducing radical and unconventional practices into business.

Principles into Practice (extracts)

Environmental policy
The Body Shop has a clear top-level commitment to ensuring environmental and social excellence. The company's environmental policy is not written in stone. It was created using a philosophy that incorporates environmental concerns into every aspect of its operation. Due to the expansion of the company these principles have now been formalized. The commitment to undertake an all-embracing environmental audit has produced an Environmental Policy Statement. The Environmental Nucleus

of senior managers has been responsible for writing the policy to ensure full commitment and understanding at all levels.

Building policy into the management structure

All departments have a departmental environmental adviser (DEA). This is an inspired member of staff who is now responsible for understanding the environmental implications of the department. In a situation where a department has several areas of major environmental impact more than one DEA has been appointed. The DEA works closely with the Environmental Department and their departmental head to implement relevant changes and provide information to ensure the company policies are upheld. This will also ensure that all departments are kept informed of recent changes in technology and legislation. The Environmental Group is responsible for seeing to it that staff understand the policies, and that adequate training and information is provided. It is also a further avenue for inspired staff to participate in the decision-making process.

Communications

It is absolutely fundamental that internal and external communications monitor and express the philosophies and practices. The Body Shop has extensive communication facilities both internally and externally (regular bulletins, videos, facts sheets, training sessions and campaign vehicles) to ensure the staff worldwide understand and put into practice these values. The senior managers meet regularly with the board of directors and shareholders, customers and suppliers are kept informed of activities and are encouraged to participate where appropriate. This is evident not least by the amount of environmental campaigning that is undertaken by the company. A suggestion box is placed in every shop, which is the basis of an invaluable link with customers. Over one thousand enquiries on environmental issues and the company's policies and practices are handled every week.

Campaigning

A relationship between environmental and human rights organizations has been developed over the past five years. The emphasis of this campaigning has been to educate both staff and the public on a variety of crucial issues. The network of shops has meant that these issues have been brought to the high street in countries whose environmental and human rights records are appalling, to say the least. In this way it is hoped that the Body Shop will become a force for social change. 'We have not chosen to stick with "safe" topics in the hope that, by example, we can encourage individuals to become proactive in changing the way society is developing.' This will continue to be a major activity of the Body Shop.

The company has given generous support to a vast range of community and environmental organizations. An on-going relationship with Friends of the Earth has increased its membership considerably due to in-store campaigning. National environmental campaigns undertaken by BSI are outlined below:

- 1986 Greenpeace: Save the whale. The Body Shop launched a new raw ingredient that replaced the need for sperm whale oil. Promotional leaflets highlighted Greenpeace and provided membership forms.

■ 1986–1988 Friends of the Earth: six campaigns focusing on a range of environmental issues illustrating what individuals could do.

■ 1988 Amnesty International: promoting the work Amnesty does in releasing prisoners of conscience.

■ 1989 Shelter: balloon race tickets sold in-store for the charity for homeless people.

■ 1989 START: Skin Treatment and Research Trust: raising funds for a charity developing test-tube skin which will have a huge range of applications.

■ 1990 Stop the Burning: petition to stop the burning of Brazilian rain forest. One million signatures delivered to the Brazilian Embassy in London.

■ 1990 Against Animal Testing: petition to stop the testing of cosmetics on animals. Five million signatures obtained. EC-proposed directive challenged. This campaign was run in several countries.

■ 1990 Refill, Reuse, Recycle: campaign to promote recycling and reuse. For every bottle refilled at a Body Shop, a tree will be planted in the next season. Some 23,500 trees will be planted by March 1991. Again this campaign was adopted by several overseas franchises.

Training and employee participation

The Body Shop has a training school in London. Induction training and personal development incorporates a strong element of awareness raising on environmental issues and codes of practice. This reaches out to all members of staff. Staff are given guidelines and encouragement to become actively involved in environmental and human rights activities. All shops fund community projects ranging from prison visiting to outdoor conservation work. These projects are also run from the subsidiary companies. One subsidiary closes the offices for an hour a week to engage in campaign letter writing. Considerable amounts of money are raised for charities and environmental organizations which frequently involves local community participation.

Purchasing standards

Those departments involved in purchasing have a close liaison with the Environmental Research Department to ensure items are selected which have been assessed in an environmental context. Guidelines are developed to examine not only the specifications of the products but also the management strategy of the supplying companies. The ultimate objective of the environmental audit will be to develop a code of practice whereby the Body Shop will only purchase from those companies whose standards of operation reflect those of the company.

Trading with developing countries

The Body Shop has an active policy of 'Trade not Aid', has developed projects in southern India and Nepal and is in the process of exploring trading links with such countries as Brazil. These projects provide a market for goods which are produced with the following principles in mind: sustainable development (both socially and environmentally), non-exploitation (i.e. payment is made at realistic levels), and wherever possible, a new resource is developed to allow increased prosperity for that community. An example of this is the Nepal Paper Project.

Waste management

The company has a policy of reducing, reusing and recycling waste wherever possible: for example, the issue of waste from distribution and post-consumer waste. The Body Shop is the first retailer in the UK to be recycling its own post-consumer plastic waste. Approximately one tonne of plastic bottles is sent for recycling each month. The Body Shop has extended its direct-link distribution from the warehouse to the shops for recovering plastic containers, plastic film and cardboard boxes for reuse and recycling:

- Reusable roll cages now distribute many products which will mean the saving of over 500,000 cardboard boxes a year.

- Cardboard cartons, when used, are sent back for reuse whenever possible and are now being reused up to four times.

- Recycled plastic crates have recently been introduced to reduce the use of cardboard cartons – these have a ten-year life span.

A full survey has recently been undertaken to examine all trade influent waste and develop a system which minimizes the quantity that will ultimately leave the manufacturing site. The need for work in this area was identified by the environmental audit. Paper is only recycled after it has been used on both sides, saving money and resources. There is an office paper recycling system that has been passed on to a number of schools, businesses and local authorities all over the world. Not only is the proper disposal of waste environmentally responsible, it also raises awareness among staff, showing the power of individual effort. Wherever possible, facilities are provided for staff to dispose of their waste in an environmentally responsible way if local facilities are lacking.

The shops

The following principles have been established for the shops. All shop fitting materials are being assessed for environmental performance. No tropical hardwoods are used, whether for construction or decoration, and only woods from sustainably managed sources are permitted. In cases of replacement and disposal of unserviceable refrigeration and air conditioning units, CFC refrigerants must be drawn off and returned to the manufacturers. Energy-efficient lighting is used.

Recycled paper till bags are used to impart information as well as being functional. The bioplastic bag is now known to be inappropriate and is being replaced by a low-density polythene which is made from recycled plastic (all film from the manufacturing process is collected and recycled by the same company that produces the recycled plastic bags). Environmentally less damaging cleaning agents are recommended. Recycling facilities are continually being monitored and improved.

Environmental audit

In September 1989, the first environmental audit was undertaken internally with the assistance of an external observer. It was an all-encompassing audit of the operations at head office in Littlehampton, West Sussex. The objectives of the audit were as follows:

- To discover any areas where systems of environmental protection management are insufficient to meet current and/or imminent regulations and the Body Shop policy requirements.

- To provide an environmental base line from which the Body Shop can measure its future environmental performance.

- To take recommendations for on-going management and working practices.

- To identify areas needing further study, research or employment.

- To broaden and further promote awareness within the Body Shop.

The methods used were a combination of interview with relevant company personnel, direct observation of working practices, the collection of samples for analysis and the gathering of data for a feasibility study into further aspects of waste recycling. In addition to these sources various outside bodies were contacted to obtain further information which would enable a more objective assessment of company working practices to be made. A full report was presented to the board of directors who gave the approval for all changes specified to be made. The report was subsequently shown to senior management who were responsible for implementation.

This environmental audit proved to be an extremely valuable exercise in centralizing information. It provided the company with a working document which has enabled the Body Shop to draw up a more comprehensive environmental strategy to be dovetailed into the existing decision-making structure. It has pointed out the company's strengths and weaknesses and highlighted areas where more resources need to be channelled.

An independent internal audit was conducted of the retail outlets, and reported in January 1991. At the same time an energy survey has been undertaken of both the head office site and a selection of retail outlets. The next stage of the audit will be a full assessment of the Littlehampton site and the retail outlets by a fully independent environmental audit team. A systemized and more thorough investigation of suppliers is planned for the new year.

Anita Roddick was 1985 Business Woman of the Year, was awarded the OBE in the 1988 New Year's Honours List and was 1988 Communicator of the Year. She was nominated Retailer of the Year (1989) and received the United Nations' Global 500 Award (1989). In 1990 the company was awarded the Queen's Award for Export and in 1991 the UK Better Environment Award for Industry.

Chemical products

The chemical industry is probably the branch most directly affected by the activities of environmental protection. It has also suffered most from public pressure. After the Rhine disaster in Switzerland, depletion of the ozone layer, the dumping site emergency, alarm over plastic packaging and the over-use of agro-chemicals, the chemical industry seemed to take on the guise of the Devil incarnate. It was forced to pay massive sums towards environmental protection, especially in Germany.

On the one hand, this sector produces about £300 billion in western Europe (global turnover, £1,000 billion). It makes a positive contribution to the economy (jobs, turnover, taxes, etc.) and its products have become an essential part of our lives. On the other hand, the production methods and the products of the chemical industry are inseparably linked with ecological problems.

The multinationals in this sector are among the largest companies in the world. In Germany there are the huge combines Bayer, BASF and Hoechst, in Switzerland Ciba-Geigy and Sandoz, in the USA Du Pont, Dow Chemical and Johnson Wax, and finally in the UK Imperial Chemical Industries (ICI). Most of these firms are referred to in this book in connection with their functional management activities.

◇ Follmann and Co.

Follmann and Co., a medium-sized company, has managed a technological leap forward in the field of environment-friendly printing colour. The company is aware of the debt of responsibility owed by the chemical industry and is determined to create a balance between economic and ecological goals. Many departments are trying systematically to replace harmful products with eco-friendly ones. Alongside its water-soluble printing colour, with which it leads the market, Follmann and Co. produces solvent-free adhesives and chemicals for the construction industry.

The transition to low-solvent and solvent-free colours required a considerable customer persuasion operation. A catalogue of arguments was produced containing statements on the advantages of water-based materials. In this project Follmann succeeded in achieving an almost complete market reversal. The company has also successfully introduced foams based on dispersion and plastisol as an alternative to PVC foam print colour.

Follmann has achieved a closed-cycle system by converting its waste output into a granular product which has been taken up by the market.

Motor vehicles

In spite of the eminent role this sector has played in the economy, its alarming effects on the environment and on human life are the subject of intense discussion. Along with traditional safety and design features the car as a product has to respond to a number of environmental demands:

- Clean air (emission standards, alternative fuels).
- Energy savings (smoother aerodynamics, reduced weight, better fuel consumption).
- Global warming (elimination of CFCs in air conditioning systems, CFC-free plastics).
- Reduced noise levels.
- Environmentally improved production methods (minimum of materials, energy, water, waste or pollution; use of water-based paints).
- Development of the recyclable car, coding of all plastic components, etc.

Without wishing to resurrect the unreliable statements and exaggerated figures which were bandied about when catalytic converters and lead-free petrol were introduced, every automobile manufacturer now sings the praises of the catalytic converter. Suddenly, converters are part of the standard fittings. It is enough to turn the competition green! Those who remember how these measures were forced on to the manufacturers now stand back in amazement.

As will be shown later with the environmental 'Blue Angel' label, the criteria for calling a product eco-friendly are often based on one aspect alone. Catalytic converters were brought in because of acid rain, and, in a sense, pushed other possible solutions into the background: for example, the use of less fuel or alternative forms of fuel. The newly recognized dangers from the greenhouse effect could lead to new interpretations of the effects of petrol consumption. One of the main causes of danger is carbon dioxide emission, and this is why there are calls to introduce a CO_2 tax. The catalytic converter has the disadvantage of leading to roughly 1 litre per 100 kilometres more petrol being used.

> It is so important to undertake everything technically possible, to use the reserves more economically and to find new, regenerative sources of energy. It is so foolish to believe that climate problems are to be solved through technology alone. For even a catalytically converted three-litre car is still a car, which, even in production, costs vast amounts in raw material. There is no way of making energy without damaging the environment. Solar and wind power are cleaner than coal fires. That much is true, but they too have to be built, maintained and renewed. (Schütze, 1988)

Opel speaks of a 'plus for the environment'; Renault feels sorry for the finance minister because his taxes are slipping through his fingers; the Environment Minister says thank you for the eco-friendliness of motor vehicles; Renault presents one model in a TV programme on the environment as 'the little eco-friend'; Mercedes-Benz offers the ecological long-distance runner; and Bosch proposes diesel as the environment-friendly way to travel. Everywhere you look things are turning green ...

First we protect the car from the environment. Then we protect the environment from the car.

100% zinc galvanised steel. 10 year anti-corrosion warranty. Lead and cadmium-free paintwork. Asbestos-free clutch linings and brake pads. 3-way catalytic converter. 75% recyclable. The new Audi 80. From £13,855. Phone 0800 585 685

In the shadow of the impending EC laws (1992), Audi goes so far as to exercise a little self-criticism: 'Given that the car industry has done the environment few favours over the years, we decided not to wait until we were forced to act.'

The protection of the environment has become very fashionable. Politicians are afraid of losing votes by accidentally sounding uncommitted. Managers are discovering that eco-arguments really do sell. A battle of words has broken out, in which everyone wants to gain the upper hand: who is the greenest in the land?

The old stereotypes don't fit any more. Leaders stand under the motto 'preserve creation', and even industry has changed its tune. One car firm has beautiful landscapes and a Louis Armstrong song in its advertisement, so that you would almost think driving an Opel was an active contribution to environmental protection. The competitors, Audi, attempt to get the British public to buy 'clean cars' with questions like, 'Be honest, hasn't the car done enough damage to the environment?' (Vorholz)

In western Europe approximately 14 million vehicles were scrapped in 1990; some two million in Germany alone, and this figure will increase to almost three million by the year 2000. It is estimated that about 10 per cent of all motor vehicles in use today will be disposed of each year.

German manufacturers were leaders in the revolution of public concern, first with conversion to lead-free fuel then with the introduction of catalytic converters designed to remove harmful exhaust emissions. Many other European markets turned a blind eye to inevitable progress.

During recent years green issues in car manufacturing have covered areas as diverse as fuel efficiency and the car production process itself. Now 'recycling' has become the latest buzz-word in the automotive arena. Manufacturers try to use materials in the design of their new cars which can be recycled as economically and ecologically as possible. Manufacturers like BMW believe that motor vehicles which, by virtue of their design, are easy to dismantle will enjoy a higher scrap value in the future. 'This fact may influence the initial customer purchase decision. As a result, the recyclability of a car may become a competitive factor. The car of the future will not be measured only by its motoring comfort, safety, economy and ease of service.' Designers are now also required to build cars which can be recycled as completely and economically as possible.

◇ Volkswagen ADAC

A pilot recycling centre has been set up by Volkswagen in its Frisian works. It is planned to recover 85–90 per cent of all materials in the scrap cars, with a possible

30 per cent recovery of plastics. In August 1990 VW was the first European car manufacturer that publicly guaranteed to take back its new Golf model free of charge. Next day Opel followed with the same offer for its new Astra, then Ford for its Escort and Orion.

In 1991 ADAC, the German Automobile Association, started similar pilot projects in Stuttgart and Esslingen. The aim is to prove that recycling is cost effective. Old cars are collected free of charge from members, and for around £20 from non-members.

◇ BMW

BMW's strategy is to face the recycling issue on two fronts:

- Dealer recycling of waste (collection and clean disposal of all waste oil, batteries, paint waste, anti-freeze, solvents and brake fluid).

- Recycling the cars themselves.

So far approximately 25 per cent of an old car goes to waste sites in the form of shredder residue: 250 kg per car, consisting mainly of plastics, rubber, glass and fluids. With the new project these figures might be reduced to 50–60 kg. Shredder residue is currently considered as domestic waste in Germany, and can therefore be deposited at waste sites. A new bill the German government is preparing will reclassify shredder waste as hazardous ('special') waste, so that the cost of depositing it at waste sites will probably increase fivefold in the next one or two years.

Due to the very limited availability of waste sites in Germany, the government is also preparing a bill which will require car makers to take back old cars from their last owners free of charge. Thus, car makers or their representatives will ultimately be responsible for the waste management of vehicles, and so recycling or the reuse of parts and materials will have utmost priority over any other concept of conventional waste management. By mid-1991 the German car industry had to submit specific proposals to legislators for establishing a system of vehicle recycling. By 1994 this system must be operational throughout the whole country. While Germany is the forerunner in Europe in taking this initiative, various other European countries are considering similar strategies.

So, how does BMW propose to solve this problem? After draining fluids from the old car efficiently, the main point is to disassemble its parts and components. In this process:

- Everything suitable for reuse as spare parts is removed.

- Parts and components can also be used as a source of materials, and can be recycled for BMW's own supply.

- Fluids are recycled for reuse, and materials which cannot be used in these ways are used for generating energy.

- The remaining body and remaining parts of the car are shredded.

BMW's concept of scrap car recycling is based on what they call a 'cascade model', which is well suited to the 'cascading' decrease in value associated with the recycling process. The model consists of the following stages:

1. Disassembly of the components which are suitable for reuse (highest values in the recycling process).

2. Parts which cannot be recycled via the first step are used as material in order to produce new parts (second highest values in the recycling process).

3. Remaining car parts are used for the extraction of chemical components.

4. Left-over parts are used to produce energy.

Plastics are still a major problem in the area of 'high-value recycling'. Two examples of how BMW recycles plastic parts are as follows:

■ Six plastic parts on the new 3-series can be made from the old, painted bumpers of the 3-, 5- and 7-series, which are cut up and reconditioned for this purpose. The rear lining in the luggage compartment is one of these six parts.

■ Further components already made from regranulated plastics and used for new vehicles are wheel-arch covers, cable coatings and foam plastic parts made of flaky compounds.

BMW plants are already recycling a number of parts formerly thrown away. In 1987 BMW became the first manufacturer to take back used catalytic converters via its dealer network, and 90 per cent of the precious metals are reclaimed and reused. Another benefit is that customers receive between £35 and £100 for each converter returned.

Such items as plastic bumpers are reclaimed and granulated; 20 per cent of the old material is incorporated with 80 per cent new material to mould new bumpers. Items such as sound-deadening material and rubber linings are also used in this way. Used oil, neon tubes, glass, packaging materials, solvents, plastic films and injection-moulded parts are also reused in the actual production process. At BMW's Munich factory the proportion of reusable waste obtained in the course of production is over 40 per cent. Even water in the painting process is recycled six times.

The new 3-series, the most recently designed model, benefits from the evolution of recycling technology. It contains many parts which are recyclable or recycled, such as the boot lining, wheel-arch lining, wiring protection, bumpers, dashboard and floor panels. Recent advertising campaigns by BMW (and also by Daimler-Benz for its new S-model) place great emphasis on the 'recycling' issue.

Since a car is a composite of 20,000 parts made in a wide variety of materials, the process of recycling is very complex. It involves dismantling the car, sorting parts into different material groups and arranging for these components to go to a specialist for recycling. Although 75 per cent by weight of most cars is capable of being recycled, in reality it is unlikely that more than 50 per cent of all scrapped vehicles will be used in another production process.

In 1990 BMW became the first manufacturer to open up a disassembly plant. Until the end of 1991, old cars from all the BMW series will be disassembled in Landsberg in six workshops: doors, roofs, interior, luggage compartment, bodyshell, engine compartment and underfloor. The main objectives of this comprehensive project are as follows:

■ To develop and improve model-specific methods of disassembly.

■ To optimize the time and cost of disassembly.

■ To develop internal and external logistics for collecting, sorting and transporting parts, assemblies, plastics, glass, etc. for reconditioning or recycling of materials.

■ To develop further-reaching waste management and recycling technologies, in particular for automotive applications.

■ To compile and complete BMW's own recycling directives to be implemented within the network of BMW factories.

■ To increase substantially each vehicle's recycling potential.

■ To compile and apply recycling and ecological standards for suppliers.

Engineers responsible for vehicle development can also draw important conclusions from this project in designing new cars suited for recycling from the outset. In addition, the project allows precise analysis of the disassembly and recycling potential offered by the current generation of cars.

BMW's recycling operations are no longer limited to the pilot plant in Landsberg, but are also undertaken at the first scrapyard, where the fluid drainage and disassembly systems are currently being installed. This scrapyard has been operating in the market for a long time and the objective is to pool BMW's experience with its own know-how. A number of suppliers are also participating in this market-orientated pilot project, taking parts that BMW has disassembled and reconditioning them for future use.

BMW's plan is to drain fluids and disassemble vehicle components in the future, not at centralized, manufacturer-specific plants, but through a widespread network of car recovery yards throughout Europe. These companies must, however, fulfil specific requirements in order to obtain a licence to be entrusted with drainage and disassembly operations by car makers. In 1991 two professional centres were operational in Germany. In the UK the BMW project team aims to establish the first independent car dismantling and reprocessing centre by the end of 1992, five regional centres by the end of 1993 and ten centres by the end of 1994. This plan will be implemented in co-operation with the Motor Vehicles Dismantlers' Association.

Power production

Power stations are near the top of the agenda in discussions of pollution. This is not the place for a full-blown discussion of the politics of energy, our wasting of fossil fuels or the advantages of regenerative energy. We will restrict ourselves to the marketing activities of some of the energy producers.

In an advertising campaign in Germany the central information bureau of the Electricity Board reports on measures for cleaning up the air. The installation of desulphuration plant in coal-fired power stations has led to a two-thirds reduction in sulphur output. By 1992 it will be three-quarters. Everywhere you look the output of nitrogen oxides is being reduced and eco-friendly power stations are receiving just praise.

OVER the last couple of years, the Greenhouse Effect has become one of the world's hottest topics.

But actually, it's nothing new.

Since the mid 1800's there have been warnings about how increased levels of carbon dioxide in the atmosphere can affect our climate.

It acts rather like glass in a greenhouse.

The sun's rays pass through it to Earth, but then it traps some of the heat that would otherwise be radiated back into space.

And this is the problem. Too little carbon dioxide in the atmosphere and we freeze. Too much and we get overheated.

Which is exactly what's been happening.

Things are hotting up.

In the last 100 years, the Earth has warmed up by more than half a degree.

That may not seem like a lot. But geologists have observed that changes of minute fractions of a degree can cause glaciers to advance or decline.

The net result could mean rising sea levels all around the globe.

Some scientists believe that a rise of between 20 centimetres and 1½ metres can be predicted by the year 2030.

Certain areas of the world would return to marsh and swampland.

A rise of just a foot would drown the sandy beaches of the US Gulf and Atlantic coasts.

A three foot rise would flood a sixth of Egypt's arable land, making 8 million homeless. Not to mention the 15 million that would lose their homes in Bangladesh.

Venice could even disappear. And parts of London would become a swamp (not unlike the Late Pleistocene period when the hippopotamus was a native of the Thames Valley).

However, this rather dismal scenario is by no means definite.

Must act now.

Just as man has been responsible for polluting the atmosphere, he should be responsible for cleaning it up.

Scientists are beginning to acknowledge that carbon dioxide from fossil fuels is the single largest waste product of modern times.

It is also a major contributor to the Greenhouse Effect.

Others include chlorofluorocarbons

We have the power to help prevent it.

are beginning to be taken more seriously, although a wind-farm the size of Greater Manchester would be needed to replace a single power station.

And what of fossil fuels?

As the majority of our power comes from burning them, can we afford to stop? Or even slow down?

The fact is, we're going to have to conserve them anyway. Because our fossil fuels won't last forever. And they're not being replaced.

Nuclear alternative?

Fortunately, we do already have a secure source of clean energy for the future.

Nuclear power.

At BNFL, we believe that it has an important role to play in a balanced energy policy for this country. Not only that, it has an important role to play in the environment.

In France and Belgium, for example, they generate more than two-thirds of their electricity from nuclear power.

This has helped to reduce their output of carbon dioxide faster than in the rest of Europe.

In Britain, we could do the same. And we must.

So sure are we of a nuclear future, that BNFL is currently investing £1½ million a day at Sellafield.

We are equally sure of the role we can play in the environment.

Naturally, we'd expect you to weigh up the arguments for and against.

Then, ask yourself a simple question: Are the others offering really workable alternatives?

(CFCs) which are found in aerosols and refrigerators. Also, methane which comes from various natural bacteria processes and the burning of tropical rain forests.

So, the simple answer to halting the Greenhouse Effect is to stop producing these gases responsible for it.

What can be done?

Naturally, this is easier said than done, but a start is being made.

Governments are trying to phase out the use of CFCs, so that by the end of the century, no products will contain them.

Further losses of the rainforests must be stemmed and new trees planted.

We must continue with energy conservation. Along with lead free petrol and catalytic converters, how about the 100 miles-a-gallon car? Current prototypes can do 80mpg.

Dams, windmills and tidal barrages

BRITISH NUCLEAR FUELS PLC.

Risley, Warrington WA3 6AS.

Nuclear power stations do not lead to the emission of CO_2, and they are regarded by some as the ideal balance between ecology and economy. Global warming is seen as the big threat nowadays, and one of the main causes is the burning of fossil fuels. This makes nuclear power appear in a more favourable light, even though problems of reactor safety and waste disposal remain unsolved.

In Britain a new campaign has been initiated. It is exemplified by a number of newspaper advertisements.

British Nuclear Fuels asks the reader, 'Just how green are you about nuclear power?' and goes on to refer to the ecology movement and its dilemma:

> Once upon a time, green was just a colour. Now it is a universal movement. And what shade of green you are says more about you than even class or status. To a lot of people, however, being green presents a dilemma: how best to safeguard the future of mankind, and accept nuclear power as playing an important part in that future. We at BNFL believe nuclear power has a role to play in both. By far the biggest threat to our future comes from the Greenhouse Effect.

Even when the facts seem clear ('Fossil-fuel power stations produce CO_2 which contributes to the Greenhouse Effect. Fact. Nuclear power stations do not. Fact.'), competitors are not convinced and stress what they claim to be their own advantages.

Without wishing to get too involved in the expert wrangles over the causes of and solutions to the accelerating greenhouse effect, we should acknowledge two problems which are continually highlighted by scientists:

- Our knowledge about ecology is constantly changing and makes re-evaluation absolutely necessary. Not so long ago CFCs or asbestos seemed almost ideal.

- The priorities of environmental politics are only ever valid and vouched for by science for the present time and state of knowledge. Abrupt surprising changes are always possible.

'One only knows truly when one knows little; with the knowledge grows the doubt' (Goethe).

Other products

The domestic goods sector usually aims to cut down on energy and/or water consumption. In particular, the washing machine industry is currently riding on the crest of an eco-wave with its advertising splash on the environment-friendly qualities of its products. Under the title, 'Environment Protection transcends Competition', German domestic appliance manufacturers have joined forces to inform the public about efforts to overcome the CFC problems in the disposal of fridges and freezers. New coolants and insulation materials are being

WE WON'T ASK
YOUR CHILDREN TO PAY
THE EARTH
FOR TODAY'S ENERGY.

Environmental pressures have forced us to all to think more about the world we leave to our children.

At British Coal we've been thinking particularly hard. And it's had reassuring results. You'd be suprised just how clean coal burning is today.

The world's modern coal-fired power stations aren't just more efficient, they can now eliminate 90% of sulphur emissions. An extensive programme of installing this technology (called flue gas desulphurisation) in British power stations has now started.

Coal-fired power stations generate 40% of the world's electricity, but contribute only 7% to total greenhouse gases (both of these figures come from OECD statistics).

And in Britain, coal produces over three quarters of our electricity. Modern coal plants are clean and safe to work in and live near.

The current technology is impressive enough. But future advances promise to provide us with 20% more electricity from the same amount of coal, reducing emissions still further.

And long-term contracts offered by British Coal to the power stations will guarantee prices well into the future.

Which all means that British Coal will be capable of generating electricity safely, cheaply and more cleanly during our own lifetimes. And those of generations to come.

Whichever way you look at it, it won't cost your family the earth.

For more information write to British Coal Marketing Department, Hobart House, Grosvenor Place, London SW1X 7AE, or ring 01-235 2020.

WAKE UP TO THE
NEW AGE OF

researched and CFCs in insulation have been cut by 50 per cent. Their message is: 'Buy this new-generation technology and help protect the environment.'

◇ AEG

AEG is certainly one of the pioneers in the field of domestic appliances with its Eco-Lavamat washing machine. By appealing to the eco-consciousness of consumers and including power- and water-saving extras, AEG was able to raise its share of the market from 11 per cent to 13.4 per cent. In recent campaigns AEG talks about 'ecosystems'. Saving is child's play, you just use less water and electricity, 'which helps your budget and the environment'.

AEG is also intensifying its efforts at recycling old machines. In the production stage, easy dismantling is being built in as a feature of new machines. Cable, for instance, is now secured only by clip, electric pumps can be unplugged and in some appliances metal parts are seamed together not welded. Similarly, manufacturers such as Grundig and Philips are beginning to code plastic components.

In 1989 AEG launched a £1.6 million advertising campaign to promote its 'white goods' in Britain. Although the market for these goods was on the decline, AEG was able to achieve a 30 per cent increase in turnover.

◇ Miele

Miele put forward the prototype for a new washing machine in 1990 which manages to wash a 5 kg load with only 38 litres of water instead of the usual 80–100 litres.

◇ Siemens

The new eco-appliances aim at equivalent performance in spite of achieving savings in energy and water consumption. This idea underlies the Siemens Eco-Plus programme. 'This concept embraces the sum total of our ideas for the environment':

- Half the water, electricity and time of older washing machines.

- Reduced noise output in dishwashers as well as savings in water, electricity and cleaning fluid.

- Reduction of CFCs in fridges and coolers and 50 per cent savings in energy.

- Pyrolitic or catalytic self-cleaning in cookers, which makes harmful sprays and cleaning fluids redundant.

- Energy saving of up to 50 per cent in microwave ovens.

◇ Bosch-Siemens/Lever

An interesting collaborative development between a detergent manufacturer and a machine manufacturer early in 1990 has resulted in a new, fully automatic washing machine with an overshot water system. The innovation is a dispensing unit consisting of four containers for a co-ordinated liquid detergent system developed by Lever. Micro-chip control of this Automatic Dosage System (ADS) prevents 'overdosing'. Some 50 per cent fewer chemicals, 50 per cent less water and 40 per cent less electricity are anticipated. The four 'skip' tanks (bleach, softener, washing fluid, conditioner), last for four to six months. They can be refilled during the introductory phase by calling out a Lever service engineer.

In summer 1990 the first CFC-free refrigerators and freezers came on to the market. Complete transfer to the new polyurethane insulation foam will take from two to four years. There will be a rise in price of about 10 per cent for these machines. Bosch-Siemens Domestic Appliances have applied for a patent.

◇ Philips

The development of compact light bulbs presents another example of energy-saving products. For almost ten years Philips has produced a bulb in which the same strength of illumination is achieved with 80 per cent less electricity than conventional bulbs. A new 20-watt bulb gives just as much light as an old 100-watt bulb, and with eight times the life expectancy. These light bulbs not only have a long life, they also contribute to environmental protection by saving more than 30 per cent on glass and illuminant, and on average 50 per cent on mercury.

Many private businesses as well as government offices have taken up this idea, replacing old light bulbs or installing entirely new systems.

◇ Osram

Since environmental protection is a major concern of the American people, the Federal energy corporations have undertaken programmes as a matter of course. An example is Operation Lightswitch in the state of Maine. Central Maine Power (a company with 482,000 customers in 330 communities) avoided the purchase of new production plant, thereby contributing to environmental preservation. Through Operation Lightswitch, which involved selling 85,000 Deluxe EL bulbs using 75 per cent less energy than normal, considerable amounts of energy are saved (currently 7.6 million litres of oil or 12,500 tonnes of coal). In addition there has been a reduction in waste. Since the life-span of the bulbs is estimated at 13 times normal, over a million fewer light bulbs will end up on the garbage dumps of Maine.

Osram was the first company to see the importance of this growth market and has been targeting it with its Deluxe EL, which is mentioned more often by energy companies than its competitors. On the strength of its high media profile Osram was able to establish itself in the minds of politicians, industry and environmental groups as the authority in energy-saving lighting techniques. The 15-watt bulb gives the same light as a 60-watt traditional bulb, and although this fluorescent bulb is much more expensive than the old incandescent light bulb, there are ecological advantages because of lower energy consumption as well as economic benefits because of lower electricity bills and longer life.

◇ Romika

Romika, the fourth largest German shoe manufacturer, has placed the Spirit of Nature line at the centre of its four 1990 collections. The products are described as 'environment-friendly shoes', because Romika see environmental protection as topic number one in the public mind, and it is currently testing market acceptance of this product line, using the slogan 'Out of Nature for Nature'. Customers are promised a high degree of naturalness based on the use of leather, cork, rubber, recycled textiles and natural fibres. The Pursoft sole is eco-friendly, and disposal is no problem because of minimal material use and tester-based plastics. In construction and shape the shoes are therapeutic and comfortable.

The prices are approximately DM10 (£3) higher than the competition. Advertising was limited to 120 TV spots from March to May 1990 on RTL Plus and SAT 1.

◇ Philips

There has been growing environmental concern over the last few years because of domestic refuse: not just the quantity, but particularly the composition. The spotlight has rested on batteries because of their mercury content. Towards the end of 1989 Philips presented the outcome of its research: the Green Line battery. This zinc/manganese dioxide battery has the following properties:

- It contains no mercury.
- It can therefore be disposed of via normal domestic rubbish dumping.
- It has a steel outer covering for maximal leak proofing.
- It has a clearly legible best-by date on the base plate.

10

Integrative approach to logistics management

◆

Never in the history of mankind has so much valuable raw material been transformed into so much worthless rubbish.

(Bavarian environment minister, 1988)

Industrial economy consists in producing worthless rubbish with a high level of entropy from valuable resources.   (Roeser)

Principles of an integrated concept

Within an integrated materials management system, avoidance and reuse should clearly take priority over disposal. This philosophy needs to be inculcated into every section of a company's activities.

Avoidance/use/disposal

Since the principle of recycling is so fundamental to the balance of the ecosystem, it is inescapable in the context of modern industry. However, the real value of recycling only emerges from the framework of an integrated system of waste management. Obviously, we should try to maximize reuse, but it is better not to create the waste in the first place. In other words, every effort must be made to avoid waste before planning disposal.

Recycling is an eminently reasonable partial solution, but it must not be allowed to disguise the existence of floods of waste material. Integrated environmental protection means planning disposal into the production process, replacing 'collecting and disposal' with 'preparation and avoidance'. Think about the end at the beginning.

> Everyone on this earth is making a grab for its bounty. It is an endless brawl. Every man for himself! (Heinrich Heine, *Atta Troll*)

The three principles are outlined in brief below.

Avoidance

The most effective way of combating the burden on the environment is to prevent it from arising at the start. Instead of setting up a purification plant as an afterthought, procedures should exist to exploit possibilities for combining processes. For example, metal recovery plants can avoid the pollution of waste water by reclaiming tonnes of heavy metal. Similarly, transferring from a sulphate to a chloride process during the production of titanium oxide facilitates the preparation of sulphuric acid from the acidic waste water. In the Bayer chemical factories at Leverkusen, production of naphthalene disulphonic acid has been transferred to a water-free process from which both sulphuric acid and solvents can be recovered. Previously, the process produced an acidic, saline waste water which had to be put through a purification plant.

It is estimated that special industrial waste can be reduced by 50–60 per cent by the year 2000 – considerably more in some branches. There are countless instances of the potential for innovative technologies in avoiding waste and emissions (e.g. aluminium salt slag, dyes and solvents from car manufacture, recovery of acids). There are cases of reclamation plant being integrated into a circulatory system of production management. In addition, there is the possibility of replacing dangerous input materials with more environment-friendly ones (e.g. solvent-free powder paint instead of paint containing hydrocarbons, or the use of organic solvents or solvent-free adhesives).

The logistics of disposal are underdeveloped compared with, say, production methods. Integrating waste avoidance can be a very long business, estimated at six to ten years on average.

Use

The process of recycling can take two forms:

● In-house materials cycles as an integrated component of production processes.
● A bolt-on to the process of production and consumption (as separate recovery and use of residues).

Recycling is often seen merely as a kind of reuse; in fact, it embraces all measures aiming to recover materials from waste which can then be fed back into the production system.

There are four basic types of recycling, depending on whether the product or substance is reused or exploited for a new use (see Figure 27). During the course of production and beyond there are many points at which recycling can be introduced.

The first cycle is based on waste from the production process, which is either fed back into the same process or used for another purpose. If this is not possible within the same firm, there are opportunities to find inter-industrial uses via a waste exchange.

The next possibility is to reuse the finished product, the main aim being to ensure that the product does not end up on the rubbish tip. First of all, one can try to prolong the life of a product or rework it in some way so that it can be used for the same purpose again (e.g. a reconditioned car engine or tyre).

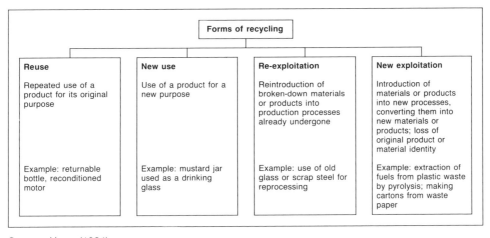

Source: Heeg (1984).

Figure 27 Forms of recycling

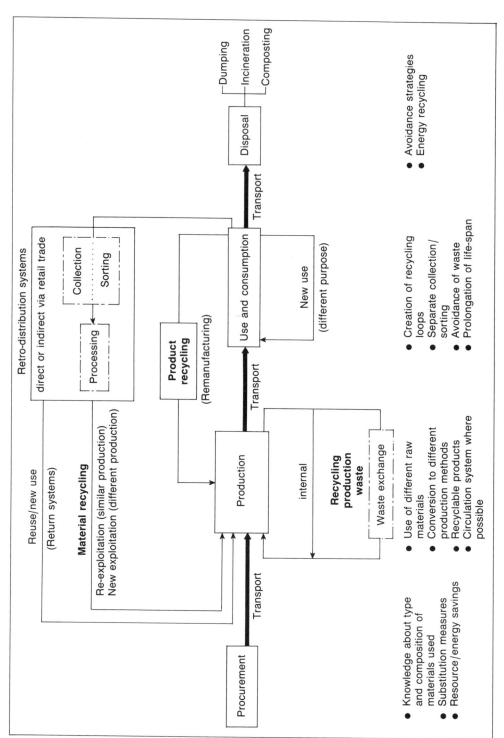

Figure 28 Recycling within the eco-product life-cycle

The last phase is to recycle the material from which the old product was made, and any residue which cannot be re-exploited must finally be disposed of (see Figure 28).

Recycling aims to make waste into useful output which can be utilized as input to another system. This means that:

● Waste must be sorted according to its possible output attributes.

● Waste must be treated to make it into useful output.

● Recycling production requires close collaboration between supplier, producer and customer.

> We must reuse or re-exploit the materials and energy left over from our existing forms of production and distribution. It is important to recognize that recycling is not the only real alternative to disposal and that it can only save very few of the raw materials we consume. Only when it is used in conjunction with prolongation of use and curtailment of the proliferation of new goods can we achieve the desired relief to our natural resources. (Schenkel, 1981)

Ecologically, recycling represents a kind of stretching of the life-span of materials. One danger is that it functions as an alibi for more painful preventive measures which could have been adopted at the stages of production or use. On principle, avoidance is better than recycling, but it demands a large time-scale for planning and implementation. Also, it does not alleviate the emergency caused by existing 'waste mountains'. Although this crisis has been predicted years ahead, political decisions have led to hesitation; in some countries the easier option has been to export garbage: 'waste tourism'.

Disposal

The higher the cost of disposal rises, the stronger the incentive will be to adopt avoidance or reusage measures instead. In Germany, the cost of disposing of 1 tonne of domestic waste has been estimated at DM40–80 (around £20). Special waste costs DM250–500 per tonne (around £120) and the incineration of domestic waste costs DM100–150 per tonne (around £40). The incineration of special waste costs about DM100 per tonne (£330), up to about DM3,000 (£1,000) for waste containing PCBs. Hitherto, environmental protection has been practised as a mere administrative exercise.

◇ BASF

At BASF total disposal duties are combined into one unit. All production residue is recorded on a data base including details of origin, chemical-physical properties, type of disposal and relevant regulations. According to the 'polluter pays' principle,

costs are paid by the departments responsible, as an inducement to explore the
possibilities of recycling.

Design for durability

The desire to be conscious of recycling at the construction stage is manifested
in two ways:

- In the list of product requirements.
- In the design stage.

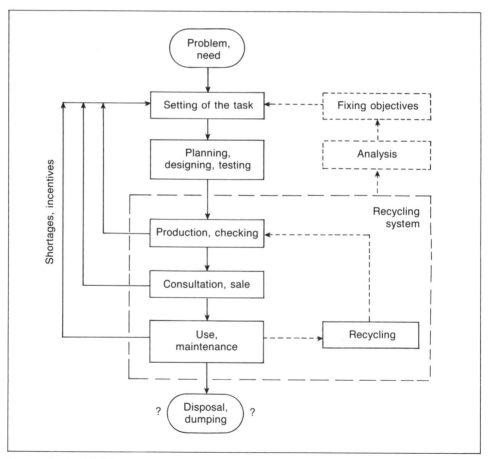

Source: Jorden (1983).

Figure 29 The cycle of product – recycling – information

The design engineer not only determines the cost of manufacture but also the way a product will be used and therefore its effect on the environment. (Jorden, 1983)

Previously, the design engineer has been regarded merely as a link in a linear chain of information. An optimal product, however, needs to be designed with recycling in mind, and so the design engineer ought to draw information from the recycling system, thereby closing the circle of information flow (see Figure 29).

Heeg (1984) has drawn up a checklist of rules for an appropriate product design procedure (see Figure 30).

Design products to be as reusable as possible
- Build long life into non-expendable parts
- Locate expendable parts for ease of dismantling
- Select bonding for ease of dismantling

Anticipate the need for up-dating
- Provide room for expansion, avoid integral construction
- Build the possibility for expansion into the technology (performance in reserve, interfaces for additions)

Provide for the possibility of different uses after irretrievable obsolescence
- Adapt exterior design for the possibility of new uses
- Make allowances for conversion

If products are not suitable for reuse, ensure that components are usable
- Combine components into functional units that can be dismantled
- Standardize components
- Arrange for easy dismantling
- Code usable components

Do not forget possible additional uses

Do not forget exploitation of raw materials

Use only one material in production or as few as possible

Plan for easy re-exploitation of materials
- Only use compatible materials
- Reduce the proportion of incompatible materials to below the permitted levels
- Design high proportions of incompatible material for easy removal
- Reliable coding of all materials used

Plan carefully the use of restricted or non-exploitable materials
- Substitution with exploitable materials
- Use only in long-life products, if possible
- Improve the quality of materials with restricted exploitability, to increase the number of usage cycles

---

Source: Heeg (1984).

Figure 30 Rules for designing recyclable products

Stahlmann (1988) sees the following additional demands for materials management:

- Selection of input materials based on recycling criteria.
- Purchasing designed to encourage co-operation and the use of waste exchanges.
- Collaboration with the design engineer to avoid combining materials which are difficult to separate out for re-exploitation.
- In dialogue with the sales department, modification of the sales programme to include reusable, long-life products.
- Listing material waste flow based on input–output analysis.
- Choice of production methods aimed at minimizing waste.
- Avoidance of possible waste at each stage of the product's life-span.

The best-known example of use-orientated product design is the returnable bottle.

- Non-returnable packaging causes 31 times the volume of waste and twelve times the weight of returnable bottles.
- From 1970 to 1985 the proportion of non-returnable bottles out of all drink packaging rose from 11.8 to 25.6 per cent.

The Association of German Engineers (VDI) has already drawn up basic rules for the design of disposal-friendly products, but they have not yet been widely adopted in production. The most important considerations for this type of product design are as follows:

- Minimizing product deterioration.
- Ease of replacement.
- Ease of assembly.
- Ease of dismantling and up-dating.
- Standardization of components to enable cross-product uses.

For products which cannot be reused, exploitation of the materials is sometimes possible, although separation of materials can sometimes cause difficulties. Heeg suggests the following measures:

- Increased use of products made from one material.
- Maximum permitted proportions for certain substances.
- Attention to material tolerance.
- Quality of material appropriate to use.

Collaboration between different stages of production will be necessary. The example of recycling old paper shows how printing ink manufacturer and paper manufacturer have to work together. Conflicts between objectives will inevitably arise. New inks used for off-set printing need good adhesive properties but must be easy to de-ink. If the printing ink designer does not take this into account, problems will arise at the recycling stage.

> The generations which follow us will look back on the egoism of twentieth-century man with bitter hatred for having plundered the planet in a hundred-year excess of greed and selfishness. For, what we devour today we remove from those who will succeed us. They will have to live on the left-overs. They will have to try to use what we found too difficult or too expensive. They will have it much harder. Exploitation of our fellow men is despised, but taking away the basis for existence from our great-grandchildren counts as a worthy deed. It brings money and honour and electoral victory. (Kuba, 1986)

The manufacturer's responsibility for disposal

Towering mountains of refuse have long been recognized as a visible sign of an unrelenting throw-away mentality in our society. Local communities are positively threatened by the task of removing waste and setting up dumping sites or incineration plants.

Retailers have an important part to play in this scenario, as 'gatekeepers' of distribution channels. For Schenkel (Federal Environment Office, Berlin), a social market economy such as that in Germany demands symmetry in this matter:

> Why should there not be a principle that whoever creates and distributes materials and products is obliged to see to their disposal? It is intolerable that electricity producers should generate and sell electricity and leave the waste products to society. The same is true of a business which offers its products in non-returnable bottles, and is only prepared to offer returnable bottles as an alternative in the export market.

Schenkel also stresses the producer's responsibility for disposal:

> This knowledge means that one cannot find the correct design for a product without solving the question of its disposal. Our future development strategy must be to find a symmetry between production and disposal. At the moment a highly effective business economy is under way, driven by all intelligence, all knowledge, all market power and economic interest. And up against this colossus a few people are standing, trying to clear away the mountain of refuse. This cannot bode well.
>
> We can only arrive at a just symmetry if producers are not allowed to shrug off their responsibility, if they are forced to pay the cost by laws, compelled to deal with their products up to the end.

It is incumbent upon marketing to create a redistribution system of materials ('reverse channel concept') in addition to the traditional flow, and to feed vital resources back into the system. Questions of eco-friendly packaging and recycling are becoming ever stronger marketing arguments.

If an effective, comprehensive programme of recycling management is to be installed in conjunction with the retail sector, we must give high priority to avoidance and reutilization strategies as well as disposal.

◇ Castrol, Germany

Castrol, the oils and lubricants manufacturer, has been offering its customers the Environment Care System since 1989. It embraces recovery, controlled disposal and appropriate use of products. Castrol has set up optimal use of input materials, maintenance of plant, laboratory supervision and staff training as part of this integrated scheme.

In coming years the disposal of computers will be a big problem. The incredible surge of PCs on to the market will draw new solutions to the problems of reuse and disposal in its wake. At present PCs or TVs can be disposed of only via local refuse collection facilities. There is no legal obligation for the manufacturers to take back the goods, but this is being discussed as the only real basis for optimum production. It will certainly encourage producers to plan reuse and disposal into new models. At present, in Germany, at least 150,000 tonnes of electronic waste are dumped, including 10,000 tonnes of computer waste, with an anticipated increase rate of 10 to 15 per cent per year.

Computer waste contains precious metals such as silver, gold and platinum, as well as iron, copper, tin and aluminium, all of which could be re-exploited. However, re-exploitation would be very difficult because of the number of different substances involved. Circuit boards contain up to 23 different metals and various plastics. At the moment, about 5 to 10 per cent of computer waste finds its way back into the recycling net. Very few manufacturers offer return services: Digital Equipment, Dell Computer and Unisys on a small scale, with Nokia Data and IBM providing comprehensive recycling concepts. Since three-quarters of all computer waste occurs outside of the maintenance and distribution systems, it is important to recover old computers in one piece and feed them back through the trade.

◇ IBM

IBM initially trialled the return of old machines in Switzerland. The machines are dismantled by hand, and individual parts are sorted according to material and distributed to relevant disposal firms. IBM is working on new concepts. It processed 600 tonnes of disposal materials in 1990 and is expecting 350 tonnes of old hardware for 1991. Since June 1990, IBM has begun to offer a disposal service to its own customers in Germany. Trade customers are expected to carry the costs themselves: between DM50 and 4,200 (£16–1,400), depending on the hardware. The company hopes to achieve as closed a circulation as possible, and at present the recycling quota is 83 per cent and as much as 90 per cent for some components. The remainder has to be disposed of elsewhere.

A haulier collects machines from IBM. They are mechanically dismantled in Nieder-Roden, and the parts are then distributed to specialist companies. The computers are broken down into five types of material during the manual process:

- Reusable parts, e.g. linear motors, certain circuit boards and network machines.

- Parts containing precious metals, e.g. control boards, cards and connectors.

- Electro-technical waste, including iron-based metals (completely reusable), non-iron-based metals, plastics and glass.

- Ecologically non-problematic items, e.g. manuals, disks, etc.

- Items needing treatment, e.g. batteries, capacitors and oils.

Particular disposal problems are caused by cathode-ray tubes and plastics. Optimum sorting of plastics would be helped by having just one type of plastic, so IBM are cutting down the number of plastics used and coding them for recognition. Coding is soon likely to be made obligatory.

◇ Nokia Data

The Swedish/Finnish firm Nokia Data presented an excellent concept for the disposal of discarded computers, terminals, printers and electronic components at CeBit 1990. A payment of about £16 is made for returned machines. The computers are mechanically dismantled and the parts are sorted into seven groups: iron and scrap metal, screen, keyboards, control boards, connectors and cable, batteries and glass. Over 90 per cent of the materials are reused. The rest – for example, glass from screens, dry cells and plastic from control boards – is scrapped.

The lighting industry in Germany developed voluntary disposal concepts as early as 1985 for the recycling of discharge tubes containing mercury. The volume of discarded light bulbs will eventually be reduced by about 90 per cent. The aim of the process is to reuse the glass, the mercury and the illuminant gas. This will fulfil new national regulations. The cost of reprocessing (about 10p per lamp) is roughly the same as the cost of traditional disposal.

Other voluntary agreements have been developed in the battery industry and the electrical goods industry, especially for refrigerators. The German superstore Quelle accepts trade-in fridges when a new fridge is bought, and guarantees recycling of the CFCs.

Establishment of recycling management

Recycling models

In terms of ecology, recycling means feeding back material or energy residue into the production process for reuse or re-exploitation. It is connected with saving resources, reducing the burden on the environment, saving energy and economizing on valuable space. In our consumer society, waste is seen as synonymous with rubbish. Waste is, however, raw material in the wrong place. In industry, crafts and commerce we need a kind of recycling culture. This would not only bring about ecological benefits but would pay in economic terms as well.

A distinction is often made between production and consumption recycling, and between internal recycling and intercompany recycling. Recycling within a holistic system of life-cycles should be applied to all three phases:

● Recycling waste from production.

● Product recycling or rebuilding.

● Recycling used materials.

Recycling is interdisciplinary, drawing on the sciences, engineering and economics, and this amount of expertise is usually found only in large companies. Logistical means must be found of combining the stages of purchase from suppliers, manufacturing control, distribution and disposal. Recycling clearly has significant growth potential.

Recycling production waste

Internal recycling

Recycling from primarily economic motives has long been established in certain branches of industry: for instance, foundries and glass works. The present discussion, however, proposes recycling as an ecological mechanism for saving resources and reusing them within the company infrastructure as far as is technically possible.

The recycling of waste from production is already used consistently in branches which produce and process raw materials. For example, material savings of about 10 per cent have been made possible in metal-processing industries by means of melting down scrap.

The idea of using unwanted remains, after processing, as components for some other production process led to co-production in the chemical industry many years ago. Bayer Chemicals has been making pigment out of iron oxides which occur during the reduction of nitro-benzene to aniline. Similarly, the co-product anhydrite from the manufacture of hydrofluoric acid is used in the building trade to make plaster and flooring compounds.

The whole of chlorine chemistry could be seen as recycling technology for chlorine by splitting NaCl to fulfil the demand for aqueous sodium hydroxide. Individual branches, e.g. manufacturers of VCs, used to produce waste which had to be burned on incinerator ships on the high seas. Nowadays, chlorolysis is the state of the art. (Schenkel, 1987)

◊ Volkswagen/Daimler-Benz

Water recycling is increasing in all branches because of rising costs for fresh and waste water. This implies that the amount of fresh water consumed per tonne of production is decreasing. The balance achieved through closed circulation systems can be seen in the following cases:

- At Volkswagen in Wolfsburg, the total demand for 355 million cubic metres of water is met with only 32 million cubic metres, in a closed circulation system. The site is fed by three separate water systems which, with the quality achieved by water recycling, allows twenty-fold reutilization.

- In the iron foundry in Esslingen-Mettlingen, Daimler-Benz has achieved savings in water consumption of 400 cubic metres per hour. This water circulation system relieves the local purification plant of an enormous industrial burden. In addition, a heat recovery plant in the heating exhaust outlet of the factory saves 1,700 tonnes of coal per year, or 900,000 litres of fuel oil. Another environment protection measure is the 'cold box' process: by installing a plant for regenerating core sand, the dumping of more than 110,000 tonnes of waste sand has been avoided.

Waste exchanges

If there is no possible way of recycling the residue from production processes within the company, certain substances can be offered to a waste exchange. In Germany, these operate on a national scale within the branch of the relevant Chamber of Industry and Commerce or Association of the Chemical Industry. The Chambers of Commerce and the DIHT (Association of Chambers of Commerce) limit themselves to establishing contact between participating companies which have to work out their own contracts. The services of these agencies are free.

At present, around 1,000 batches of industrial waste are dealt with by the German waste exchanges, and about 700 firms make enquiries about particular waste products. On average 3.6 replies are received per offer, and four offers are made in reply to each request. Once enquirer and supplier have found each other, there is no obligation for them to continue to use the services of the chamber, so the figures cited do not give a true reflection of the achievements of this service. The possibility of intercompany exchange of waste materials considerably raises the potential for recycling and indicates the importance of intensifying this form of business co-operation.

Since 1980 the DIHT has been the co-ordination point for production waste from across Europe, and in 1989 the European Computer Database was expanded correspondingly.

Product recycling (remanufacturing/rebuilding)

Recycling is a form of circular thinking. Hitherto, it has been applied only to production and disposal phases to create a new input material. The intervening phase of use is, however, becoming more important. For instance, a car need not be scrapped but can be refurbished for another use, which has the great advantage of leaving the production value partly intact.

This kind of work has previously been carried out within companies as a kind of maintenance. Especially in the USA, series production of reconditioned products has been developed further. Around 2,000 firms with more than 150,000 employees are said to be engaged in rebuilding or remanufacturing. Industrial reconditioning can be regarded as a useful instrument of market upkeep in the face of increasing disposal difficulties.

Recycling in the car industry is well established in Germany. The gearboxes, dynamos, starter motors and so on represent 10 per cent of new production. Huge numbers of engines are reconditioned: at present 200,000, making a saving of around 40,000 tonnes per year. There are familiar examples of countless other recycled products, such as electric razors, tools, office equipment, industrial robots, cigarette machines and so on.

A certain amount of product recycling can be carried out in-house or it can be transferred to independent companies as part of after-sales. There are possibilities for small to intermediate companies here. According to Steinhilper (1988) worldwide purchasing organizations act as suppliers of 'raw materials' to such firms in the USA.

Series product recycling embraces five production stages: dismantling, cleaning, testing, component repair or replacement, and reassembly. High costs are incurred during dismantling and component repair. The Fraunhofer Institute for Production, Technology and Automation has developed a flexible dismantling unit and a research programme, RECOVERY, to promote the use of recycled components.

◇ BMW

BMW has been involved in recycling for 25 years under the name of 'reconditioning'. Mechanical parts have been returned to BMW plants and reworked to give the same service as a newly manufactured part. The advantage to the consumer is one of reduced cost, but to the global community it offers the benefit of reusing scarce resources. Each year BMW reconditions 16,000 engines, 8,000 transmission units and 13,000 starter motors.

By disassembling, reconditioning and reassembling the old engine, BMW is able to build an exchange engine virtually equivalent to a new product with a 30 per cent saving to the customer. The company does the same kind of reconditioning on the rear axle differential, starter motor, alternator and water pump. In addition, it has developed and introduced a process for recycling catalytic converters. The converters are cut up and the various materials separated from the monolithic body. A raw materials company then recovers platinum and rhodium from the monolith at a rate of about 80 per cent.

Using the most advanced technologies, each exchange unit is reconditioned and subsequently examined according to strict quality standards at BMW's Recycling Centre, at the Landshut factory. Currently, the range of exchange parts and components comprises approximately 1,700 different items. Since such exchange units are absolutely equal to new parts in their function and service life, they come with BMW's usual new parts warranty.

Recycling used materials

A product should not be considered as 'waste' after the use/consumption stage. It is better to regard it as used, raw material for future multiple uses. This presents not only a technical problem, but also a marketing issue, because suitable markets for recycled products have to be found. There is not much sense in aiming at ever higher quotas of recycling if there are no stable market outlets. The onus is on the government to lead the way in this respect, as it is potentially a large consumer of this type of product and can impose taxes on primary resources and exert direct legal pressure on industry, commerce and consumers.

The *Warmer Bulletin* (22/89) describes this as the 'golden rule' of recycling: 'Growth in the volumes handled is limited by demand for the reclaimed product rather than its availability. Until a market is found, the recovered material can only be considered as waste.'

In Germany, the circulation of raw materials, particularly from one-substance products, or those which are easy to separate out, has reached a viable level:

- Iron/steel 90 per cent
- Used tyres 80 per cent
- Paper 40–50 per cent
- Tinplate 40 per cent
- Glass 45 per cent
- Plastics 33 per cent

In single-product areas the rate can be as high as 95 per cent (e.g. lead storage batteries; aluminium, copper and zinc scrap from used cars; aluminium tops on returnable bottles).

In a voluntary agreement on the disposal of batteries (September 1988), in which manufacturers undertook to reduce mercury content, a new symbol and a pledge to accept returned batteries was taken up. All batteries with mercury content above 0.1 per cent of the total weight display a recycling symbol, three arrows in the form of a circle. The batteries are sorted into separate return cartons and processed by various firms.

Positive development of the recycling market is borne out by the figures. According to the German Association of Paper Raw Materials (BVP), 5.3 million tonnes of used paper found their way into the recycling banks in 1989. The figure worldwide is about 75 million tonnes, and for the EC is around 18 million tonnes.

Of the 10 million tonnes of paper and cardboard produced in Germany per year, only about 160,000 tonnes are made from 100 per cent recycled paper (i.e. closed circulation). However, nearly all types of paper do contain a large proportion of used paper. New pulp and used paper are mixed according to the quality of paper required. Recycled pulp cannot be used indefinitely because the fibres become shorter each time they are processed.

The paper industry has expanded its capacity for recycling, and Germany, with 1.2 million tonnes of export volume, is the largest exporter of recycled paper in Europe. Used paper recycling quotas for the world average 32 per cent, and for the EC 47 per cent. In western Europe the quotas are very variable. The leaders are the Netherlands with 49.3 per cent and Germany with 43.8 per cent. Britain and Italy are lagging behind with 30.4 per cent and 25.8 per cent respectively (source: DRI/McGraw-Hill).

In 1988, 37.8 per cent of toilet paper in Germany was made from recycled paper, 60 per cent of newspapers, 91 per cent of packaging and 100 per cent of grey or brown corrugated cardboard. But the average German still uses 191 kg of paper and cardboard per year, mostly in packaging. The highest demand is for paper for use in catalogues and magazines, which contain only 5.1 per cent recycled paper.

The use of recycled paper for routine office paperwork has become standard practice. One-fifth of the 1 million tonnes of paper purchased for office use in Germany consists of 100 per cent used materials. The market leader for high-quality recycled paper is Steinbeis-Temming Paper Ltd, but countless small companies also offer eco-friendly paper, which must meet strict processing regulations: for example, no chemical bleaching, and closed-circulation water consumption.

◇ Federal German Postal Service/Bavarian Co-operative Bank

The German Postal Service, the biggest customer for recycled paper, uses 630 million sheets (15,000 tonnes of printing paper, 3,200 tonnes of DIN A4 sheets). Since the Postal Service started using 100 per cent recycled paper for accounts, envelopes and telephone bills, the Bavarian Co-operative Banks followed suit in February 1989 by printing their statements on recycled paper. In local banking in Bavaria alone, over 250 million bank statements are issued. This initiative has since been taken up by other institutions.

◇ Europa Carton

The Europa Carton company, which manufactures corrugated cardboard in Hoya exclusively from used paper, will be testing customers' readiness to take cardboard cartons to the recycling bank, and a recycling symbol for the cartons is being designed.

There are also high quotas for recycling glass. In Germany, 50 per cent of glass jars find their way back to the glass industry. This fulfils the regulations for recycling glass packaging. Only wine bottles fall short of the ministerial requirements. There are 70,000 bottle banks in Germany which are relatively accessible to 97 per cent of the population. Glass recycling enables great savings in energy – approximately 100–120 kg of fuel oil per tonne of broken glass.

Recovery (collecting, processing and sorting) is the first stage of re-exploitation. A general problem in recycling is keeping the materials separate. Impurities confound the production process. Efficient separation and the introduction of differentiated collection systems would considerably raise the recycling quota, and some local communities are running trials in this essential area.

In Britain, there are various street collection projects under way: for example, in Bury, Cardiff, Dundee, Leeds and Sheffield. In Milton Keynes, as well as disposing of normal rubbish in plastic sacks, householders collect plastics, glass and metal in a blue box and used paper in a red box. These are emptied every week. Although recycling in England brings in more than £2 billion per year, only 2 per cent of domestic waste is exploited.

The world organization for recovery and reuse, Bureau International de la Recuperation (BIR), reports that, for 1990, around 200 million tonnes of re-exploitable material worth $16 billion were collected by its societies. Already 44 per cent of world steel production, 36 per cent of copper, almost half the lead and one-fifth of the paper is produced from recovered materials.

There is a long tradition in the recycling of scrap metal. It has become a separate branch of industry with about 3,500 businesses in Germany and a yearly turnover of DM4 billion (£1.3 billion). Scrap metal is also a key export. Approximately two million cars per year are converted into 1.4 million tonnes of steel.

Catalytic converters

Recycling of catalytic converters is on the cards. They contain platinum with a total value of around DM200 million (£67 million) and also rhodium and palladium, which make recycling well worthwhile. The adoption of catalytic converters began in earnest in Germany in 1975, and only a few tonnes of waste were recovered up to 1988, but by 1992 there will be hundreds of tonnes per year.

The companies operating at present in Germany (Thyssen Sonnenberg/ Walter Trupp Rohstoffe, Deutsche Autokat Recycling, etc.) represent only an interim stage in the process. They dismantle the converters, resell the stainless-steel casings as scrap and pass the ceramic parts to refineries (e.g. Degussa Ltd) for re-exploitation. Of the 41 tonnes of platinum used in catalytic converter production in 1988 only 5 tonnes were recycled metal, although a boom is expected in the next few years. The main problem is setting up a nationwide collection network. In addition, a logistics concept still has to be worked out between car manufacturers, supplying industries, scrap dealers and refineries.

Problem plastics

Disposal cycles for scrap metals, paper and glass have been virtually completed. The problem with plastics, however, remains a worry for environmentalists; particularly integrated plastics. At present there are very few strategies for dealing with polymers. Society acknowledges plastics as an invaluable material resource and recognizes the disadvantages in the disposal phase.

A holistic manufacturing approach must explore the possibilities of environmentally guided exploitation of resources. Material recycling is preferable wherever possible. In cases where it is not possible, recyclers may resort to 'energy recycling', using the energy potential of plastics released during incineration.

The introduction of a coding system will greatly simplify the problem of separating different types of plastic. As with other forms of recycling, the development of appropriate technologies and the establishment of a market for the recycled material are important to its success. Legal and hygiene restrictions must also be considered. In Italy, children are already playing with toys made from recycled plastic.

According to a study by the Berlin Federal Environment Offices approximately 1.8 million tonnes of plastic are deposited in dumping sites. This will rise to 3 million tonnes by the year 2000. In the USA only 2.2 per cent of the 60 million tonnes of plastic waste are recycled. Since this occupies over a quarter of the space available for waste disposal, it has led to furious debate on how to raise the proportion of plastic recycled. The chart published by Werra Plastic (Figure 31) gives a quantitative overview of the possibilities for recycling plastics.

Delmart suggests strategies for feeding plastics back into the economy (Figure 32). The process involves either breaking down certain plastics into their

Exploiting plastic waste		
	Approx. tonnes per year	Exploitation aim
Total of pure and mixed plastic waste	2,500,000	
From this quantity the following are exploited:		
a) Preparation of own product waste	500,000	recovery of raw materials
b) Material recycling	400,000	recovery of raw materials
c) Energy recycling. In Germany, 5 revolving drum incinerator plants are adapted for pure, non-exploitable, mixed, thermo-plastic waste incineration. Additional mixed plastic waste is incinerated in the remaining domestic waste incinerators, around 6%.	500,000	energy production
d) Pyrolysis method	...	energy and raw material recovery
Total	1,400,000	tonnes/year
Currently non-exploitable mixed plastic waste	1,100,000	tonnes/year

Source: *Unternehmen und Umwelt*, March 1989.

Figure 31 Exploitation of plastic waste in the Federal Republic of Germany

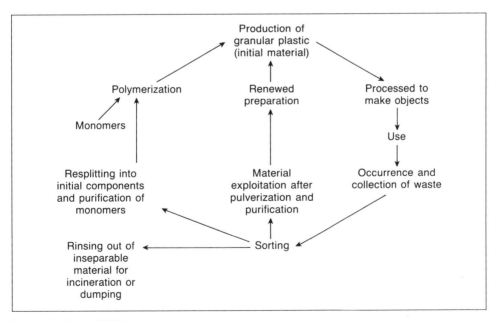

Source: Dehnert (1989).

Figure 32 Plastics circulation

molecular components and cleaning the monomers, or material exploitation after pulverizing and cleaning, and it presupposes the availability of specialized technology. In future, the question of separation must be addressed at the manufacturing stage.

A significant rise in the required quotas is not likely until the second half of the 1990s. Pure granules are relatively easy to feed into reuse cycles, but mixed materials present great problems. Even when high-quality granules can be produced, the fly in the ointment is the cost of water and energy needed for these processes.

Recycling plastic is plagued by major technical difficulties, and countless methods such as pyrolysis, hydrolysis, hydrocyclonics and compression are currently under trial. The bulk of domestic waste is just not clean enough or separable enough to be recovered. Mixed and soiled waste gives low-quality secondary recycling products which can only be used for sound proofing, garden furniture, insulation, flower pots, etc. These products cannot normally be recycled again. While new bottles can be made from glass waste, polyethylene teraphthalate (PET) waste is suitable only for making the opaque bottoms of bottles.

In general, plastic from recycled bottles is used for low-quality goods. The American Food and Drug Administration (FDA) has banned the use of recycled plastic in food packaging for reasons of hygiene. Some firms, such as Coca Cola in collaboration with Hoechst, and Pepsi with Goodyear Tire and Rubber, are working on technologies which will meet the strictest hygiene standards.

Pure granules are relatively easy to feed into reuse cycles, but mixed materials present great problems. Even when high-quality granules can be produced, there remains the problem of the cost of water and energy needed for the processes involved.

◇ Du Pont

- Du Pont will suspend by the end of the 1990s all production of CFCs, which bring the company about $750 million a year.

- It recovers about £1 billion of polymer and polymer feedstocks per year from recycling.

- It has eleven reclamation centres across the USA, which recover nearly £200 million of high-value materials with more than £55 million in sales (*Financial Times*, 16.3.91).

- It formed a joint venture with Waste Management to sort and recycle plastics from solid waste throughout the nation.

- It formed a Safety and Environment Resources Division to help industrial customers clean up toxic waste.

◇ Storopack

Styropor and Loose Fill packing chips are the first plastics for which there is a national recycling project in Germany. This is not because of the chemical composition of the plastics, but because of their volume and eye-catching whiteness which stands out in every dumping site. Storopack, Europe's leading manufacturer of expanded polystyrene chips, wishes to increase the recycling quota of the 35,000 tonnes of chips produced annually. The high-volume packaging can be returned via delivery drivers, given back directly to Storopack by the sack-full, or collected at central collection points where it is taken back to Storopack as a complete load. The returned material is either milled and used for making new chips or regranulated.

Of the 30,000 tonnes of Styropor produced annually, 1,200 tonnes are recycled, which represents 4 per cent of the total market. The Federal environment minister has called for a return quota of 25–30 per cent, which could only be achieved with much greater commitment. With this in mind the Industrial Union for Plastic Packaging and Foils has set up its own committee.

Motor vehicles are also developing into a problem area (see Chapter 9). While the scrapping and shredding of cars has caused relatively few problems so far, the use of plastics instead of steel in car body work is beginning to cause recycling difficulties. The average proportion of plastics used in cars has increased from 2 per cent in 1970 to 11 per cent (around 80–150 kg). A limit of 15 per cent has been proposed.

◇ GM/Du Pont

The exception which proves the rule is probably the General Motors Cadillac. The mud-guard, which used to be made of plastic, is now being made of steel again. In stark contrast, Du Pont, one of the biggest plastics manufacturers and suppliers to the motor industry, presented plans for a five-door limousine as part of a vehicle research study: 30 per cent of the total 1,100 kg was made of plastic.

It is anticipated that most of the body work of cars in the future will consist of polymers. The use of glass-fibre toughened plastics in particular has also increased.

There are, however, positive aspects to the increased use of plastic. It prolongs the life-span of the product, cuts down the total weight of the vehicle and therefore also reduces the fuel consumption. It is characterized by a high degree of safety and durability and low maintenance. The negative side is that the mixture of different types of PVC, polyethylene and polystyrene cannot be reused.

Production design must be conceived so as to facilitate the separation of different types of plastic, which should all be coded. In general, dismantling should be borne in mind much more in the construction of cars.

Politicians in Bonn have been seriously considering incorporating a scrap charge into the price of cars, or imposing an obligation on manufacturers to take back old cars. The objective, of course, is to increase pressure on designers to develop eco-friendlier cars. In 1988 the Federal Association of German Scrap Merchants (BDS) called for a disposal fee from manufacturers whose materials are left over after shredding. This currently represents 520,000 tonnes of waste from two million cars, for which DM50–100 (around £25) per tonne have to be paid for dumping and transportation by someone who did not cause the waste in the first place.

Collaborative efforts are being made by the motor industry to reduce the number of different plastics used from the present 20 or so. Cars which are reasonably compatible with recycling are not envisaged for 10–15 years because of the long development process and the increased average life-span of the cars.

◇ Opel

Opel has come up with one solution to the problem of liquid coolants. It is installing recycling plants for the coolant Frigene, which contains CFCs, with its dealers across Europe. The recycling plants make it possible to exchange coolant without releasing pollutants into the atmosphere.

Environmental packaging policies

Functions/environmental impact

Packaging has come under ecological scrutiny because of the unstoppable growth of refuse mountains, the detritus of our throw-away society. Recent discussions about a packaging tax have brought the matter into even sharper focus. Each individual spends an average of DM500 (about £170) per year on packaging, and about 6 per cent of food prices pays for packaging. Indeed the heaviest use of packaging materials is made by the food industry (47.2 per cent), the chemical industry (22.4 per cent), and other processing trades (18.7 per cent), according to figures published by the IFO. The turnover of the packaging industry in Germany alone is DM31 billion (£10 billion) per year, and it provides employment for 500,000 workers.

Packaging which is thrown away represents the main cause of the refuse crisis. This is particularly true of 'overpacking'. Most packaging finishes up in the dustbin, representing 50 per cent of the volume and one-third of the weight, and then in dumps or incinerators. It is therefore vitally important to reduce packing and intensify recycling, although it is useful to bear in mind that even the best recycling will only deal with 35 per cent of domestic waste.

The following points will help to put the discussion in context:

- There could be no self-service without packing, and 95 per cent of all goods are sold via self-service.
- Packaging is an essential part of a proprietary brand product.
- Packaging fulfils a variety of useful functions, such as protection during transportation, stacking, storage, conservation, sales and information, portioning, food regulations and so on.
- Packaging is supposed to be cheap.
- Packaging has to fit into the highly automated production process.
- Packaged goods, especially food, can be offered in relatively small portions suitable for single-person households.

Since the cost of refuse disposal will rise in the 1990s, avoidance and reduction strategies must be sought. The food industry will have to bring more environmental considerations into product and marketing strategies. An eco-packaging policy would have to respond to a number of notions:

- New technology for storage and transport.
- Saving material by limiting wrapping.
- Saving resources through weight reduction.
- Introduction of reusable packing, e.g. returnable bottles.
- Introduction of reusable materials and improvement of recycling potential.
- Recyclable package design to facilitate return.
- Avoidance of portion packaging.

The provision of eco-friendly packaging depends on acceptance by retailers and the customer. The shopkeeper, for example, has to be willing to set up and maintain redistribution points, while the customer has to decide to take part in recycling and to use a shopping basket instead of throw-away plastic bags. The first attempt to introduce returnable milk bottles at the food store Tengelmann had to be abandoned because of lack of customer response. However, a come-back was possible in 1987. Similarly, Toni circulation jars needed a second run-up (see p. 184).

◇ McDonald's

McDonald's is exploring new directions, specifically in those countries where consumers are sensitive to the growing flood of packaging waste. It has launched a 'green' initiative aimed at reducing waste by 80 per cent. Forty-two different measures have been announced, including the following:

- In 1990 polystyrene 'clamshell' hamburger packages in the 11,000 restaurants in the USA were replaced with parchment-like quilted paper cartons. These were introduced by rival Burger King some time ago. By December 1991, corrugated boxes containing at least 35 per cent recycled paper were to be used exclusively. Ironically, an environmental impact study by the Stanford Research Institute, carried out in 1976, had recommended abandoning the paper wrappings used until that time. However, public pressure in the 1980s proved too strong to resist.

■ In a pilot project involving 450 New England restaurants, customers were asked to separate foam and plastics from other waste. The polystyrene collected from this project is used by a recycling firm.

■ Since January 1991 polystyrene packages in restaurants in Germany have been replaced by cardboard packs containing around 75 per cent recycled paper. From 1992 all refuse arising from McDonald's, Germany, will be subjected to a special fermentation process developed by a Munich company. The new method produces 70 per cent compost and 30 per cent bio-gas.

■ After McDonald's announced its intention to buy $100 million in recycled materials for use in building and remodelling its restaurants, a toll-free number was arranged (McRecycle USA Registry Service), under which the manufacturers of recycled products could register as potential suppliers.

■ A joint task force, together with the Environmental Defense Fund, is seeking new ways of reducing refuse, and a marketing agency has been given the job of presenting McDonald's environmental efforts to the public more persuasively.

It is not enough for consumers to show interest. They must learn to take action. For instance, too many consumers who claim to be in favour of environmental protection continue to wrap presents extravagantly and lend their support only to measures which do not involve them directly. However, as a survey by the Allensbach Institute for Demoscopy shows, there is growing pressure from consumers on trade and industry to find alternative forms of packaging.

◇ Bischof and Klein/Werra Plastics

Bischof and Klein, one of the leading European packaging manufacturers, sees its job as helping to take the product from the producer to the customer. The company philosophy is based on the principle, 'Products come and go, but functions are here to stay'. This implies that the function of packaging can and should be achieved on the basis of ecological principles. Many manufacturers recognize the need and ask Bischof and Klein to find eco-friendly solutions to their particular problems. Transferring to an ecological business concept has meant that the input of raw materials could be cut by 50 per cent. It was possible to double the proportion of secondary materials without limiting the efficiency of the wrapping material itself.

Some 62.5 per cent of production waste is reprocessed into marketable products, and combined with externally treated waste. This means that a total of

90 per cent of the waste materials are fed back into the production cycle. Energy recycling is also used in the case of wrapping foils.

In 1989 Werra Plastics, a subsidiary company of Bischof and Klein, set up an innovative material circulation in combination with a Danish firm. Silage sheeting is made from recycled plastic waste and sent to Denmark. After use, the sheeting is collected and reprocessed by the Danish partner. It is then sent back to Werra Plastics, which makes it into silage sheeting again, thus completing the material cycle.

◇ **Henkel**

Industrial hygiene is increasingly concerned with green issues, and Henkel is one company which has extended its business along ecological lines. Natural raw materials, sparing use and easy-disposal packaging are all included. Bag-in-box packaging, used for a range of cleaning products, consists of a cardboard box which can be recycled with a double-strength plastic bag inside. The plastic bag becomes part of normal domestic waste, but it represents a saving of 20 per cent space compared with a bottle or canister. A dispensing tap encourages sparing use of the product. Packaging with an automatic dispenser for cleaning concentrates is also space saving.

Fully biodegradable surfactants were developed in this context because of the solvent properties of their natural ingredients. Coconut oil is the basis of the soap cleaner, and the soap is made from natural fatty acids.

In 1985 Henkel introduced the environment logo 'Dem Schutz der Umwelt verpflichtet' (dedicated to the protection of the environment) as an assurance from manufacturer to customer. Shortly afterwards the eco-certificate came out. Henkel's own scientists carry out extensive tests in their ecology institute and their standards are higher than the legal requirements. The certificate gives customers clear information about the very varied environmental properties of the products and their ingredients.

Testing packaging for environment compatibility should be carried out in a holistic study of the effects on recovery of raw materials, production and disposal. The use of raw materials and energy needs to be monitored at all stages, as well as pollution of air, water and land. Even if it is possible to acquire most of the necessary information, almost insuperable difficulties can be encountered in evaluating the effects on the environment. Who can say whether a given quantity of one toxin is more or less eco-damaging than another? Legal regulations are helpful with individual types of pollutant, and the concept of quantities 'approaching critical level' is widely used (Switzerland/Germany). Investigations into packaging have been carried out by the Swiss Federal Office for Environmental Protection (BUS), by the Migros Association with the aid of a specially designed computer program, and by the Institute of Ecology in Berlin.

Even a comprehensive balance sheet of material and energetic properties comes up against difficulties. The results are often contradictory, as in the case of the controversy over whether to pack Swiss yoghurt in returnable glass jars or non-returnable plastic containers. Divergent results are no surprise as it is impossible to account for all factors, and interpretations vary widely. Hocking, for instance, in his study of the environmental effects of paper and polystyrene cups, comes out in favour of the plastic. He was investigating the whole life-cycle from the raw material needed to make one cup, through the utilities required per tonne of material, to final disposal methods (*The Times*, 14.2.91).

The Fraunhofer Institute for Food Technology and Packaging is working on the design of a unified environmental and economic analysis for testing eco-friendliness in packaging.

Bauer and Müller (1988) illustrate these problems with an example. Figure 33 shows a typical comparison of the effects of a certain form of packaging on four aspects of the environment. In a second stage (Figure 34), the flow of materials and energy is assessed on the basis of ecological value. Even when only quantitative values are used, there are large discrepancies between the results. A is based on data from TA Luft, B on the Swiss BUS and C on the work of Müller-Wenk.

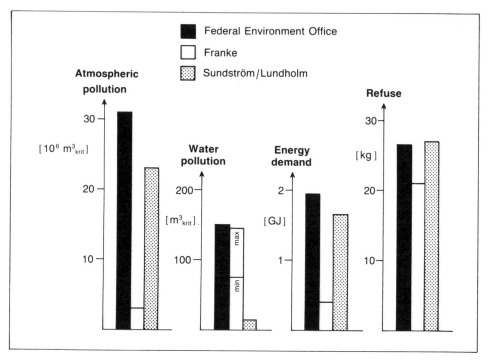

Figure 33 Material and energy balances: various research findings for a given packing material

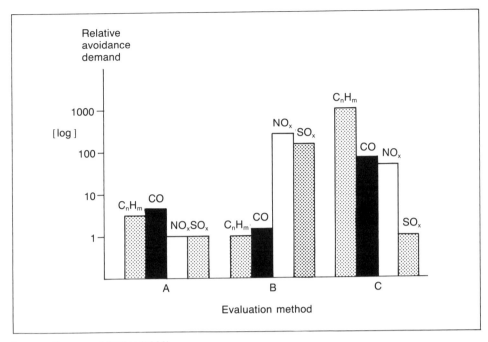

Source: Bauer and Müller (1988).

Figure 34 Ecological evaluation of atmospheric pollutants

The call for an eco-tax on some forms of packaging, such as cans, plastic bottles, Tetra-Paks and aluminium foil, has led to controversy. The various interest groups are making wide use of publicity on the environmental advantages of certain forms of packaging. The German Association of Aluminium Processing Industries (VAV) is up in arms against the disqualification of aluminium as a packaging material. Aluminium foil is represented as indispensable for food packaging. It is true that aluminium can often be recycled with very little loss of quality. However, processing the raw material uses vast amounts of energy.

◇ Alcan

Since late in 1989, Alcan has been running the largest recycling plant for drinks cans in the world. It is situated in Kentucky, USA. A maximum of 65 per cent of the recycled material is permitted in each new can. The largest fully operating plant for recycling aluminium cans in Europe is in Britain.

Alcan Aluminium has installed 5,000 containers for used soft drink cans to boost recycling in Ontario in Canada.

Four out of five drink cans, in a total world market of around 130 billion, are made of aluminium. The overall recycling quota for aluminium cans is 50 per cent, making the cans the most widely re-exploited containers for beer and carbonated drinks.

There are, however, differences from country to country. In the USA, for example, the quota is 61 per cent. In Britain, where over one billion cans are recycled per year, the current Save-a-Can campaign is attempting to raise the quota above 50 per cent. In Sweden the figure is 85 per cent, reflecting national regulations on returnable containers. In Germany, for reasons of tradition, only 15 per cent of cans are made of aluminium, the vast majority being tinplate. This has prevented the development of a fully fledged, nationwide recycling system. Aluminium has the distinct advantage that it allows an almost continuous recycling chain, each can being recycled to make another can. The reintroduction of old cans into the production process requires only 5 per cent of the original energy used.

In Britain, at least five billion plastic carrier bags are used per year. Since most of them end up as litter, retailers have started up various successful projects. Marks and Spencer has its 'reusable shopper' and firms like Sainsbury, Tesco, Gateway and the Co-op have been trialling biodegradable bags. Incidentally, biodegradable bags are obligatory in more than ten states in the USA, and are under trial in the Australian supermarket chain Franklins. These bags are considerably more expensive.

The Ecological Materials Research Institute at Brunel University comes to a positive judgement of these projects, whereas others favour intensified recycling. The use of a shopping basket, or reusing plastic bags, is clearly the best solution, and this is supported by the German Federal Environment Office.

◇ Hertie

As an alternative to the plastic bag made from improved, thinner plastic, Hertie has been offering customers cotton carrier bags at cost price in the food department since 1989. By early 1990 more than 100,000 bags had been sold. A donation of 30 pfennigs per bag was made to an environmental charity (BUND).

Companies striving to respond to ecological demands have experienced great difficulties because of the impossibility of evaluating environmental compatibility on a single scale for different systems. Different interpretations lead to different results.

In the conflict between glass, cardboard and plastic, various attempts have been made to draw the superiority of returnable bottles into question. Publications by the Association for Cardboard Packaging of Liquid Foodstuffs, or by Tetra-Pak in the EMPA study, *Milk Packaging in Comparison* (December

1989) or by the Swedish Environment Profile (1986) are examples of this conflict. The Institute for Ecological Recycling also played its part by drawing up an eco-balance sheet of the pros and cons of returnable glass and one-way PET. (*Natur, 7/88*).

◇ Unilever

Under the auspices of the 1989 Dutch National Environmental Plan, Unilever has made proposals for the avoidance of packaging waste. By the year 2000, it aims to eliminate the dumping of packaging waste. A whole series of questions remain unanswered as to how this goal can be achieved, mainly because of the lack of reliable data. Flow diagrams and data on energy and bulk of waste are needed to facilitate the choice of environmentally friendly packaging materials.

Late in 1988 the Cologne court forbade the Co-op advertisement 'Returnable bottles are eco-friendly' on the grounds that it undermined competitiveness. The slogan was regarded as misleading and the opinion of the court was that 'The statement in this form is incorrect because there is no general environmental superiority over one-way packaging.' With regard to the quantity of waste, and the saving of raw material and energy, the returnable bottle 'possibly' has advantages, but its weight, transport and cleaning problems create a strain on water, waste water, roads and fuel consumption which is greater than with one-way systems. 'Neither returnable nor any other system of packaging is generally environmentally friendly.'

Reuse of packaging materials

Recycling of packaging is hampered by the increasing use of plastics. Paper and card are still more common, but their proportion is decreasing. In Germany, the ratio has fallen from 46.3 per cent in 1970 to just below 40 per cent. Plastic has risen to 30 per cent, metal has remained stable at 21.5 per cent and glass has fallen to 7.8 per cent.

Each year, between 1.5 and 2 million tonnes of plastic packaging are discarded; from yoghurt pots to carrier bags. Only a few thousand tonnes of this are recycled, largely because of the no man's land of combined plastics. Collection and sorting represent the biggest problem because there is still no effective obligation to mark the different types of plastic.

In Germany, in 1990, dramatic steps were taken to stem the flood of waste packaging, reduce the amount of one-way packaging and raise the quotas for recycling. Of the 32 million tonnes of domestic waste which land on the tips, around 11 million tonnes are packaging waste. The German government packaging regulations will give industry a difficult choice:

- Either the retail trade will be legally bound (from 1 January 1993) to accept returned packaging from customers (at the point of sale), and a compulsory deposit will be payable on all drink containers.

- Or the affected groups of industry (manufacturers, retailers and disposal agencies) will have to set up nationwide collection systems for exploitable materials, with containers for every household. The containers will have to be collected and sorted, and maximum reuse of the waste will have to be guaranteed. Definite targets have already been fixed for the immediate future.

Naturally, the retail trade is vehemently opposed to being degraded to the status of a refuse collection and sorting service. They claim that waste disposal is a public service and not their concern.

The proposal for a 'dual disposal system' is generally seen as a better alternative, since the principle of co-operation is so central to German environmental policy. The idea of a 'dual waste economy', which should unburden the public waste services by about 30 per cent, involves allocating the disposal of packaging waste to the private sector and all other waste to public authorities.

Installing this system, which was launched early in 1991, will cost between DM1.5 billion and DM2 billion (around £0.6 billion). The cost of packaging will go up by about 2 pfennigs, or less than 1p per item. Recyclable products will be identified by a green spot and the first of such products is already on the market.

One worry is that there is no built-in incentive for the consumer to avoid packaging waste. Consumers may come to think of themselves as quite eco-conscious enough simply because they place their 'green spot packaging' into the correct container.

◇ Neff

Various measures in the field of packaging have been undertaken by the company Neff:

- Return and reuse of packaging materials from customers.
- Transfer from plastic to cardboard packaging for some products.
- Trial of returnable packaging via mail-order.
- Exclusive use of polyethylene for plastic packaging.
- Writing to all suppliers to send only articles wrapped in polyethylene.

◇ Johnson Wax

The combined efforts of the research and development and manufacturing divisions has facilitated the production of a plastic package for its Shake 'n' Vac product made entirely from recycled material. The blow-moulded bottle can be made from post-production polyethylene to the same standards expected from virgin material. The polypropylene cap is also produced from recycled material, as is the paper for the labels. This is a first for the bottle as a mass-marketed consumer product.

◇ Migros

Migros has disposed of the outer cardboard package for toothpaste, with a saving of 40 tonnes of cardboard annually. After initial difficulties this was eventually accepted by consumers. Many cosmetic products have followed suit.

◇ McDonald's, USA

McDonald's avoids the use of 30 million kg of plastic packaging by having concentrated cola syrup pumped directly into the drink-mixing machine from the delivery lorries. The syrup used to be delivered in heavy-duty plastic bottles.

McDonald's has also cut down on waste by using 220 per cent lighter drinking straws, and thinner polystyrene in their packaging. This measure has cut down refuse by about one million pounds weight per year. Napkins at all stores are now made from recycled paper, as is office paper at corporate headquarters.

◇ Karstadt/Kaufhof

At Karstadt combine, the largest department store chain in Europe, they are eager to reduce packaging during the transportation of goods to regional centres. Trials are being undertaken with clothes on hangers to save on packaging. This does not apply to light-coloured clothes, for obvious reasons. Some suppliers have also agreed to package-free transport. With items like shoes, which need boxes mainly because of stacking, cartons are not used for transport to the branches. Reusable containers have been used for this for some time now. They are collapsible plastic boxes and can be stored in space-saving racks for the return journey. Any other packaging material is collected and handed on to recycling firms when possible.

Kaufhof are also in the process of sorting through the 13,000 articles in their range with packaging and the environment in mind. Around 800 suppliers have already been approached for advice.

Degradable plastics

Research work is being carried out in several projects (for example, at the Battelle Institute) investigating biological and physical-chemical degradability:

- Biopolplastic, a thermo-plastic produced from sugar beet and corn, is degradable to CO_2 and H_2O. It has recently been unveiled by Wella Cosmetics and ICI Biological Products as a brand new concept in plastics. This polymer plastic can be used for making sheeting or bottles, but the cost is still eight times that of traditional products. However, Castrol, Hamburg, is using it for its two-stroke oil bottles.

- Water-soluble Belland plastic.

- The inclusion of additives in PE sheeting to enable photo-chemical degradation.

- The addition of modified starches to plastic sheeting.

In 1989 a new hybrid product consisting of part-plastic, part-natural materials was brought on to the market in Italy. A free, self-assembly watch was given away with the children's magazine *Topolino*. It was made of plastic based on maize starch with other natural softeners. These biodegradable plastics are two or three times as expensive as traditional plastics.

In the USA 16 states stipulate that the plastic sleeves on six-packs of beer cans must be made of biodegradable plastic.

It has recently been suggested that such measures are leading down a blind-alley. On the one hand, these plastics are not, with present knowledge, reusable. On the other hand, the organic compounds which arise from their decomposition are not always above suspicion.

◇ Wissoll

At the last International Confectionery Fair, edible packaging was welcomed from Wissoll, the chocolate and sweets subsidiary of the Tengelmann Group. Collaboration with a waffle manufacturer has led to the introduction of packaging in vanilla-flavoured waffle pastry instead of plastic for four types of chocolate. Although 'only' 180 tonnes of plastic will be saved per year, this innovation does provide inspiration for new ideas in packaging. This year Wissoll is to abandon artificial colourings and replace remaining PVC packaging with the more eco-friendly polypropylene.

Recycling alone is not the solution

From an ecological viewpoint, recycling is clearly a positive step. It minimizes the drain on natural resources, cuts down on emissions and avoids disposal. For example, a tonne of used aluminium requires only 5 per cent of the energy for resmelting that would be required for initial extraction from bauxite. For every unit of used glass a 0.2 per cent energy saving is made in melting.

Similarly, the manufacture of recycled paper needs less than half the electricity used in making white, wood-free paper, and only one-fifth the water. In addition, dumping space is saved because for every tonne of recycled paper 1.12 tonnes of waste paper are used up.

One should bear in mind that treating emissions also requires an input of work, in the form of energy and water consumption. This follows the second law of thermodynamics, which holds that a higher level of order (lower entropy) in a system can be reached only through the input of energy. Recycling also causes emissions itself. Dust, sulphur, carbon dioxide, nitrogen oxide and sulphur-based emissions are all given off during glass recycling. The water used in the cleaning process is polluted with sodium hydroxide salts and surfactants.

Often the raw materials are denatured through recycling ('down-cycling'), although not all products need top-quality raw materials. The typical example of this loss of quality is paper recycling, where the fibres become too short after a certain amount of processing and need to be enriched with fresh raw materials.

If environmental relief factors are weighed against pollution, the overall result is positive for almost all recycling processes because resources are extended and time is gained to plan new avoidance strategies.

One thing, however, is absolutely clear: these technological delaying tactics on their own can achieve only a postponement of resource depletion and pollution. Recycling is merely a curative tactic. In the final analysis only a 'reduction in the flood of material and energy we use, and a qualitative change in our way of life can bring about lasting effects on the environment' (Stahlmann, 1988a). Recycling is an alternative to waste disposal; that is its main ecological significance. Real progress, however, can be achieved only through limiting consumption. Recycling is always only the second best way. The best way is to save.

Intensifying recycling techniques instead of building up strategies for avoidance is problematic for two other reasons:

- On the one hand, consumers interpret their contribution to environmental protection wrongly. They see no reason to change their buying habits, for they already consider themselves 'green enough' because they take their bottles to the bottle bank.

- On the other hand, recycling favours re-exploitation of materials rather than reuse of products.

This latter point can be seen quite clearly in the conflict between returnable and non-returnable bottles. In terms of ecological balance, the returnable bottle is far superior to the one-way bottle and the PET bottle. Admittedly, plastic bottles are lighter and cheaper than glass, but in other respects such as energy and water consumption they are ecologically inferior. All forms of political incentive should therefore aim to increase the proportion of returnable systems.

Even measures such as putting a 50 pfennig (16 p) deposit on all plastic bottles between 0.2 litres and 3 litres (introduced in Germany in 1989) do not alter the basic facts. On the contrary, the deposit falsely raises the status of the plastic bottle and puts it on a par with the real returnable bottle. But plastic bottles cannot be refilled, they can only be recycled and transformed into new low-quality products.

The introduction of reusable plastic bottles which can be refilled up to 20 times is planned for the not too distant future. This really would place PET bottles in direct competition with glass as the deposit regulations would not apply to them.

According to figures from Klöckner, the largest manufacturer of refilling plants, 43 per cent of the 4 billion hectolitres of drinks sold worldwide are packaged in glass bottles, 15 per cent in metal cans, 15 per cent in barrels, 15 per cent in cartons and 12 per cent in plastic bottles. In the USA, almost 80 per cent of all drinks are sold in aluminium cans.

The EC Commission sees, in the German obligation to return bottles, a form of trade discrimination against foreign suppliers. A nationwide system of return facilities and transport of empty bottles (mostly to France) would cost millions. Currently, the market occupied by French imports is gradually being clawed back. Some 200 German companies have formed the Association of German Mineral Springs (VDM); its members use a 'bottle pool' for the standardized German bottle. So far, the pool deals with 93.5 per cent of returnable mineral water bottles. Foreign manufacturers wishing to join the system are greeted with not a little hesitation. The first effects are already discernible: for instance, the Belgian mineral water manufacturer Spa has announced a transfer to 1-litre returnable glass bottles.

In its newly planned regulations for drinks packaging, the EC Commission demands a rise in the proportion of returnable bottles. 'Returnable' implies: for the purpose of refilling, recycling or incineration. All packaging for liquid foodstuffs will have a compulsory deposit to support voluntary action.

Methods of waste treatment

Are we facing a waste disposal emergency – or are we already in the middle of one? A glance at the daily paper would suggest the latter. Our welfare society is seeking new ways to divide up these problems, and the lion's share falls to industry in general and management in particular.

The costs of industrial waste removal will inevitably increase. There is less and less space available in dumps, and technical processes are becoming more expensive, while tighter legislation is assigning a greater proportion of materials to the class of 'special waste', needing costly treatment.

The problem of refuse disposal is becoming globally urgent. Even in countries where the problem is not yet a crisis, the following points are valid:

- An acute shortage of suitable landfill sites. Existing reserves will be used up in very few years. This and stricter laws determine the cost of disposal.

- An increase in incineration facilities is not necessarily an environmentally better solution. In many countries it is not even feasible because of public opposition.

- 'Waste tourism' is becoming more difficult because of EC regulations.

- Great effort is required to increase recycling quotas.

- The need for avoidance of refuse is vital. In some countries, especially Germany, drastic legislative steps are being taken.

◇ USA

According to figures from the Environmental Protection Agency, the American refuse mountain for 1988 weighed 150 million tonnes and it is expected to increase to 193 million tonnes by the year 2000. This refuse is divided up as follows (figures for the year 2000 are given in brackets):

- Dumping grounds: 120.1 million tonnes (96 million tonnes).

- Recycling: 17.4 million tonnes (48.5 million tonnes).

- Waste-fired power stations: 20.5 million tonnes (–).

A typical American discards 590 kg of garbage (38 kg of plastic) a year, and uses 140,000 litres of water. In the USA 16 billion disposable diapers are used, 1.6 billion ballpoint pens, 2 billion razors and blades and 220 billion tyres, to mention just a few examples.

◇ UK

The Confederation of British Industry estimates that industry and commerce in the UK produce over 100 million tonnes of waste per year. Of this, about 90 per cent finds its way into infill sites compared to 20 per cent in Switzerland and 30 per cent in Japan.

A survey from Marketing Strategies for Industry (UK) estimates that the total waste in Britain for 1989 was 503 million tonnes. The total cost of disposal for 1989 was £3 billion and this will probably rise to £7 billion by 1992.

The *Financial Times* survey 'Waste Management' (26.9.90) quotes a figure of £16 billion for waste disposal in western Europe, consisting of 60 per cent industrial refuse and the remainder domestic waste. Paribas, the international stockbrokers, believe 'that this annual cost is likely to rise to £32 billion by the end of the 90s and that three-quarters of this will go on industrial refuse'.

◇ **European Community**

The problem of refuse has become a major priority in EC environmental policies. An investigation by the EC authorities in Brussels in 1987 estimated that within the Community, with its 341 million citizens, 2.2 billion tonnes of refuse occur each year, of which 30 million tonnes are harmful. About 60 per cent of domestic waste goes into landfill sites, 33 per cent is incinerated and 7 per cent recycled. A much higher proportion of industrial waste (60 per cent) is re-exploited. More than two million EC citizens are employed in industries connected with waste disposal, and these industries have an estimated turnover of ECU200 million.

Waste can be treated in the following ways:

● Recycling.

● Dumping, with or without biogas.

● Incineration, with or without recovery of heat energy.

● Composting.

If waste is viewed as a potential raw material instead of worthless rubbish, then we must obviously aim for as high a recycling quota as possible. To make full use of this 'rubbish' we need the means to separate different types of waste, specific definitions of minimum quantities and a highly developed logistics of resource recovery.

An ecological overview is as important in waste recycling as in other forms of recycling. Any cleaning process uses up water and all recycling consumes energy. New problems are arising because of the increased use of plastics, and our present inability to sort and separate. Plastics are valued highly in waste-fired power production because they release stored energy and leave little residue. However, the possible toxic effects from emissions are not at all clearly understood.

Unavoidable refuse and raw materials which cannot be recycled any more finish up on the dumping grounds. And when the dumps are full, there is always the dubious prospect of transporting or exporting the waste. Biodegradable materials are no problem and degradation caused by micro-organisms in biogases or in compost can be accelerated.

Newsweek reports that in the USA 28,000 tonnes of garbage per day take to the roads. The increasing popularity of recycling is seen as 'an outlet for a wide range of environmental angst'.

And still the volume of garbage keeps growing – up 80 per cent since 1960, expected to mount an additional 20 per cent by the year 2000. Excluding sludge and construction waste, a total of 160 million tonnes of refuse are tossed out by Americans each year – enough to spread thirty storeys high over a thousand football pitches; enough to fill a bumper-to-bumper convoy of garbage trucks halfway to the moon. (*Newsweek*, 27.11.89)

◇ Berlin Isar-Amper Works/Teuftal

First steps have been made towards recovering gas from garbage. This source of energy is used at 50 of the 550 dumps in Germany. The gases are used commercially at Europe's largest dump in Wannsee in Berlin. In March 1990 Isar-Amper Works opened a small power station which supplies energy to 600 households in the village of Markt Indersdorf. The power plant is fuelled with a mixture of methane and carbon dioxide from a nearby domestic refuse dump. The gases are sucked from the tip through a condenser to feed a gas motor which drives the generator.

In the largest landfill in Switzerland, at Teuftal, a network of pipes collects the gases. They feed 2,000 cubic metres per hour of gas to the power station, where four gas motors drive the generators. The Electricity Board in Bern claims that the power station produces 13 million kilowatts per year, which is equivalent to the power from 9 million litres of fuel oil.

Incineration is proclaimed by some as the only way out of the increasing refuse emergency. Some countries, like Switzerland, favour thermal conversion. The USA also has 155 plants in operation, 29 under construction and 64 being obstructed by local residents. In Germany, political parties are discussing the pros and cons, with scientific support for both sides. Many people believe that avoidance strategies would be undermined by incinerators. There are also fears of dioxins produced by incineration, and of the high cost. One plant costs between £13 million and 133 million.

The American love of acronyms has led to the following descriptions of the anti-incineration syndrome:

- NIMBY: Not In My Back Yard.
- GOOMBY: Get Out Of My Back Yard.
- LULU: Locally Undesirable Land Use.
- NIMEY: Not In My Election Year.

The syndrome could be applied equally to the siting of dumps.

Composting breaks down organic waste, by means of microbial conversion processes, into a product with high humus content. Ideally, the waste should be as unpolluted as possible.

In Upper Franconia, 'green barrels' for vegetal waste have been set up in residential areas without private gardens. In a project in Wye in Kent, organic materials are collected for composting. The project is run under the auspices of Wyecycle, together with Controlled Computing Systems Ltd, and it represents a development of the project begun in 1989 to collect newspapers, glass, metal, plastic sheeting, cardboard, batteries and used engine oil.

11

_ironmental marketing: more than just a green label

◆

We call it the Green Bubble. Is it going to burst? (Porritt, 1989)

Marketing with social responsibility

Growth-intensive marketing concepts are frequently blamed for a number of negative effects on the environment:

- The wilful exploitation of natural resources, especially as a result of obsolescence strategies.

- Too little regard for the actual needs of the consumer, producing goods which are harmful to health and the environment.

- Demand creation: the promotion of dubious patterns of consumption.

- The tendency towards waste, through advertising incentives, product differentiation and shortening of product life-span.

Meffert sees marketing as partly responsible for damaging the environment because 'The activities of marketing have increased consumption and the use of raw materials.' For this reason it is clear that businesses will have to heed the

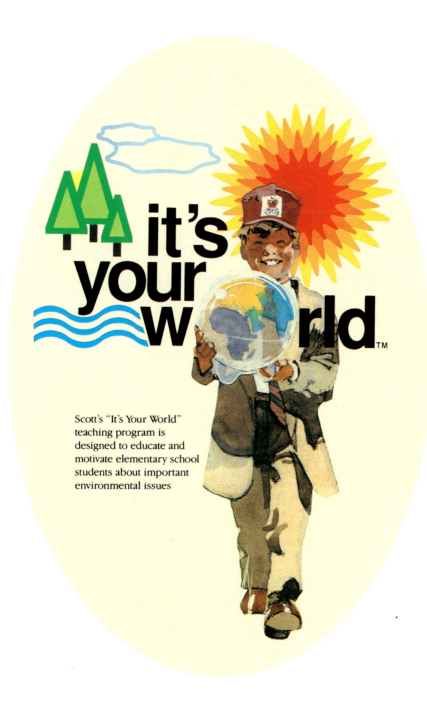

it's your world™

Scott's "It's Your World" teaching program is designed to educate and motivate elementary school students about important environmental issues

At Elida Gibbs, we believe our motto

'Caring for Health and Beauty' includes our environment.

New Sanara haircare from Wella. As kind to water as it is to your hair.

You'll notice how kind new Sanara is to your hair. See it. Feel it. Sanara's naturally derived formulations bring out the shine and smoothness in your hair, leaving it manageable and healthy. You won't actually see how kind Sanara is to the environment – but it's nice to know that the whole range is biodegradable, so it doesn't pollute water or the soil. And, naturally, the packaging is recyclable. **Sanara. Kind to you, kind to nature.**

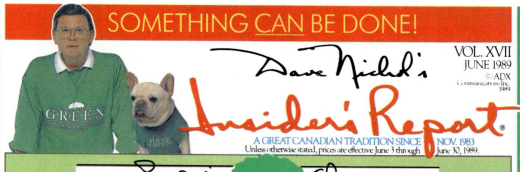

SOMETHING CAN BE DONE!

Dave Nichol's

Insider's Report®

VOL. XVII
JUNE 1989
© ADX
Communications Inc.
1989

A GREAT CANADIAN TRADITION SINCE NOV. 1983
Unless otherwise stated, prices are effective June 3 through June 30, 1989.

President's Choice

G·R·E·E·N ™

An Open Letter To Canadian Consumers about President's Choice G·R·E·E·N Products

Over the last year, while travelling the world looking for new products, I was astounded at the level of consumer interest in environmentally friendly products. For example, the best-selling book in England last year was an environmental handbook ranking retailers and their products.

Back in Canada, I noticed that every public opinion poll indicated that the environment was the number one concern of Canadian consumers — confirming what my mail had been telling me for at least a year.

Convinced that this concern was genuine, the Insider's Report team met with executives of many of Canada's leading environmental groups and asked them what products they would like to see us create that would in some way help to reduce pollution. Their guidance was the genesis of the G·R·E·E·N "Environment Friendly™" product program and in many cases we actually worked with these groups to develop specific products which they then felt confident in endorsing.

At the same time we also began development of "Body Friendly™" (low calorie, high fibre, low fat, low cholesterol, etc.) products under the G·R·E·E·N label. This Insider's Report highlights the first wave of our new President's Choice G·R·E·E·N product program.

Here are a few points of clarification about the program.

1. With few exceptions, President's Choice G·R·E·E·N products are priced at, or below the price of the national brand to which they are an alternative.

2. We do not intend to censor products that some may feel are "environmentally-unfriendly." We see our role as providing a choice so you may decide for yourself.

3. Protecting the environment is a young and therefore, imprecise science. As a result, not all groups agree on what the best products are to help control pollution. For example, some advise us to use paper pulp trays for all eggs while others say recyclable, ozone-friendly foam trays made with pentane instead of chlorofluorocarbons (CFC's) are a better solution. We accept the fact that it is inevitable that not all environmental groups will agree with all of our President's Choice G·R·E·E·N products.

4. Some may accuse us of being "environmental opportunists." WE SEE OUR ROLE AS PROVIDING PRODUCTS THAT PEOPLE WANT. That's why we created No Name products when Canada's food inflation was running at 16%. That's why we created President's Choice products when a demand for superior-quality products arose. And that's why we've created G·R·E·E·N products when the overwhelming concern of Canadians is the environment.

We invite you to read about our new President's Choice G·R·E·E·N products in this Insider's Report and decide for yourself whether or not they fill a real need in our society.

5. A number of our G·R·E·E·N products are products that we've carried for years (such as baking soda). Putting them under the G·R·E·E·N label was in response to environmental groups who chided us by saying, "You have a number of products in your stores right now that could help fight pollution but you have to bring them to your customers' attention and then explain how to use them."

We acknowledge that we are not environmental experts and we readily admit that we do not have all the answers. However, we feel strongly that these products are a step in the long journey toward the solution of our enormous environmental problems. If G·R·E·E·N products do nothing more than help raise awareness of the need to address environmental issues NOW, and give Canadians hope that SOMETHING CAN BE DONE, then in the end, they will have made a positive contribution.

Dave Nichol

David Nichol, President
Loblaw International Merchants

 zehrs Loblaws the super centre no frills

Selected products also available at Mr. Grocer, valu-mart® freshmart™ and Your Independent Grocer®.

interests of public opinion as well as the drive for economic growth (Meffert *et al.*, 1986). The call for 'awareness of social responsibility' will entail the following measures:

- Abandonment of unhealthy products or production methods.
- The use of environment-friendly packaging.
- Abstention from processing environmentally harmful raw materials.
- Taking on board the social costs arising from production.

It is very important to respect the social dimension in marketing. Long-term corporate objectives can obviously not be satisfied without catering for customer needs as a whole: 'The social aspect of marketing demands that marketing decisions are made in the context of a wider social system' (Meffert *et al.*, 1986). Marketing should no longer be construed solely as a way of fulfilling sales-orientated company policies. It must be expanded to embrace decision-making factors pertaining to ecology.

- Eco-marketing should be guided by the limitations on resources and not by the creation of consumer needs.
- Eco-marketing should attribute greater importance to stabilizing the ecosystem and energy consumption than to the production of throw-away products.
- Eco-marketing should seek alternatives which prevent the devastation of nature and redress the damage done by the industrial age.
- Eco-marketing should promote ecological product design, minimize packaging and develop recycling concepts.
- Eco-marketing should aim at decentralizing, for the stability of the system: initially by transforming industry, and then by developing local forms of industry on a small scale. (Schreiber, 1983)

The complexity of marketing decisions within this framework will certainly require a comprehensive system of information:

It is extremely difficult for business adequately to fulfil its social function because the means of analyzing the social effects are unavailable, and because economic objectives are far more clearly formulated than social and ecological needs. The social commitment of a company is limited by the wishes of shareholders and by its relationship with competitors. An environmental orientation of marketing which is not profit motivated, such as the Human Concept of Marketing, is hardly likely to be practicable. (Meffert *et al.*, 1986)

◇ **Esprit**

A unique approach to environmental issues was initiated by Esprit. In addition

A PLEA FOR RESPONSIBLE CONSUMPTION

SO OFTEN OUR needs are defined by things that don't get us much: the comfort of having lots of stuff, the image we want to portray, the social pressure to appear to be affluent, the bizarre idea of having something new for its own sake, like a new car or new TV or the latest fashion. For years, we have spoken to our customers about the difference between fashion and style. We've tried our best to encourage style and reinforce the concept that style isn't a fad. It comes from your imagination and is developed slowly. It's a reflection of your values.

Today, more than ever, the direction of an environmentally conscious style is not to have luxury or conspicuous consumption written all over your attire. This is still our message. We believe this could be best achieved by simply asking yourself before you buy something (from us or any other company) whether this is something you really need. It could be you'll buy more or less from us, *but only what you need*. We'll be happy to adjust our business up or down accordingly, because we'll feel we are then contributing to a healthier attitude about consumption. We know this is heresy in a growth economy, but frankly, if this kind of thinking doesn't catch on quickly, we, like a plague of locusts, will devour all that's left of the planet. We could make the decision to reduce our consumption, or the decision will soon be made *for* us.

We are optimistic that we can change course and avoid the disastrous destination toward which we're heading. We also believe that there are many events occurring throughout the world right now which support this outlook. We've experienced big changes in people's attitudes about some extremely important philosophical issues and values: racial, feminist, and economic systems such as what we're witnessing in Eastern Europe.

Our purchasing habits have enormous influence. By changing the things that make us happy and buying less stuff, we can reduce the horrendous impact we have been placing on the environment. We can buy for vital needs, not frivolous ego-gratifying needs. We do need clothes, yes, but *so many?*

While we're lobbying for responsible consumption, we want to suggest one more idea. What you save, if you do, through changing your purchasing habits, consider contributing to one of the thousands of social and environmental organizations that are working to correct, repair, preserve or halt the damage to which our consumptive ways and economic system have led us.

We all have to work together to preserve the continuity of natural cycles and processes. If we don't, we'll have no inheritance to bestow to our grandchildren. All will be gone. Our place in history will be that of the greatest mismanagers of the Earth, not such a loving way to be remembered!

A COMPANY THAT IS TRYING

Esprit statement of responsibility

to many other activities such as eco-sponsoring, a special green 'hot-line' and recycling (Esprit received an environmental award for its spring 1990 catalogue: the first retailer to print its catalogue on recycled paper), the company is now attempting to modify its advertising and communication strategies towards 'responsible consumption'. Consumers are asked to consider whether they really need the product before they purchase it. They are asked not to follow every fashion, but to develop their own personal style.

Environmental awareness and the consumer

Marketing is concerned with communication between partners. There is no doubt that knowledge about ecological questions has increased over recent years. However, it cannot be inferred that this knowledge has actually had an effect at the level of the consumer. Gierl (1987) outlines the conflict with the help of the following questions:

1. Will a green consumer be prepared to pay the cost?
2. Do consumers who hold general ecological views believe in the eco-friendliness or health benefits of ecological products?
3. Are ecologically minded people prepared to accept certain sacrifices in the subjectively perceived quality of ecological products?
4. Are sales figures for green innovations related to sales for the standard product, or do green attitudes govern people's buying habits?

The central result of a recent empirical survey was that:

> ecological attitudes or knowledge of ecological constraints only explain the sales of eco-products to a small extent. Ecological consumer behaviour can only be understood in terms of product-specific variables. People only buy green when they are also willing to expend greater effort in obtaining these products: for example, information, availability, price. This readiness to pay more varies from product to product. (Gierl, 1987)

As far as marketing is concerned, it is not enough to determine the number of environmentally motivated people in the target area. Measures for removing product-specific barriers must be incorporated into sales policies. For example, reasons can be given for higher prices or for changes in quality and distribution. Since business intends to fulfil long-term consumer needs, the consumer's ecological awareness is of vital importance. In other words, if consumer behaviour is to be changed, business must learn to adapt in line with it.

Environmental awareness among consumers implies the following:

- Consumers being informed about the ecological consequences of their buying habits. This depends on market transparency.

- Consumer insight into the consequences of purchasing behaviour, understanding the problems and disputes connected with the product.

- Readiness to change habits, to contribute to environmental solutions by adaptation.

All forms of environmental protection which cannot be based on a corresponding awareness on the part of the consumer are destined to fail. Ecologically orientated marketing has the responsibility for opening up consumer awareness of the environment.

Various studies of altered awareness have been made on the basis of behavioural theory. In particular, the three dimensions, cognitive, affective and conative, are relevant. A study undertaken by Bruhn between 1977 and 1985 shows a clear increase, in fact a doubling, of the ecologically aware segment of consumers to 37.6 per cent in Germany. A growing market segment includes consumers who are guided by their ecological awareness when they purchase products. If the trend continues there should be an increase in the sales of eco-friendly products.

The change in demand is connected with modified consumer behaviour patterns. Consumers must be prepared to support the idea of recycling or to take part in retro-distribution systems, sorting waste, or supporting environmentally kind chemistry by painting their houses with biodegradable paint.

By using the findings of empirical research, companies are in a position to identify ecologically relevant consumer groups as separate market segments and to respond to this new challenge through differentiated marketing. However, in defining green segments of the market we should be mindful of the divergence between existing eco-awareness and actual buying habits. The conversion of personal responsibility into action is slowed down or prevented by non-environmental motives, such as comfort, pleasure or the lower performance standards of the product:

> Contrary to popular belief, the majority of consumers are not sensitive enough to green issues. Admittedly, environmental protection has risen on the scale of values, but there is still a great chasm between general attitude and personal conviction. Only the smallest minority is consistent enough in its interest in the environment to allow this to express itself through actual purchasing behaviour. (Bremme, Tengelmann)

Be that as it may, recent research does indicate a consistent trend towards greater environmental awareness and a corresponding adaptation of customer buying habits. According to surveys by G & I Market Research, the core of environmentally aware people has already risen to 32 per cent. Members of this group are usually quite young and have high spending power and good qualifications. The number of environmentally harmful products in the households of this group is below average, while eco-friendly products are clearly in evidence.

Raffée sketches a vicious circle in which the hedonistic, egocentric urges of some consumers arouse more and more intensive marketing. As a result, eco-friendly behaviour is often working against the current. Voluntarily controlling buying habits to protect the environment, or keeping within speed limits, are quite rare behaviour patterns. The growth of eco-awareness so often cited in surveys and public willingness to make sacrifices clearly do not always find expression in action. This contributes to the reluctance of many companies to consider ecological manufacturing strategies if they would involve higher costs. The general lethargy in introducing eco-friendly marketing springs from the lack of real incentives to do so.

There is a degree of consumer uncertainty because of the extreme complexity of ecological data. Above and beyond the activities of various environmental and consumer organizations, the manufacturer has a responsibility to inform and advise. The retail trade also has an important part to play in eco-marketing.

The growth in demand for green alternatives is generally described as 'the ecological pull effect'; pressure from the government to internalize environment

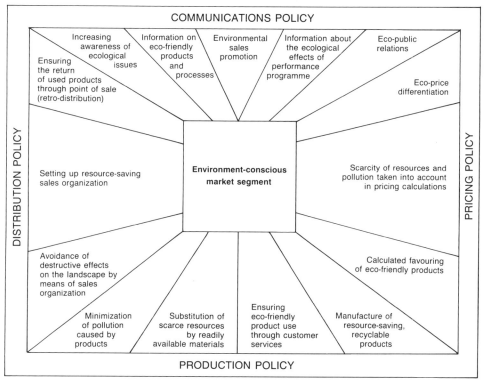

Source: Meffert *et al.* (1986)

Figure 35 Environment-orientated marketing mix

protection costs is described as 'the ecological push effect'. Ecologically induced market behaviour will be discussed here with reference to product policy, pricing policy, communication policy and distribution policy (see Figure 35).

The marketing mix: environmental (re)design

Product policy

A questionnaire undertaken by the magazine *Absatzwirtschaft* and aimed at the marketing managers of leading companies asked about the most important themes and investment decisions for 1990. The salient feature of the results was the high ranking accorded to the manufacture of eco-friendly products and packaging. Marketing strategies are generally a response to consumer sensitivity about environmental or health issues.

Product policy includes responsibility for putting new products on to the market and modifying existing products and production methods. Meffert *et al.* (1986) make the following suggestions for ecological product improvement:

- Products should meet the requirements of a neutral agent.

- They should be subjected to a test of environment compatibility.

- Eco-friendly products could be marketed under a unified eco-brand name.

- Recyclable products should be placed in the foreground.

- Customer services and advice to retailers ought to be intensified to ensure eco-friendly use of products.

- Design of packaging needs careful consideration of factors like reduction of materials or multiple use.

The development of an eco-friendly product ought, in general, to show regard to the material and energy consequences of the whole life-cycle of the product. In short, an eco-friendly product fulfils the same function as a more damaging product, but with respect to its whole life-cycle it is less harmful to the environment (see also Chapter 9).

Product policy measures within the programme could address the following issues:

- The improvement of existing products by modification and differentiation. Can a harmful product be designed to be more eco-friendly? Should an eco-friendly alternative be offered?

- The elimination of existing products. Is an environmentally harmful product endangering the company's image?

- The introduction of new products. Can new markets be opened up by innovations? Can diversification lead to new uses for the company's product? Can our internal knowledge of the environment protection market be exploited?

Alongside the manufacturer's responsibility to provide information and advice, the idea of disposal services will become a significant sales argument in the future. The more difficult it is to dispose of a product at the end of its life-cycle, the higher the status of this customer service would be.

Disposal services of this kind are already successfully practised by some refrigerator manufacturers. With their Babcock Environment Services Ltd, the German company Babcock and Co. is able to supplement desulphuration plants with the appropriate service for disposing of the plaster residue. The precept 'out of sight, out of mind' applied to after-sales will soon be a thing of the past. Pressure on manufacturers to take back used goods is intensifying. Early in 1990 the German Industrial Union for Metals and the chairman of Volkswagen called for an obligation on industry to accept returned goods for recycling and re-exploitation of materials, to replace the old practice of used cars going for scrap.

Distribution policy

Ecological criteria impose the need for new directions in product distribution. In some branches, the system of distribution has been designed around the concept of returnability. The traditional one-way flow of goods is being replaced by a two-way flow. The less the consumer is willing to bear the cost of disposal, the more the manufacturer is forced into seeking solutions. There is a need for a retro-distribution system for products and packaging after the phase of consumption or use. Consumers may well favour manufacturers who take responsibility for disposal, and only buy a new product if their old one is taken in part exchange (e.g. fridges, computers, batteries and cars).

Co-operation with the retail trade is extremely important, especially as taking on this responsibility will cause several problems for stores, such as higher personnel costs and use of floor space. Increased contact with customers, however, will operate as a positive compensation.

Distribution policy also encompasses environmental logistics, which must include resource-based factors such as energy and raw materials, as well as environment-based factors such as emissions and waste. Measures such as the reduction of packaging materials or the choice of alternative transport are typical examples of this. An environment-friendly company will equip its fleet with 'lead-free' cars and use rail transport for long-distance haulage. Particularly in sales, criteria of speed and coverage of the market area must be fulfilled alongside ecological criteria.

Collaboration between several market participants is the absolute prerequisite for the successful setting up and running of a retro-distribution system. Consumers, retailers, manufacturers and environmental organizations must all work together.

◇ Toni Milk Association

A typical example of this model is the Toni returnable jar for yoghurt, which was introduced by the Toni Milk Association in Winterthur in Switzerland, well over 15 years ago, at a time when plastic packaging was up and coming. After a successful six-month market trial, Toni agreed to the purchase of an industrial glass-washing

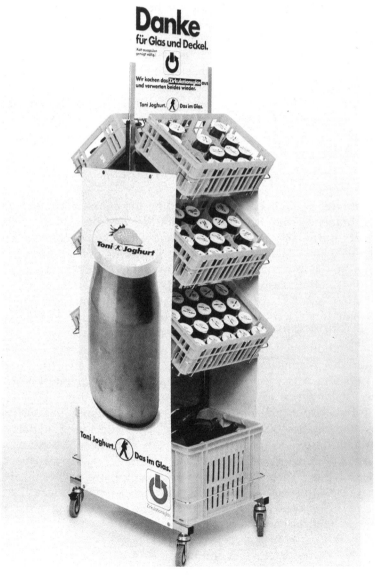

Toni circulation jars in their new collection stand

plant. After a surprisingly high return quota of 40.3 per cent (without deposit!) during the trial period, the quota rose to 51 per cent in 1976, and then began a steady decline. The nadir was reached with 32 per cent in 1981, when sales were also stagnating, if not regressing. Although everything seemed to indicate the imminent collapse of ecological and marketing strategies, it was decided to relaunch.

A new recyclable plastic lid was designed to replace the aluminium top and a special collection stand was installed in retail outlets, as shown in the photograph. The relaunch with these 'new' jars in March 1982 was a tremendous success. The return quota began to rise again, and reached 56 per cent in 1983. It has remained level at around 68–70 per cent since the mid-1980s, and it reaches 92 per cent when a special drive is put on. The relaunch was supported by a completely new form of advertising campaign with special promotions (see pp. 194, 210–11).

In 1985 the Toni light-jar, with 15–20 per cent less mass, came into being. It brings about a saving of around 700,000 kg of glass. In the same year, an environmental charity (Händ Sorg zur Umwelt) was founded. It quickly became accepted, and in special annual return drives small donations from each returned Toni jar are made to the charity.

Pricing policy

As a rule, intensified investment in environmental protection will be accompanied by higher costs. According to a survey conducted in Bavaria, environmental protection led to increased business costs of 70 per cent in 1984. Additional costs arise particularly in connection with newly developed eco-friendly products because of intensive R & D work, conversion of production methods, or expansion of communications policies. Also, in the early stages, low sales and production rates will be experienced. In some areas, though, there will be energy savings and reductions in cost.

The company is likely to try to pass the rising costs on to the consumer. This requires a sophisticated information policy to legitimize the price of the new product. According to a survey by Emnid, 75 per cent of those asked would prefer eco-friendly products even if they were relatively more expensive. Positioning the product in the high price bracket reflects the readiness of the consumer to pay in this market segment. Our case studies frequently bear this out. If it is not possible to adapt to a suitable price, the possibility of differentiated prices should be explored, using a combined calculation across the whole range of products.

Wicke (1990) points out that these products are often more attractive to consumers anyway because of savings in energy, waste reduction, and cost of materials, and because of the availability of replacement parts. He considers this to be the case for the following 23 products selected from the 47 which currently bear a Blue Angel environment label.

● Retreaded tyres.

- Returnable bottles.
- Spray-cans without CFCs.
- Eco-friendly paint.
- Powder paint.
- Recycled paper.
- Plant-pots and similar products made from used plastic.
- Low-noise and long-life silencers for cars.
- Car washes with low waste water.
- Eco-friendly pipe descalers.
- Returnable capsules for cream-whippers and soda-siphons.
- Reusable packaging for food.
- Reusable packaging for use during transportation.
- Reusable industrial packaging and pallets.
- Products made from recycled materials.
- Water-saving cisterns.
- Electronic controls for showers.
- Wallpaper from recycled materials.
- Building materials made from recycled paper.
- Low-formaldehyde products.
- Water-saving flow controllers.
- Water-saving pressure dishwashers, etc.
- Building materials based on used glass.

Communication policy

Ecological communication policy seeks to transmit an environmentally informed company image and to convey messages about the product to prospective customers. This is achieved by means of advertising, sales promotion, public relations and other new marketing instruments. It encompasses communication with external and internal interest groups. Public relations drives serve to strengthen ecological awareness and to build up an eco-competent image in the eyes of target groups.

The goal of communication policies, then, is to create an unambiguous corporate identity for the company. This basis of confidence presupposes a harmonious relationship between the other instruments of marketing. Clearly, the overall marketing mix must correspond with the desired environment image. Superficial, short-term communication policies which are not accompanied by complementary product policies will always be met with disbelief. A credible environment concept must pervade the company holistically and strategically.

Holistic thinking and actions in conjunction with an objectively testable communication policy are vital because the 'environment' can also provoke negative associations. Communication policy has to deal with this potential for mistrust. The fear of being misunderstood or pushed into the wrong corner could perhaps explain why some companies are very hesitant, and try to keep a low profile in connection with their environmental activities.

Market information can take two forms:

- A defensive communications policy which strives to counteract a poor image. Industries with a high profile, such as the chemicals industry or energy producers, tend to give information about their achievements in the field of environmental protection and to emphasize their social responsibility.

- A proactive communication policy which sees the ecological challenge as an opportunity to build up long-term success potentials in the market. Attempts are made to strengthen the awareness of ecology and to respond to consumer behaviour with a long-term concept.

Advertising

If the idea of eco-friendliness was once no more than an added extra, it is now gaining in importance as a sales argument at a breathtaking pace. One day, it could become the absolute prerequisite to saleability.

Advertising green products should never be a superficial pushing forward of eco-friendliness as a sales argument. The boom in products with the unattested adjective 'ecological', 'biological', 'organic' and so on, rouses suspicions that some manufacturers are jumping on the green bandwagon. They seem to think it sufficient to follow the fashion without having a clear environmental strategy. Short-term eco-drives are seldom successful because the complexity of the subject demands thorough preparation.

Environmental packaging and a touch of green seem to make for better sales so there is no shortage of pseudo-ecological marketing visible in the shops. A survey by the German Environment Office shows how easily green advertising can mislead the consumer: 72.5 per cent of shoppers believe, quite wrongly, that reference to ecological issues in adverts is officially controlled in some way. A green label alone, however, can be met with incredulity from customers, as the current green wave in several countries amply testifies.

In recent years, jumping on to the green bandwagon has led to the use of slick, pseudo-eco-marketing to capitalize on green consciousness among consumers. More than a quarter of the 12,000 new household items launched in 1990 in the USA boasted green virtues of one sort or another. The periodical *Advertising Age* describes the phenomenon as 'green overkill'.

A bigger problem though is product hype. Green marketing's greatest potential to the planet and to the economy is the development of serious, ecologically positive products, which will, in one way or another, reduce pollution and be a net environmental plus. But some marketers are making small, well-meaning gestures toward environmental consciousness only to trivialize their efforts – and the seriousness of the problem – by blowing their contributions grossly out of proportion. (29.1.91 p. 26)

Bob Garfield also puts the idea aptly:

When declarations of environmental righteousness become a gimmick, a fad, a cynical device for exploiting the consumer – which, so far, seems to be the case most of the time – green marketing threatens to die aborning. A lot of marketers had better think twice about eco-appeals, or consumers will get fed up very, very fast. They're already separating their cans from their bottles, and they'll quickly separate the enviro-chic from the frauds.

He concludes with the following comparison: 'Everybody wears green on St Patrick's Day, too – but it doesn't make them Irish.'

A survey by Mintel shows that the majority of consumers were confused about green claims. Almost half of US consumers dismissed the labelling as 'mere gimmickry'. Most consumers also believe that it is just an excuse for putting up the prices. Dissatisfaction can be diagnosed from various symptoms:

- In Germany, Europe's greenest country, the president of the Federal Environmental Protection Agency warned manufacturers early in 1991 against the excessive use of eco-friendly labels.

- In Britain, Friends of the Earth publish annual 'green-con-awards'.

- In the USA, the term 'green collar fraud' has been coined. A coalition of attorney-generals from eleven states has set up a task force to take proceedings against unjustified environmental claims and improve 'ecological standards'. As industry's attempts at self-regulation have been unconvincing, the US Federal Trade Commission aims to provide assistance.

The British Advertising Standards Authority (ASA) recently expressed the fear that exaggerated advertising can make the customers feel they are being duped: 'The cynicism of the majority is undermining the good work of a growing number of companies.' The Incorporated Society of British Advertisers (ISBA) has issued a warning against such practices. There are also plans to modify the Trade Description Act to curtail false advertising claims on environmental issues. Advertisers have been warned 'not to make unwarranted environmental claims about products in an attempt to cash-in on the green customer boom' (*The Times*, 10.1.90).

Friends of the Earth gave out 'Con of the Year Awards' over the last ten years and the first prize was won by British Nuclear Fuels for 'Just how green are you about nuclear power?', followed by Higgs Furs with 'Environmentally friendly furs, by Higgs'.

◇ General Motors

There is something particularly cynical in the bold claim at Earth Day 1990 that 'General Motors marks 20 years of environmental progress', especially because automobile companies like GM have been exercising pressure for decades to slow down clean air action, and only now that the laws have changed are they suddenly changing their tune. Denis Hayes, chair of Green Seal Inc., has described this technique, which is based on the theory that attack is the best form of defence, as, 'Praising Caesar instead of burying him' or, putting it even more bluntly, as 'eco-pornography' (*Advertising Age*, 29.1.91).

Environmental advertising ought to present arguments in a wide context, not forgetting practical use. Environmental considerations are occasionally in conflict with consumer aims such as comfort, but in general eco-friendliness is a supplementary component and should be treated as such. Real green advertising will present information about the product, aimed at the target group in question. This kind of informative advertising is difficult to prepare as a complex range of data have to be presented in an accessible way. A successful campaign should satisfy both the company and its customers that a real contribution to the environment is being made.

Careful positioning and differentiating of a product on the basis of eco-friendliness, as well as other strengths such as social recognition and prestige, can be especially successful at a time when products are closely comparable in terms of price, quality and terms. Attention to ecological aspects of packaging and product design is often the key to success. It is also useful to supplement eco-friendliness with other practical advantages: the convenience of concentrates, the health dimension of biodegradability or the financial advantages of cheaper refillable detergents.

The changeover to products with ecological advantages should offer a particular opportunity to proprietary brands. Customers are likely to reach out for the security of the proprietary brand in the confusing thicket of eco-labels; there are fewer difficulties in establishing acceptance because of the continuity of the name. Unfortunately, this ready acceptance is also an opening for misuse, and manufacturers of proprietary brands tend to be anxious that they may be forced into a 'green corner'. As a result they keep a low advertising profile and may be reluctant to give detailed information on products and contents.

There have been many successful eco-advertising campaigns from all branches of industry. Several were presented in Chapter 9 and some more appear at the end of this section. First of all, we will look at one or two more unusual examples.

◇ Opel

In November 1989 Opel was the first company to receive the award of the German

Association for Communication. It was granted for outstanding achievement in the field of environment and economics. In the award-winning TV advert, shots of an unsullied nature backed by the Louis Armstrong song 'What a Wonderful World' advertised a product which remained unseen. When Opel decided to put three-way catalytic converters in all their cars, the news was broken to the consumer in a graded communication concept. The changeover was celebrated with a press conference in Bonn (to show the connection between environment and politics), and an advertising campaign on the environment. The successful relaunch of the old hit song was accompanied by a new release sponsored by the Opel dealers.

◇ AEG

In 1988 AEG announced an art prize on the subject of ecology. One hundred art students took part, submitting 150 works. The contest was so successful that it has been continued in following years.

> Art, ecology and industry: three disparate concepts, but also a field of forces which can give birth to new motivation, new ideas. For AEG, it is a new dimension in which not only thoughts but also feelings can be expressed. A dimension which can support and inspire the process of inner change.
> The art prize 'Ecology' offers the chance for a dialogue between a new generation of managers and hopeful young artists. It has a wider influence too as the winning entries will be shown to AEG staff and to the public in a touring exhibition. (Exhibition brochure, 1989)

The first prize went to a work of action art, 'Poppy Red and Lizard'. The female artist had sown wild poppies in the form of a lizard 100m long into a corn field, 'There, where massive doses of herbicides were supposed to stop the growth of this weed, but where other forms of animal and plant life too strive to exist.'

◇ Bischof and Klein

Bischof and Klein, one of the first German companies with a holistic conception of eco-management, announced a competition entitled 'Packaging and Environment' in 1987. Entrants had to submit graphic or artistic designs for a plastic carrier bag made from the environment-friendly material polyethylene. The design had to promote eco-friendliness and also the company.

> In discussing packaging we do not encourage confrontation, but rather co-evolution. We try to make our ideas transparent and talk about them in critical groups, like young students. We make progress that way, and that is how we came up with the idea for the competition. (Extract from catalogue)

Environmental labels/eco-logos

Presentation of environmental information can gain considerable credibility from the support of independent, neutral testing. A predominant place in this context is occupied by the Blue Angel. Based on the environment emblem of the United Nations, this quality seal has been awarded by the German Institute for Quality Assurance, in collaboration with the Federal Environment Office, since 1978. The purpose of the symbol is to assist consumers in purchasing, and as a complementary function the label motivates manufacturers to supply environment-friendly products.

Goods with the emblem are noticed by consumers. According to a survey in 1989, around 75 per cent of those questioned prefer to buy environment-friendly products. Since there are no objective criteria, it is very difficult for consumers to judge which products are really less damaging to the environment. After a slow start, manufacturers are now queuing up to obtain the award and to fit it into their communication policy. Surveys show that the symbol is known by a very large percentage of the German population, almost 80 per cent. There are currently almost 4,000 products with the award from around 630 different companies, including about 10 per cent non-German firms. Many manufacturers attribute leaps in turnover of up to 40 per cent to this environmental distinction.

The Blue Angel award for recycled paper

Some companies have introduced labels themselves, but this is not advisable because of lack of neutrality. The array of labels on supermarket shelves across Europe is quite bewildering at the moment: Migo del ozone; Amici dell'Ambiente; Melien Vriendlyk; protège la couche d'ozone; Umweltfreundlich; and many more. The EC Commission in Brussels has now introduced an EC eco-label which will be valid throughout the single European market after 1992. The symbol will probably depict a daisy and is to replace national labels.

Many other countries have national labels, and suffer a certain amount of confusion as a result. In the USA, for example, there is an eight-state union striving to develop unified regulations for environmental protection, but two rival factions are competing for control: the Green Cross and the Green Seal.

To acquire the German Blue Angel, which is valid for three years, the manufacturer must prove that the product is more environmentally friendly than other comparable products, while achieving the same performance standards. Particular attention is paid to noise pollution, emissions, waste, waste water, harmful ingredients and recycling. The test is based on special criteria for each product type, and since these are changed in line with current technology, they act as a motivation towards innovation.

The symbols can, however, be misinterpreted by consumers. A product bearing the symbol is not environment friendly in itself, but only by comparison with other traditional products. A useful supplement to the environment seal would be a product test, but the difficulty of setting up this type of test should not be underestimated. In some countries, for example, different criteria are selected, which removes any possibility of comparability. However, critics of the award fail to realize that there clearly are good and bad qualities present in the range of products it caters for, and that it does encourage competition to improve environmental performance.

Because of the relative nature of the award there are strict legal constraints governing its use in advertising. Paragraph 3 of the German law on unfair competition forbids the use of the symbol in misleading ways. However, there are no general regulations on environmental advertising. The consumer's assessment of the effect of an advertisement is therefore particularly important, and high demands are made on the advertisers' duty to inform and explain.

The use of the phrases 'biodegradable' and 'environment friendly' to describe the lavatory cleaner 'bio-Fix' was condemned by a court as misleading because consumers might think it contained only natural ingredients. (The main difference between bio-Fix and traditional products is that formic acid has been replaced by citric acid.) It is important that advertising statements about compatibility with the environment can stand up to testing.

There has also been a legal prohibition of shelf-signs which try to draw attention to products with the Blue Angel Award. The court decision was based on the fact that the award was given on the strength of one property alone, and that the shelf-signs gave the impression that all articles on the shelf near the sign were eco-friendly.

◇ Mobil

A classic example of the problems associated with environment-friendly products is the marketing nightmare experienced by Mobil USA, when they introduced Hefty degradable garbage bags. Several state attorneys-general sued Mobil with charges of 'deceptive advertising' and 'consumer fraud' over degradability claims for the trash bags. Since refuse is usually disposed of in covered landfill sites the degradation process is hardly ever able to take effect. Along with other information, the labelling on the new Hefty bags gives an explanation of the term 'degradable'.

The attorneys-general multi-state task force has reached an agreement with American Enviro Products which will stop them making degradability claims for their Bunnies disposable diapers. Dow Chemical has also agreed to withdraw its claims for Handi-Wrap plastic tool wrap. The task force recommends 'green guidelines' to create 'national advertising standards' for the future. A corresponding suggestion from the Environmental Protection Agency is anticipated by the end of 1991.

Sales promotion

Sales promotion drives offer special short-term incentives to purchase at the point of sale. They are directed at the consumer through customer services and retailer.

◇ Hertie

The department store giant Hertie is running a comprehensive sales promotion for the second time. The motto is 'Live with conscience, buy with conscience, and we'll save our shared environment'. The promotion will be mounted in Hertie's 60 or more stores, and involves a prize-winning game with German rail tickets among the prizes. The eco-friendly products to be promoted are introduced by cryptic questions:

- What has a jogging suit to do with a cat fish in the Rhine?
- What has the WC to do with pine forests?
- What have jeans to do with the pond in the park?
- What has changing the wallpaper to do with our health?
- What has coloured washing to do with the chestnut tree?
- What has house cleaning to do with your seaside holidays?

The 16-page prospectus, printed on recycled paper, was distributed in millions.

These activities are attempting to change the views of suppliers, customers and staff by providing information, better presentation and a corresponding offer in order to help the customers decide in favour of environment-friendly products. A donation of one Deutschmark was made to an environment charity for each reply coupon returned.

◇ AUGE

In 1989 a public relations drive called 'Environment-Friendly Household 1989' was mounted under the auspices of the German environment minister. It involved distributing around 35 million questionnaires and brochures, and prizes from a lottery were offered to the most eco-friendly households. The promotion was realized by the Action Association for Environment Health and Food (AUGE) and supported by various firms, including AEG, Commerz Bank, Co-op, Opel, Otto Versand, Procter and Gamble, Tetra-Pak and Neuform. The way in which this promotion was misinterpreted by the Consumer Centre in Hamburg as 'unfair advertising with environmental views' gives an idea of how sensitive an issue eco-promotions can be.

◇ Toni Milk Association

A new advertising campaign was also accompanied by sales promotion measures. Product information was distributed to the trade, and special promotions were directed at the consumer. In 1987 customers were offered a Toni yoghurt bath towel on return of 30 Toni yoghurt labels plus 15 Swiss francs. The offer was publicized on double-sided inserts in newspapers and magazines, and altogether 38,000 bath towels were sold.

◇ Johnson Wax, UK

In 1988 Johnson Wax launched the 'plant a tree' promotion with the Woodland Trust. When the consumer sends in a wrap-around band from one of four million aerosol cans, Johnson donates 25p to the Woodland Trust. With three purchases, a tree is planted in the customer's name. When donations reach £20,000 the Johnson Wax Forest will have been planted. This will help to rebuild woodland ravaged by the October 1987 storm.

◇ Océ

The office copier manufacturer Océ launched a successful sales promotion in Germany. In an 'air and odour' show, customers had to identify odours and were sensitized in this way to the problem of office atmosphere. At the same time, the importance of the human senses, even while photocopying, was brought into focus in an unconventional way.

This had a very direct impact on Océ copying systems because the company wished to emphasize the value of investing in the environment. Océ had been aware for some time of an increasing interest in ecological issues, and it sponsored research by industrial doctors and scientists into the medical, ergonomic and environmental hygiene aspects of their products. The results of their research were disseminated to around 1,000 organizations and purchasers.

◇ Woolworth

Since 1989 Woolworth, whose main target group is families with children, has been trying to put across their environment-protection ideas to children and encourage them to behave in an eco-friendly way. It has a butterfly symbol and a children's environment club with its own magazine and environment hot-line.

Public relations

A key position in company communications will be taken by public relations. The role of PR is to promote the whole company and especially its involvement in green issues. It is not enough to use PR as a diversion from inadequate environmental measures.

After a hesitant start, some branches of industry were able to use PR drives to place themselves almost at the forefront of the environmental movement. One need only think of catalytic converters and CFC gases. However, it is easy to alienate customers, making them see advertising as merely cosmetic, and produce negative responses by arousing mistrust about company commitment.

The only way to restore and create public trust is to build up a public relations system which is consistent with a real environmental concept. Good PR goes further than just establishing a positive company environment image. It should arouse awareness and sensitivity in the consumer and provide reliable information.

Winter (1990) recommends 'maxims of truth, clarity and unity of word and deed', and offers the following examples:

- Only make PR statements about the environment which can stand up to some form of test.

- Do not speak about the eco-friendliness of a company, but only about concrete activities; not intentions, but deeds.

- Make sure that the media report company activities in the context of a wider plan. Welcome reports about innovative behaviour.

- Involve the public in green issues. For example, invite the public to staff seminars on the environment, and extend the use of industrial waste disposal facilities to the public.

- Publicize progress in disposal, recycling, working conditions, research and development, and even the fulfilment of legal requirements.

- Address the widest range of target groups: staff, customers, all age groups, one's critics and one's admirers.

Staff and their families provide a good vehicle for promoting the company image. Local residents are another important target group as they sometimes have negative feelings about a neighbourhood industry. Environmental groups and those with a special interest in ecology deserve particular attention. In some ways, dialogue with these experts is easier, but different perspectives can lead to animosity. A sceptical or critical attitude on the part of the company is almost certain to lead to confrontation with such groups.

Attacks launched by environmentalists against the management are all too common at general meetings. At the general meeting of Bayer Chemicals in 1988, heated arguments arose on the subject of environmental protection, started by critical shareholders. Open dialogue about the different viewpoints is the only sensible way of dealing with this sort of occurrence. Management ought to be able to affirm their position in conflict; to accept the existence of pollution and be prepared to discuss it.

◇ Johnson Wax

The American company Johnson Wax, one of the largest privately owned companies in the world, specifies in 'This We Believe' (the corporate statement of its business philosophy) an obligation to five groups of people to whom the corporation believes it is responsible, and whose trust it has to earn. The five groups are employees, consumers, the general public, neighbours and host countries in which the company operates, and the world community.

> The corporation states that it cannot operate in isolation from any of these groups. To do otherwise would be to deny its perceived role, which is one based on 'partnership and obligation' and not on any corporate self interest.
>
> The philosophical basis of this belief is that in taking resources from society with which to flourish and make profits the company incurs a compensating obligation to put back into that society some of the fruits of our endeavor. To fail to respond would be morally wrong. It explicitly perceives capitalism as dynamic and benevolent and not introspective and selfish.

The passage 'Working Together' is also interesting because dialogue is sought with other sectors of the population.

> Industry has a poor public image on environmental issues and there will probably be continued pressure for stronger consumer and pollution legislation. There is also evidence that consumers are increasingly interested in wider issues than just product performance, and they will not be taken in by companies which attempt to jump on the 'green bandwagon'.
>
> A consistent approach to all of a company's activities will pay off in the long run as consumers ask more questions about such issues as waste disposal, recycling, social and community policies.
>
> As a means of staying close to customers' and consumers' needs, companies should develop links with environmentalists to consider issues of

common interest. Failure to do so will perpetuate the current unproductive and adversarial relationship between industry and the Green Movement. This is in no-one's best interest, least of all the consumer. The reality is that the environment is something in which we all have a direct, personal interest.

At Johnson Wax we believe it is possible to work in industry and be actively concerned about improving our environment. 'Wherever we go the community should be better off because we're there' appears frequently on our company literature; more than a theme, it is a way of doing business that is instilled into every generation of Johnson Wax managers.

Responsible public relations should take account of the following points put forward by Nickel in 1990:

● Talk about what you are doing.

● Ask others if they agree with it.

● Explain the motives behind your actions and plans.

● Include the interests of others in your decision making.

The organization must develop a clear concept in order to formulate its goals. It is useful to think of 'threads of dialogue' in building up a system of public relations. Nickel proposes the following general principles for a framework of dialogue with staff and external groups:

● Social obligation: recognizing contrasts between company interests and the interests of others.

● Obligation to inform: responsibility of the communication system.

● Obligation to legitimize company activities.

● Obligation to listen: gather other opinions and ideas.

● Obligation to take corrective measures: allow criticisms to influence decision making.

In the realm of environmental protection the company must use PR work to make it quite clear that:

● It is striving towards a balance between economic and ecological interests.

● Public opinion is often divided over green issues: for example, the concept of individual responsibility, and the discrepancy between thoughts and actions.

● Every economic activity is associated with risk.

Schuh (1990) has referred to the difficulty of adequately interpreting environmental burdens. Exaggeration and overreaction are to be expected in this area. While some speak of 'chemophobia', things are not moving quickly enough for others. The reactions of the media, politicians and scientists are often in violent contrast to each other. There is also a noteworthy difference in national reactions to the same phenomenon. The radioactive gas radon arouses a great deal of attention in the USA, but not in Germany. Schuh calls for a comparative evaluation of risks, and cites experts who question the need for many of the sanitation measures undertaken at great expense.

Dyllick highlights the development of social acceptance as the central responsibility in securing the future, because market forces are not the only influences on business:

> This becomes only too clear when companies find themselves in public altercations which are of great importance for their survival and where the problem is not their economic performance but their activities in sensitive areas like ecology, safety or health. Conflict of this kind underlies the need for a higher political and moral profile, not just in society at large but within the company itself. The image which emerges here is one of society and its problems growing in on business, and business, through its activities and their effects, reaching outside of itself. (Dyllick, 1989a)

In contrast to the process of strengthening strategic success potentials, securing public acceptance is concerned with building up trust and understanding between business and the various social groupings. With various case studies showing which social interest areas impinge on business, how central a role the media play and how a power base emerges, Dyllick shows that public relations are based upon moral positions.

A public, media image can rapidly develop its own dynamic and can quickly erode the basis of trust. This kind of internal dynamic applies particularly to the sensitive area of environmental protection. From a certain point in public discussion it becomes unimportant whether the accused has really brought blame upon himself, or whether reproaches are justified or not.

Löwisch describes credibility as an ethical category, which therefore presents a considerable problem for private business because management does not sufficiently cater for the staff's and the public's need for an ethical orientation. 'To counter public protest with informative PR exercises alone is about as ineffectual as the recent vigorous emphasis on business philosophy and business culture was in solving internal industrial problems.' What is required is general responsibility from individual companies as a *sine qua non* for management in difficult times. This general responsibility must embrace a wide spectrum of particular responsibilities for staff, corporate goals and so on. The important thing for Löwisch is to strengthen the dimension of generality in management, since this dimension has contact with the world outside of economics; with welfare, ethics and culture.

The classic instruments of public relations are eminently appropriate for the task of eco-public relations:

- Press conferences and bulletins.
- Lectures, environment seminars.

- Business reports, social balance sheets, expanded social reports.
- Internal environment reports.
- Company newspapers.
- Open days.
- Environment hot-lines.
- Eco-sponsoring.
- Environment and nature charities.
- Collaboration with associations, e.g. WWF, BAUM, Future, etc.
- Environmental management, e.g. staff training, environment officer, suggestion box, etc.

The most important way of influencing public opinion is doubtless managing the media because of the wide coverage available.

The energy production and chemical industries provide useful examples of broad public relations drives over the last few years. The chemical industry, in particular, has launched huge campaigns to counteract its bad image. Personification is used to give the abstract appearance of chemistry a more human face. Presentations and information about environmental steps taken by the industry emphasize perceived responsibilities. This is especially true in Germany, where pollution of the Rhine has left its traces in more ways than one. Chemical companies have changed over from a reactive, defensive, passive role to an active, assertive representation of themselves.

◇ Bayer

Competence and responsibility are both given equal weighting at Bayer Chemicals. In advertisements, a problem is raised, information is disseminated and company actions are listed.

- Nature must be protected. It is our responsibility not to let the environment come to harm.
- The danger of toxic residues haunts all types of production. It is our responsibility to see that they remain under control.
- Dilute acids are an undesirable by-product. It is our responsibility to recover usable materials from them.
- Business must make a profit, but it is our responsibility not to think of ourselves alone.

◇ BASF

At BASF, staff are introduced to the public through advertisements and anyone interested can arrange to come and meet the member of staff at work or receive information. For example, Heinz Zimmerman wishes to show the following:

- How his bacteria eat 220 tonnes of dirt per day.
- Why he has collected three million data items about our water.
- How he had the team carry out 35,000 water tests per year to protect the Rhine.
- How he incinerates 100,000 tonnes of waste annually.

The kind of information offered is open to ambiguity. It does provide insight into investment costs, but it also tends to obscure because of one-sided and incomplete data. Waste water purification is all very well, but how much and exactly what is fed in? Could the incineration of 100,000 tonnes of waste leave unknown residues?

These efforts are accompanied by wide-reaching work on the part of the Association for the Chemical Industry, which tries to give the impression that chemists are actively engaged in areas such as the search for alternatives for CFCs. 'Chemistry has learnt from its mistakes.' A special environment report was published for the first time in 1988/9. It gives a complete summary of achievements in environmental relief and refers to future plans, so that individuals can make a fair judgement of the endeavours of the chemical industry. In addition, environment guidelines can be ordered.

Crisis management

The main purpose of public relations is to create trust. A 'crisis plan' should be set up to make sure that company credibility is not endangered in the event of an accident or other crisis, and to help avert a media disaster. Unprofessional PR work can do untold damage in the case of scandals, flops or malicious rumours. Fast, informative action is needed to avert any unnecessary escalation. Crisis PR has become a separate discipline within public relations as a result of this need.

Internal regulations governing action during a crisis and a plan of action can be useful, but there is no patent recipe for crisis management. Tortella (PR agency, Burson Marsteller) suggests as an emergency plan a detailed analysis of risks and weak points together with communication responsibilities kept in a handbook, supported by practice crisis drills. The best security must be extensive risk management which aims to reduce all possible sources of risk within the business, under the aegis of a preventive hazard control policy (see Chapter 15).

Schulz (1988) envisages the following questions in cases of crisis:

- What exactly has happened?
- Are there any casualties, human or material?
- Have hazardous substances been released?
- Is there any danger to man or nature?

- What self-protection measures are possible?
- Is the crisis over or under control?

A superficial PR job can ruin carefully nurtured confidence in a very short time. The consumer must be satisfied that the company accepts its responsibilities. This is far more important than the presentation of fine statistics. Company commitment also means sharing anxieties with the public.

The company should respond as speedily and thoroughly as possible to public and media needs for information on crises. Defensive information policies in the salami style (slice-for-slice response to increasing pressure) are to be avoided at all cost. The real dilemma is that the public wishes to be informed as quickly as possible, but often only unverified information about the scale of the damage is available. Constant corrections of precipitous announcements always have a negative effect. In some cases, silence really is the best policy.

◊ Sandoz/Exxon

The Rhine catastrophe of 1986 and the tanker disaster off the coast of Alaska in 1989 were classic examples, in the negative sense. Sandoz had to correct or withdraw statements several times, and the PR operation 'Lieber Fluss' ('Dear River') was placed very unfortunately.

After the collision of the *Exxon Valdez*, the management of Exxon kept a very low profile; even their whereabouts were only disclosed several days later. The 'giant' was pilloried in the media as a helpless, incompetent monster. When this was apprehended by Exxon, the company changed to an assertive stance. Alongside comprehensive press coverage a programme of cleaning coasts was mounted at the cost of over half a billion pounds. The world's largest chemicals combine is currently awaiting a tidal wave of civil law suits.

It is particularly important in large businesses with a high degree of specialization and division of responsibilities that crisis planning should prevent unco-ordinated action or panic measures and ensure that the organization remains functional. Bad environmental protection is the most likely cause for public criticism. The new forms of wide-ranging dialogue which are so vital in this context will be outlined on the basis of Haller's suggestions at the 1989 Environment Conference. He called for 'risk communication' because the public cannot be influenced by 'scientific or economic rationality'.

- In potentially dangerous undertakings, find out how the risk is perceived by the surrounding population and discuss it in public.
- Establish the connection between awareness of danger and controlling it.
- Work out on a neutral basis the conflicts arising from existing decisions.
- Promote a general readiness to discuss.

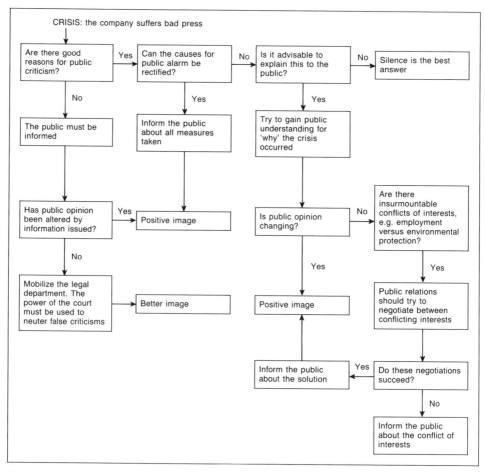

Source: Schulz (1988).

Figure 36 Assertive environmental information policies in times of crisis

- Set up internal departments to develop the dialogue on risks.

- Collaborate with groups within society which have similar aims.

- Establish research and development programmes which incorporate risk communication.

This form of risk communication should lead to enhanced internal and external dialogue. The confidence built up should help minimize damage in case of a real crisis. Preliminary preventive work prepares the way for a spontaneous reactive response to events as they happen.

◇ Perrier/Milupa

The importance of effective crisis management is shown in the example of Perrier, which in 1990 tried to save its image by calling back bottles of mineral water in which benzol had been found. Even though the first news bulletins about the benzol were confusing, management quickly took control and withdrew 160 million bottles from the market.

The public is particularly sensitive over health issues, and short-term financial savings can ruin confidence which has taken years to build up. Some years ago there was a similar withdrawal of 500,000 tins of Milupa baby food. An anonymous threat to poison tins was answered assertively because trying to hush things up could have caused serious damage to Milupa's image. The withdrawal was supplemented with a media information campaign, and mothers were informed through the distribution of hundreds of thousands of information leaflets.

◇ McDonald's

When McDonald's was confronted with a petition signed by 6,000 opponents to the opening of a new restaurant in Ravensburg, the company responded assertively and quickly because environmental protection is seen as a key factor in its image. Each signatory of the petition was sent a letter in which the charges of destroying the rain forests for meat and adding to the refuse mountain with packaging were addressed. Record sales were made even in the first week after opening.

Working with external groups

Countless institutions have set the preservation of the environment as their main purpose, and as a result of their influence they represent one of the factors which must be acknowledged by corporate management. Dyllick (1989a) speaks of the 'management of environmental relations' and calls for new forms of dialogue with these groups to secure social acceptance of business activities.

Although some of these organizations misuse their activities for political purposes, their influence on the economy is undeniable. Numerous corporate decisions and plans have had to be revised because of public pressure generated by these environmental groups. Even large enterprises are forced to respond: take, for example, the pressure on Bayer from Greenpeace to stop the disposal of dilute acids into the North Sea; the pressure from the Robin Wood group on the ADAC automobile club to stop the Wallberg motor racing; and the activities of the Bundschuh group against the Daimler-Benz test track. While some groups operate through direct activities, others aim to inform the public about environmental problems.

The need for new forms of collaboration brings business into more direct contact with people and lends credence to the activities of environment groups. Many groups have turned their sympathies against industry and the consumer

CAPYBARA
Hydrochoerus hydrochaeris.

YELLOW-HEADED AMAZON PARROT.
Amazona ochrocephala.

SWALLOWTAIL BUTTERFLY.
Papilio lychophron.

GIANT ARMADILLO.
Priodontes maximus.

These animals live in the rain forests of the Amazon.

Their existence is at risk because, as we all know, the rain forests are being destroyed.

And the rain forests are being destroyed partly to make grazing for cattle.

The rumour is that McDonald's use some of the beef to make hamburgers.

We have even seen it reported as fact.

But it's not a fact.

None of the beef we use, anywhere in the world, comes from the area of the rain forests.

It never has.

All of the beef we use in Britain comes from the E.C.

(While we're on the subject, our hamburgers are made with 100% beef. And we use only whole cuts of fore-quarter and flank, with no binders, fillers or additives.)

Nor do we use trees from the rain forests to make any of our packaging.

They are mostly hardwoods. We use mostly softwoods.

Our polystyrene packs are made with an inert gas which has no effect on the ozone layer.

We stopped using CFC gases two years ago.

In telling you this, at a time when many companies are only too eager to show how green they are, we are not claiming to be perfect.

It is not, after all, a perfect world.

We're just doing our best to preserve it.

Contrary to rumour, we do not kill them to make hamburgers.

society. They call for closer identification with ecology and a stronger emphasis on a quality of life which is not measured by material values alone.

It is difficult to assess how much positive influence the protest activities of these groups have on managers, politicians and consumers. There is no doubt, however, that they have had an appreciable impact on the political landscape and have therefore sensitized large sectors of the population to green issues. There can be no long-term development of environmental questions unless they are seen in a wider ethical and educational framework. Green demonstrations sometimes seem like a fire of straw which needs constant fanning with new, ever more spectacular protests. However, at the moment, such demonstrations seem irreplaceable as a means of shaking things up and posing awkward questions.

Similar reservations about the effect of the media are, surely, also appropriate. Ever more scandals and fires of straw serve to blunt public sensitivity. Yet they can have prodigious consequences on the economy. Certain organizations, however, do direct their efforts towards a steady change of values based on education and the dissemination of information. More and more people allow their purchasing behaviour to be influenced by the findings of institutions such as Warentest or Eco-test in Germany. The work of consumer centres is also more widely heeded. The Environment Office in Munich records around 160,000 visitors annually, with 30,000 consultations and enquiries and 22,000 phone calls. Increasing demands on environment organizations also seem likely in the future.

An inestimable number of institutions exist and are currently active:

- Federal, regional and local authorities.

- The churches.

- Private environmental groups.

- Media and specialist periodicals.

- Scientific, educational and consultancy groups.

Dialogue with these groups is sometimes obstructed by mutual fear of contact, with one or the other side anxious about losing its independence.

Because of its international importance, Greenpeace will be discussed briefly at this point, as an example of environmental groups and their activities.

◇ Greenpeace

Greenpeace carries out a great deal of informative and consciousness-raising work. Measurable results have been achieved through creating public pressure on politicians, for example, in the areas of atmospheric nuclear testing, discharging of acid waste and commercial whale fishing.

Certain cases are deliberately made media-worthy through spectacular activities. These usually non-violent demonstrations aim to draw attention to various environmental abuses in an imaginative way and to arouse discussion and awareness. Together with its main themes, 'against nuclear testing and for the survival of whales', Greenpeace concentrates on other burning issues such as nuclear waste dumping in the sea, the use of chlorine-bleached cellulose in paper, the disposal of poisonous waste in the North Sea, and the setting up of an international nature reserve in Antarctica.

Greenpeace originated from a small group of Canadian peace campaigners whose slogan was 'Let's make it a green peace', and its first demonstration was to penetrate a maritime nuclear testing area in a chartered boat. At present Greenpeace has 2.5 million members and offices in 20 countries, which makes it one of the largest international organizations in the world.

Environmental sponsoring

While the sponsoring of sports and cultural activities is a well-established instrument of business communication, eco-sponsoring is only just beginning to take off. Sponsorship must be rooted in a sound, integrated business culture and philosophy to provide a basis for credibility. A company should try to establish an identity for itself as a socially responsible body by means of socially conscious marketing and management.

The rapidly growing importance of this innovative instrument of communication can be seen from a survey of 100 businesses which engage in eco-sponsoring (Bruhns, European Business School). Bruhns estimated eco-sponsoring in Germany in 1988 at between DM30 million and DM70 million, and predicted DM100 million by 1992 and DM200 million by 1995.

There are examples of eco-sponsoring in all branches of industry, and a few examples will show the range:

- Daimler-Benz supports the European National Heritage nature protection project 'Nestos'.

- American Express is engaged in the preservation of important monuments (e.g. the Mystical Lamb in Ghent).

- Artists United for Nature (AUN) is active in the protection of the rain forests.

- IBM is supporting the German Game Preservation Society in its concern for the last of the wild grouse species.

- Lufthansa is sponsoring the German Association for Bird Protection to protect cranes.

- Ford sponsors the European Environment Prize.

- Wella is supporting a bird protection campaign.

◇ Worldwide Fund for Nature

The Worldwide Fund for Nature (WWF) receives donations from many different sources. In Germany, eco-sponsoring accounts for about 10 per cent of the total income and this is expected to rise to 20 per cent. The WWF is the largest private nature protection organization and has supported or instigated over 4,000 projects in 140 countries since its foundation in 1961. The fund, which is politically and scientifically neutral, pursues an assertive promotion strategy offering tailor-made projects for each of its sponsors.

For the sake of their reputation, environmental charities must have a very clear idea of their sponsors' activities. This also ensures that sponsoring is not used as an alibi by companies with a guilty conscience. Great care has to be taken over choice of sponsors so that money received does not start to infringe on the independence of environmental organizations. Some charities, like Greenpeace, have closed their doors to large-scale industrial finance.

The details of any particular eco-sponsoring commitment should be studied carefully by the sponsor too, because in return for taking on social responsibilities, the company should expect public recognition, sympathy, confidence and status. In the USA there is already a reference work, *Rating American Corporate Conscience*, with an analysis and ranking of the ethical attitude and social commitment of 131 companies. Without environment-friendly behaviour 'at home', the sponsor loses all credibility.

Sponsors can either be mentioned directly in the projects, in information bulletins and press reports, or they can integrate the sponsorship into the framework of their communication policy, mentioning the commitment in advertising. Pro Natur mounted a bird protection project which is mainly financed by the sale of a book published in various languages. Sponsors were sent advertising material before the publication date so that they would be able to superimpose their own advertising logos. The Würzburger Hofbräu brewery designed a two-page advertisement with the slogan, 'Why are we drinking to bird protection?' On the second page was an order coupon for the book tastefully combined with the brewery logo.

◇ Holsten Brewery

Holsten Brewery was one of the first companies to introduce comprehensive eco-sponsoring. At Holsten, they see the environment and nature protection as the responsibility of private business. Active commitment to the environment around the brewery's original home is a major component of Holsten's corporate philosophy. Environmental protection is carried out in close collaboration with the WWF.

- The Holsten Nature Fund has been involved in various projects since 1984: for example, purchasing land for a nature reserve.

- The brewery promotes individual projects from active members of the local community by awarding a prize.

◇ IBM

IBM has been involved in social and ecological projects for many years now. As well as giving financial aid to the WWF since 1985 and awarding various apparatus grants, an interesting variation is IBM's Secondment Programme. Since 1984 IBM staff have been lent out for a period of two to three years to work on mutually useful enterprises. At the moment there are projects on qualitative, sustainable economic growth, environment information systems, the sanitation of the Elbe and the compilation of a databank on the Elbe sanitation scheme.

> With its 30,500 staff, IBM wants to be integrated into its social surroundings and to find a new relationship between company and society. For us, social responsibility is more than just giving financial help to environment protection, medicine and the disabled. It means putting our special know-how into real and personal commitment. (Henkel)

Many companies have founded their own environment funds or award environment prizes. The Océ–van der Grinten Prize for outstanding scientific achievement, awarded since 1975 by Océ, Germany, is the oldest and best-endowed environmental contest in Europe; the Karl Schmitz-Scholl Fund and the Elizabeth Haub Foundation also give invaluable support to environmental projects.

◇ Alpirsbacher Klosterbräu

The success of the Alpirsbacher Klosterbräu brewery depends upon a flawless communications concept in which social commitment plays a central role. Based on ecological and social responsibility, the brewery has developed various initiatives in the fields of culture and nature. Particular emphasis is placed on the quality of life in the Black Forest. The close connection between product, advertising and public relations work can be seen from the way in which a special symbol reminiscent of the brewery logo has been designed for each of the various schemes. The marketing conception is as follows:

- The principle of quality aims to create a psychologically credible image with clear positioning of the product. 'Alpirsbacher Klosterbräu ... with the famous spring water from the Black Forest.' Pricing policy places the brewery in the high-price bracket.

- Communications strategy has to guarantee the company's goals. In the field of culture the objectives are to secure the 'high-price policy' and 'build up social connections with the environment'. The underlying philosophy accepts the fact that cultural commitment implies absolutely sound principles. Cultural involvement offers an enrichment of the area which feeds back into the reputation of the company.

■   In the field of nature there are two goals: securing the natural resources required for the brewery, and allowing nature to live on unmolested. As a company which is intimately connected with nature, any commitment of Alpirsbacher Klosterbräu to nature serves these goals.

The brewery channels 10 pfennigs for every hundred litres of beer sold into natural protection measures. The Alpirsbacher Nature Fund has been financing projects since 1980. Books and studies have been sponsored. A gravel pit has been purchased and converted into a nature reserve, and a twelve-point plan to clean up the Black Forest is under way.

◇ Hypo-Bank

This major German bank has sponsored very successful exhibitions on the theme of the environment over the last few years.

■   The touring exhibition 'Green between the houses' has been shown in 47 towns since 1984 with around one million visitors. Bavarian TV is broadcasting a twelve-part series about the exhibition.

■   The exhibition 'A park needs green neighbours', which is about the English Gardens in Munich, was displayed in the foyer of the central Hypo-Bank.

■   The project 'Green business: ideas for more green in the world of work' consists of an exhibition in the main Munich branch and the publication of a book.

◇ Co-operative banks

The International Youth Contest run by 25,000 co-operative banks in Europe and Canada is the largest of its kind. It takes the burning issues of the age and raises the awareness of young people, and through them the rest of society. Several times it has focused on themes from nature and environmental protection. In the last contest 'Love animals – protect animals', 1,994,000 entries were received! The motto for the 1990 competition is 'Air is Life'. The theme for the contest is accompanied by excellently prepared background materials. Some 50,000 copies of the 127-page book on the topic 'Air', and a 70-page pamphlet for teachers, have been produced.

Examples of total communication concepts

The following two case studies provide examples of successful changes in market relationships which have been brought about through consistent marketing of ecologically designed products.

◇ The marketing concept of the Toni Milk Association, Winterthur, Switzerland

Background
The yoghurt market in Switzerland used to bear the typical signs of levelling out of supply in a relatively saturated market: high quality; hardly any possibility of differentiating supply; no assertive marketing. In addition there were factors specific to Switzerland, such as legal limits on the area covered by milk associations. In this situation Toni had no really ambitious goals when, in 1974, it introduced a new returnable jar for its yoghurt. Even this system had no effect on the stability of the market. Things only started to move with the appearance of a new advertising agency on the scene.

Intentions and objectives
The following list of intentions was drawn up:

- Advertising objectives (quantitative): increase market recognition to 90 per cent.

- Advertising objectives (qualitative): increase market status by improving image.

- Behavioural objectives (commercial): cause consumers to change brand in favour of Toni.

- Sales objectives: increase turnover by at least 10 per cent per year and increase market share.

- Trade objectives: increase distribution quota by means of communications.

- Behavioural objectives (ecological): stimulate better return quotas from Toni circulation jars.

Strategy and conception
As with all food products, the decisive factors controlling image are quality (freshness, health, naturalness) or taste. These arguments are always interchangeable. The Toni plan, however, is based on indirect suggestion: high-quality packaging associated with high-quality contents.

The ecological aspect of the new circulation jar seems subsidiary, but as a call for voluntary environmental action it is quite compelling to consumers. The jar becomes a visual proof of quality.

Positioning statement: Toni yoghurt is different and more valuable. This can be seen even from the packaging.
Slogan: No packaging is too good for optimum quality.
Claim: Toni Yoghurt. The one in the jar.

This strategy continues to be carried out uncompromisingly. In total contrast to conventional food advertising, no claims are made on 'appetite appeal', or directly on the quality of the product. Everything is left to suggestion by the quality of the packaging.

Introduction and follow-up

The given sales area in eastern Switzerland caused one initial media problem because nationwide advertising was not possible. To begin with, advertising was limited to local newspapers and advertisers. It was expanded to wider press and TV coverage only after trading had begun to open up. The essential feature is that the whole marketing campaign was activated and concentrated:

Advertising: Adverts ring the changes on the theme: 'no packaging is too good...' Allusions to the special packaging and what it stands for become freer.
Sales promotion: Targeted support of local dealers and special promotions (bath towel, Prix Toni).
Pricing policy: Positioning in the high-price range.
Distribution policy: Retro-distribution system with special stands policy for return of jars at point of sale – a repeated point of contact with customers.
Product policy: New packaging design: glass, not plastic; reduced weight of jar; resealable plastic lid.
PR work: Very high intensity for foodstuffs, using professional specialists. The superiority of circulation jars, in terms of energy use and ecology, stands in the foreground.

Results

Sales in the first year after the relaunch almost doubled; in the second year there was another 50 per cent increase. Combined with this was a larger share of the national market, rising from 3.9 to 7.2 per cent in the first year and 10 per cent in the second year, and moving from third position to first. The market share in the east of Switzerland rose from 9.8 to 22.2 per cent. Toni contributed 80 per cent to the 10 per cent growth in total market volume. Distribution was expanded outside the local region, and return quotas were raised to 63 per cent by means of return stands in all retail outlets. Beyond the statistical level there are many other indicators of success: counter campaigns by rivals, reactive marketing, me-too launches, large-scale media reaction and direct consumer reaction.

'Communication has become part of the life of the product. The advertisers' dream of direct dialogue has come true. The public understands the point of all our adverts and people have even started to suggest new ideas.'

◇ The 'Frosch' product line by Werner and Mertz

The speed with which a certain eco-friendly frog hops up the ladder of success is ample evidence of the fact that even a relatively small company can cause a stir with environmental marketing. In just three years the little frog was able to leap into second place in the cleaning products market, against giants like Henkel (General/Dor), Colgate-Palmolive (Ajax) and the market leader Procter and Gamble.

The idea

The chemical industry is in a dilemma. On the one hand, the consumer expects a certain performance from a product; on the other hand, chemical products are now required to cause as little damage to the environment as possible. This calls for a new outlook. In 1984 the family business Werner and Mertz, a cleaning products manufacturer, set off in a new direction of product development. The company had become aware through research findings of a possible pathway to new customers.

■ Consumers wish to make a contribution to environmental protection, i.e. using fewer cleaning materials and choosing them carefully.

■ For ecological reasons they would like to use fewer cleaning materials but to have the same performance.

■ Young, better educated housewives, who see housework as a necessary evil, are particularly aware of the environment.

■ The total need for cleaning materials in this sector is quite low. There are market opportunities, but only where the product agrees with customer expectations.

Research at Werner and Mertz developed alternative preparations which comply with consumer awareness of environmental protection. The company has produced universal cleaners which are tailor-made for non-fanatical cleaners. Everything which is not essential, such as elaborate packaging, has been removed. Contents and packaging are environment friendly, and full details are given on the packaging.

The innovative 'Frosch' product line, introduced in 1987, managed to achieve growth in a stagnant market. With an 8 per cent market share it contributes significantly to the turnover and success of the company. The products are based on historical recipes which have been reworked with modern technology. In 1988 a spirit-based glass cleaner, a washing-up liquid and a vinegar-based toilet cleaner were added to the existing neutral cleaner and vinegar cleaner.

The special achievement of the Frosch series consists in being able to offer a healthy balance between eco-friendliness and cleaning power. The frog logo, which used to be exclusive to Erdal shoe polish, is now one of the best-known brand names in Germany. Because of its high degree of recognition (98 per cent), the series is likely to be extended in the near future.

Environmental positioning

The secrets of success for the Frosch products were widespread public awareness of green issues, and the subsequent integration of this change of values into company and product policy.

The products

The OECD classification 'readily biodegradable' is also surpassed, with a score of 98 per cent. Ingredients such as ethanol or vinegar (acetic acid) are combined with modern, eco-friendly raw materials. Colouring and perfumes are used only in cosmetic products. All products are phosphate-free and contain no other complexing agents. All packaging consists of polyethylene, a transparent plastic which does not undergo any harmful degradation process after disposal. Substances which might be damaging to the ground water are not formed. Similarly, with incineration, substances which might alter the pH value of ground water do not occur.

Advertising

None of the Frosch products is intensively advertised, and so advertising costs are kept relatively low. The goal of the advertising strategy is to create an honest image and take account of consumer needs, while providing information on the products. Expensive TV and radio advertising are not used, advertisements being confined to selected print media, including magazines such as *Natur* and *Eco-Test*, where less eco-friendly competitors would fear to tread.

Altogether one-third of company advertising is via print media. The advertisements feature the friendly green frog as the hero: 'The frog as connoisseur of the environment', 'The environment loves the frog'. These advertisements are supplemented with sampling promotions, and brochures are distributed giving information about the environment as well as the products.

Public relations

Under the auspices of the Federation of German Housewives (DHB) and the Association for Home Economics, there are regular meetings at which environmental aspects of cleaning materials are discussed, and workshops are organized where practical hints on eco-friendly housekeeping are given. In these and similar events, Frosch products are often seen to provide the best solution to the problems of green cleaning.

Distribution

Distribution is via the classic Werner and Mertz sales channels of grocery retailers and drugstores.

The price

Pricing is in line with the market but not too high: that is, 5–10 per cent cheaper than the market leader for any type of product.

The results

The Frosch concept is very successful. According to the Nielson Study of Market Differentiation, the brand shares sixth place with Mercedes and BMW, beating

Maggi, Nivea, Gillette and VW. This really is success if one considers that the green frog was only introduced as a consistent marketing concept in 1986. Honesty, environmental awareness and target group orientation are the basis of this outstanding marketing success.

In 1989 Frosch products had a sales volume of around DM62 million. The majority of this was from neutral cleaner and vinegar cleaner. The 'frog' corners 16 per cent of the entire domestic cleaning market and is number two in the market for this type of product. Next in importance in the range are washing-up liquid, vinegar toilet cleaner, ethanol glass cleaner and scouring cream. These items represent 23 per cent of the total DM260 million turnover at Werner and Mertz as a whole.

Opening up new markets under the Frosch brand name

Traditionally, the Erdal-Rex company produces and sells cleaning and care products for shoes, floors, cars, baths, toilets and general purposes. Under the aegis of the strong Frosch name, it has been possible to create new markets and nudge into unexplored territory. Since 1986 the previously insignificant market for neutral and vinegar cleaners has been steadily expanding. Today it is so important that no one in the cleaning materials market can afford not to be represented with their own products in this sector.

The Frosch name has proved to be transferable to completely new markets. Ethanol cleaner, washing-up liquid and scouring cream have been introduced. The company is able to operate with a significantly larger retail turnover than five years ago. The most recent new introduction under the Frosch name is a detergent. The estimated retail turnover for this market is DM1.6 billion, which makes it the most important market in the cleaning materials sector. This new product remains true to the Frosch concept. It is eco-friendly and is presented honestly and informatively. Here too contents, packaging and promotion come together in a coherent marketing strategy.

The consistent absorption of environmental concerns throughout the company

Werner and Mertz has recorded its special concern for the environment in the company guidelines and this philosophy permeates all fields of company activity. For every measure which has a bearing on the environment, an impact assessment is drawn up. Products are tested for their environmental impact and adapted to the new demands. Comprehensive, informative customer advice is also given high priority.

12

Environmental thinking and the organization

◆   ◆   ◆

The organization of environmental protection

The internal organization of environmental protection requires an integrated perception of environmental protection as a management responsibility, rooted in holistic strategic thinking. The function of environmental protection can be carried out through:

- A staff position.
- A central management department.

The individual form of these roles will be determined by the surrounding organizational scenario.

    The first possibility will be most suitable for medium-sized companies; in many cases this responsibility is transferred to outside consultants. In large companies a central department usually combines other neighbouring functions such as technical safety (Siemens), safety at work (BASF) and energy (Philips).

    While staff appointees generally have to combat acceptance problems, central departments run the risk of being over-formal. Thomas (1988) sees the advantage of departments in the variety of specialist disciplines they can encompass, and the following goals are listed:

- Co-ordination of responsibility for environmental protection throughout all areas of the company.
- Definition of company environment policy.

- Promotion of commercial and technical innovation.

- Pre-emptive activities, e.g. responding to subtle warning signals.

- Combining company expertise on the environment in a mutually beneficial dialogue with the outside world.

There are a number of further reasons for centralization:

- A central department offers the possibility of direct access, cutting down on bureaucracy.

- It shows that the company gives high priority to environmental protection.

- It offers a clearer perception of supporting and consultancy functions than remote directives.

- Communication with licensing and supervisory authorities gains from central position and long company experience.

- In emergencies appropriate measures can be quickly communicated to all levels of management.

As we shall see from the case studies in this chapter, central departments in large companies can be expanded to include sectional departments.

Environmental officer

An environmental officer is a legal requirement in Germany only in the following specified cases:

- Officer responsible for emission.

- Officer responsible for waterways.

- Officer responsible for industrial waste.

In close connection with this, there have been officials responsible for safety at work for many years now.

In practice, the appointment of an officer is handled in a variety of different ways. Either the responsibilities are carried out separately by a number of people or, more frequently, one member of staff is given responsibility for all three areas. The appointment itself is decided upon by the management, and management is solely responsible for its success. With official permission the responsibilities can be devolved to outside agencies.

In general, the responsibilities of the environmental officer include the following:

- Advising and informing the executive (especially on new investment projects).

- Supervising the observance of regulations (and reporting shortcomings).

- Protecting company liabilities.

- Informing and motivating staff.

- Presenting suggestions for improvement.

- Reporting on possible measures.

The environmental officer is not empowered to make executive decisions but only to give advice. Teamwork and the ability to establish contact with outside authorities is therefore essential. The environment officer has a special role to play:

> Increasing technology in our relationship with work and the environment places this responsibility somewhere between consultant, controller and executive. Similar roles already exist or are in the making: for example, the data protection officer or the safety officer. These functions are still a fly in the ointment of all organizations. They must still fight for the recognition of their activities. (*Karriere* magazine, 2/1988)

In larger companies there are various alternative ways of fulfilling the legal requirements. As a rule a number of officers are appointed with various responsibilities, including environmental protection. At a higher level, management takes responsibility for some of these issues. For example, Siemens employs about 250 staff with responsibility for the environment and related areas. Almost 850 staff are employed in environment and safety at work at BASF, at a level directly below senior management.

Because of their position, managerial staff are automatically responsible for the environment and for compliance with regulations. The environmental officer, however, usually has to have expert knowledge, educational qualifications and practical experience.

◊ Siemens

Siemens has a typically decentralized structure. In each of the one hundred or so factories in Germany the works manager is directly responsible for the appointment of the environment officer. Consultancy and exchange of experience are available through senior sectional managers, and at corporate level the central Department for Environment and Technical Safety takes responsibility for the following:

- Advice to the board and other management levels.

- Assistance in emergencies.

- Advice on safety and company transgressions.

- Exchange of experience between sectional officers.

- Specialist advice on chemical safety, radiation and fire hazards.

- Seminars on emissions, waterways, waste disposal, radiation and fire hazards.

- Databank on hazardous substances: SIGEDA; STS.
- Advice to inland companies.
- Advice to overseas subsidiaries.
- Contact with authorities, political parties and associations.
- Public relations, lectures.
- Publications (quarterly magazine).

◇ Mannesmann

In the Mannesmann combine the Technical and Environment Office is directly accountable to the Technology Board. On the staff there are specialists for recycling, waste water, noise pollution, emissions and filtration technology, existing waste, input materials and environmental statistics. Altogether there are 65 officers.

New forms of organization

Environmental affairs officer

The positioning of the environment officer in the technical area – that is, fulfilling a curative function – is of very limited usefulness in the kind of proactive environmental management we have been discussing. There is a need for new comprehensive organizational solutions. Environmental management can be brought about either by means of a qualitative expansion of the already existing structures or through the creation of new structures.

Environmental thinking and action must be anchored firmly within the organization. The responsibility of this specialist post is to instigate preventive environmental management, to support ecologically based decisions and to give assistance to all areas. This presupposes a high level of interdisciplinary education and training. The person appointed should not see environmental protection in isolation, as a technical problem, but needs to appreciate its wider significance. To be realistic we are still a long way from this ideal, but examples of the first steps towards a new orientation are outlined below.

The environmental affairs officer should undertake the following:

- Promote environmental ideals throughout the company.
- Advise on the development of eco-friendly products.
- Plan and supervise the introduction of technical eco-measures.
- Collaborate with development and investment projects.
- Fix regular minuted meetings.
- Arrange appraisal procedures with the committee chairperson.

● Assess the costs of environmental protection.

● Respond to regulations and oversee payment of external duties.

● Deal with questions of product liability.

● Set up environmental information and control systems.

● Carry out environmental PR work.

● Plan and accompany environmental audits.

● Act as an agent for change.

● Take part in strategic planning.

● Provide an ecological dimension to training programmes.

By contrast with the type of environment officer implied by the legal framework, this new role is greatly expanded in terms of communicative skills. It requires competence in the area of economics as well as the traditional scientific/technical training. Stahlmann *et al*. (1989) have designed a comprehensive catalogue of fields of activity for this new kind of environment officer, and it is set out in Figure 37.

The examples from IBM and Elida Gibbs show how far this position has developed in practice. At Philips too the role of environment protection officer includes consultancy, control, documentation, initiatives, influencing and developing processes and products as well as checking the environmental implications of investment, budget and changes of policy. The officer also has a major responsibility for disseminating the idea of environmental protection among the staff.

The ideal place for this key post within the organizational structure of a company is near to top management level. Stahlmann and Beschorner (1989) favour a strong connection with the materials management department because of the direct rapport with resources and the possibilities for introducing innovations. Environmental management as an overall concept, embracing every area of logistics, can have a profoundly beneficial effect on savings and recycling.

As an organizational manifestation of our awareness of energy, an energy officer has the following additional responsibilities:

● Securing the short- and long-term provision of energy.

● Execution of energy-saving measures, with the support of interdisciplinary teams.

● Planning emergency programmes for energy crises.

It is also worth considering the idea of a special environment committee as a focus for information and advice. Several companies in Germany have already taken up this option with a member from every department sitting on the committee, which deals with eclectic, not necessarily technical environment matters.

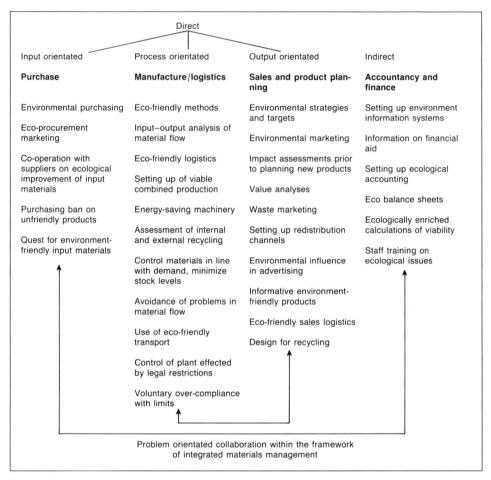

Source: Stahlmann *et al.* (1989).

Figure 37 The responsibilities of an environment officer

◊ IBM

At IBM, Germany, the job description for 'Officer for Environment Protection and Chemical Co-ordination' sets out primary and specialist responsibilities for the post.

The position

■   The officer must ensure that legal and company regulations on environmental protection are complied with.

■ As Country Chemical Authority (CCA), the officer must ensure that legal and company regulations affecting the licensing, procurement, storage, transport, distribution and use of chemicals are complied with.

Specialist responsibilities

■ Jurisdiction over sectional environment officers and chemical co-ordinators.

■ Co-ordination and supervision of the above with the aim of ensuring unified procedure.

■ Supervision of the observance of regulations and duties on emissions, water-way protection and waste disposal. Reporting back to management.

■ Powers reserved for the appointment of sectional officers.

■ Yearly review of sectional environment programmes, stock audits and research, on the basis of self-audit results.

■ Checking all official licences and duties pertaining to the environment.

■ Checking the observance of regulations and duties on licensing, procurement, storage, transport, distribution and use of chemicals.

■ Checking and reporting on all international testing agreements and investment decisions which have a bearing on environment protection (in agreement with sectional officers).

■ Influencing the development and manufacture of eco-friendly processes and products at IBM.

■ Influencing the development and application of appropriate techniques for waste treatment with particular reference to recycling.

■ Reading, interpreting and evaluating the regulations and laws. Advising and supporting sectional officers.

■ Advising and supporting the senior management of IBM, Germany, on all environmental and chemical matters.

■ Controlling and supervising environmental impact assessments (EIAs).

■ Checking and releasing all EIAs for projects affected by international agreements (FILS 117/118), IBM products and process transfers.

■ Keeping in touch with environmental issues affecting projects on IBM premises.

■ Permanent membership of Safety at Work Committee.

■ Non-executive competence for paragraph 4 of the chemo-technical regulations and regulations for safety at work.

■ Training and advising IBM staff.

■ Organization of meetings for environment officers and chemical co-ordinators.

■ Close collaboration with national and international experts (specialist support and exchange of experience).

■ Participating in the production of international regulations.

■ Producing and publishing internal executive and specialist instructions.

- Collaboration with external specialists in influencing the future development of laws and regulations relevant to IBM.
- Specialist responsibility for the IBM chemical data-sheet system.
- Formal notification of 'new substances' according to chemical regulations.

◇ Environmental organisation at Elida Gibbs

Name	Composition	Responsibilities
Senior environment management team	Chairman Technical director Marketing director Environment officer	Develops environmental strategies, decides on suggestions from the management team, decides on relevant changes to products or company structure, e.g. ban on certain raw materials or packaging, compliance with internal limits, conversion procedures
Environment management team	Managers from: Purchasing Sales Production technology R & D Marketing Environmental officer	Establishing contacts with critics among: Consumers Science Retail trade Media Collection of information, including 'ideas-exchange' Evaluation and conversion into concrete activities
Product appraisal team	R & D Marketing Purchasing Environmental officer Quality control	Critical appraisal of all materials, packaging and products, with particular emphasis on responding to critics. Deciding on input or conversion
Emissions officer	As a voluntary measure. The company is not bound by law because of its size	Consultation on development and introduction of eco-friendly manufacturing and disposal methods
Editorial team 'Green Report'	Young members of staff under the leadership of the environment officer	Communication on all environment/health-related issues

Name	Composition	Responsibilities
Organ of communication: 'Green Report' appears at least four times a year and is directed at all Elida staff	Another important aspect is the organization of an ideas pool	Ongoing discussion about environment and health issues e.g. technical discussion, sales conferences, meetings between development and marketing
Environment officer	Initiates, co-ordinates and controls all relevant measures within Elida-Gibbs; organizes and leads senior environment management team, environment management team, product appraisal team and 'Green Report' team. Has the right of veto over production with harmful raw and packaging materials; can stop production. With veto must bring in senior management	Conceives environment/health strategy of the firm and initiates measures for implementation. Co-ordinates individual measures to prevent conflict. Initiates information network. Initiates and supervises the ongoing actualization of policy. Decides on environmental profile in advertising and on packaging

13

Personnel policies

This is a story about four people named Everybody, Somebody, Anybody and Nobody. There was an important job to be done and Everybody was asked to do it. Everybody was sure Somebody would do it. Anybody could have done it, but Nobody did it. Somebody got angry about that, because it was Everybody's job. Everybody thought Anybody could do it but Nobody realized that Everybody wouldn't do it. It ended up that Everybody blamed Somebody when Nobody did what Anybody could have done.

Staff involvement

Eco-management is ultimately heading for the void if it fails to influence human behaviour. Meeting the demands of the environment is not possible without the active participation of as many staff as possible. One does not need to be a pessimist to see that we are still a long way from having motivated all staff and management in this endeavour. Moreover, the influence of business is relatively restricted. Industrial training can affect basic attitudes, but these are generally formed during schooling and through personal and social development. Bearing in mind the saying 'You can't teach an old dog new tricks', one cannot begin too early with environmental education.

Neither should one view human behaviour in too idealistic a light. The same member of staff from whom one expects eco-friendly behaviour at work may find it quite normal to make a personal contribution to the 130 billion cigarettes consumed annually. It is also worth remembering that 95 per cent of all industrial accidents can be attributed to human error.

Staff behaviour can be influenced on several levels:

- Creating an eco-friendly working environment.

- Integrating environmental ideas into industrial training.

- Integrating environmental ideas into appraisal and incentive schemes. For example, Management by Objectives systems could incorporate quantifiable eco-goals such as energy-saving percentages.

- Encouraging discussion of ecological improvements.

- Company contribution to the development of relevant industrial training programmes.

Increasing commitment to company eco-initiatives, participation in seminars and courses and many other instances provide evidence for growing interest in green issues. It is particularly important, however, to progress in easy stages, and to avoid 'too much, too soon'. The inevitable frustration of trying to impart information about a complex and ever-changing subject is all too familiar to environmental activists.

It is quite insufficient to consider environmental protection as merely something for the bosses; to expect motivation from above. Each and every member of staff shares responsibility for this vital task. Nevertheless, the role of management in creating a business culture through visible, symbolic actions, and the effect of this on staff, should not be underestimated.

Employee incentives policies

A practical way of inviting staff involvement within an employee incentives policy is to instal a 'green' suggestion box in a prominent place, as a supplement to the environmental notice board. These simple measures should provide staff with a stimulus to express positive ideas.

◇ Ernst Winter and Son

At Ernst Winter and Son suggestions for improvement have been taken seriously for many years, to the benefit of the company and its employees. Suggestions range from lowering production costs to simplifying processes. Suggestions on 'Energy Saving and Environment' are rewarded at a rate of 30 per cent of the value of all savings over two years, compared with 20 per cent of savings from non-environmental suggestions. For general environmental ideas there are special post boxes with the heading 'Environment tips ... for a better life'.

◇ Siemens

Environmental suggestions are also rewarded at Siemens. In 1989 a member of staff in the Gladbeck telephone factory was awarded DM25,860 (£8,500). The suggestion had effected considerable savings of water. By improving the performance of pumps, more cooling water can be pumped into the recovery plant and the demand on mains water falls. Previously, around 200 cubic metres of cooling water per day were lost as waste.

◇ Bayer

Since 1988 useful suggestions on environmental protection have been rewarded with an Environment Prize. Environmental protection takes third place behind improvements in production and energy saving, with a clearly upward trend. Examples of the many ideas received are: new uses for nickel-plated high-pressure pipes which are no longer needed, instead of scrapping them; recycling valuable substances in waste water directly back into a rubber production process; and minimizing breakdowns in the exhaust fume incineration unit.

Environmental protection and vocational training

Environmental protection has been integrated into industrial training programmes in Germany, particularly in the industries most obviously associated with pollution: the chemical industry, electricity producers and the metal industries. It is a question not only of inculcating specific knowledge and understanding about ecology, but also of establishing environment-friendly attitudes and behaviour.

According to a survey of technical, trade and commercial training managers, environmental protection is dealt with in more than half the in-company technical and trade courses, and in one-third of the commercial courses, with a strong increase anticipated. The following pedagogical goals have been highlighted:

- Widening understanding of the dynamic relationship between ecology and economy, and developing solution strategies.
- Developing knowledge of environmental technologies such as recycling, energy saving and waste treatment.

- Transferring environmental knowledge into industrial reality.
- Providing information about the 'polluter pays' principle.

Since 1987 the Federal Institute for Industrial Education (BIBB) has been striving to integrate environmental protection into the curriculum for training courses. This has already been achieved in some areas such as the metal industries and the retail trade. Most training curricula contain a standard package, 'Safety at work, accident prevention, environment protection and the rational use of energy', within which several learning objectives may be fulfilled.

The integration of environmental themes at the level of in-service training and at training colleges is also of great importance.

◇ **Henkel**

In 1987 Henkel plc developed an environment planning game which has subsequently been run more than 20 times with over 500 trainees.

◇ **Hoechst**

In collaboration with the BIBB, Hoechst has contributed to a project on 'Environment Protection in Industrial Training' by developing materials for science and chemistry modules. These materials have since been made available nationally for training in the chemical industry.

◇ **Ernst Winter and Son**

Trainees at Ernst Winter and Son are given ample opportunity to gain first-hand experience of environmental issues. Recent examples of course components make this quite clear:

- Ground water works in Hamburg: a lecture on water extraction and the protection of waterways.
- Federal Environment Office in Berlin: information on waste treatment and atmospheric decontamination.
- Specialist lectures for 'Green Week' on municipal greening and healthy eating.
- German Society for the Protection of Birds: advanced course on biotopes and species protection in marshland.
- Visit to the planetarium in Hamburg.
- Slide-show on hedgehogs and lecture about life in mud-flats.
- Visit to Eekholt game park: insights into eco-cycles and systems.

◇ Carl Nolte

Apprentices with Carl Nolte are encouraged to initiate and organize their own environmental projects. In 1989 the new apprentices acting as 'environment managers', set up a project for separating plastic waste. They are currently planning a local 'greening scheme'. A representative of the apprentices sits on the environment committee to ensure co-ordination of the various initiatives.

Staff development

In many companies environment protection has already become an established component of management training. Effective environment protection calls for a broad interdisciplinary training, which has not hitherto been available.

As the inclusion of environmental protection is well established in most courses for apprentices, it is necessary to follow this up with specialist extension courses for as many staff as possible. The implementation of environmental objectives requires the full support of staff and management.

◇ Mannesmann

The environment officer at Mannesmann has to be prepared to provide training materials for staff. Seminars are given for trainees and staff at all levels.

These training schemes can be supplemented by traditional awareness-raising measures such as brochures, posters and articles in the company magazine.

Environmental training is often carried out in conjunction with safety at work. Staff are required to:

- Recognize the long-term effects of their activities.
- Develop the skill to perceive the consequences of their actions and avert hazards of any kind.
- Maintain awareness of the risks associated with work.
- Develop preventive habits through repeated practice and training.
- Acknowledge and fulfil legal requirements.
- Accumulate facts and understanding to promote the creation of a better working environment.
- Respond to incentives, e.g. competitions and awards.

- Keep up to date with new information.
- Respond actively to company suggestions.

In small and medium-sized companies it is not possible to provide an appropriate qualification without outside help.

◇ Bayer

Certain groups of staff, such as works managers and master craftsmen, are obliged to attend regular training sessions. Since individual staff each have their own responsibilities, a new in-service training concept has made the following measures obligatory:

- Around 40 graded, targeted seminars covering a wide range of subjects.
- Annual training days catering for 7,500 participants.
- Annual exchanges of experience for all employees.

The overall goal is to design and control production so that 'Unnecessary burdens on the environment or in the workplace are avoided. We are aiming at a scenario in which safe, environment-friendly actions are fostered.'

Information and training is organized in the phases: knowledge, understanding, commitment and application. A broad basis of agreement is created by involving management in this process. A special working party has been formed from the Economic Committee to ensure the flow of information.

◇ Ciba-Geigy

Environment protection and safety form an integral part of in-service training courses for all staff at Ciba-Geigy. Personnel spend 5–10 per cent of their working hours in training of some form. Suggestions from staff are rewarded, and environmental suggestions constitute 20 per cent of the total.

Implications for personal life

Company responsibility is not limited to the workplace, but extends to raising staff awareness of environment-friendly behaviour in the home. Ernst Winter and Son financed a pilot project 'Environment Consultancy for the Home' in 1985–6. The idea was that manufacturers in turn would have to adapt to environment-friendly domestic behaviour and the massive demand for suitable eco-friendly products and services. The company placed specialist staff at the disposal of the project and partly paid for their employment at the Federation for Environment and Nature Conservation.

Many other firms offer seminars, usually calling in outside speakers. For example, staff households can be assessed in terms of energy saving and eco-friendliness using computer checklists, as with the scheme set up by AUGE.

◇ Follmann and Co.

Follmann and Co. has organized computer-aided budgeting advice, in conjunction with an individual investment and profitability plan. Based on the experience of this and several other schemes, it appears that average savings of DM800 per household per year are possible.

Healthy eating in the canteen

Staff awareness of health is increasingly seen as a part of company environment philosophy, and the availability of a nutritionally balanced diet in the staff canteen contributes to this.

◇ Christof Stoll

From the start, wholefoods have been available in the works canteen at Christof Stoll. Since it has become increasingly difficult to purchase suitable food for over 200 meals per day, Frau Stoll has wasted no time in deciding to grow her own organic vegetables for the canteen. Two hectares of market garden are devoted to this project. Full agricultural recycling, including the exploitation of waste by two pigs, is practised. Any raw materials which have to be purchased undergo strict scrutiny. The canteen kitchen has now become so famous that it is visited by kitchen managers for training purposes. The Stoll VITA charity publishes a wholefood cookery book with recipes from the works canteen. Neither cola nor lemonade is on sale (not even in machines), but free vegetable soup is available during the morning break.

Community and school support

Many companies have realized that changing consumer consciousness must begin early, and they have consequently prepared copious information and lavish teaching packs for schools.

◇ Safeway

Following consultation with teachers and advice from a top environmentalist, Safeway has produced a Schools Environmental Pack which is completely free of charge. It contains notes and ideas to assist teachers, and children aged 7–12 years in environmental studies. The pack comprises an inflatable globe, 'I'm On Earthwise Patrol' stickers and an audio cassette, giving animal noises for children to identify. The reverse side of the tape advises teachers how to make best use of the pack. There is also a series of detailed fact sheets and teacher's notes. A large number of packs have already been sent out to schools.

The pack covers five main topics: reusing and recycling; organic living; energy; pollution; and conservation. It also makes suggestions for 'actions' related to each topic, for further investigation either at school or at home. Each of the topics covered is linked to attainment levels for the national curriculum in England and Wales. The pack also includes details of how schools can win one of 38 prizes in a £6,000 competition designed to focus pupils' attention on practical ways to help protect the environment. The information in the pack has full copyright clearance.

◇ Scott

Scott, the largest manufacturer of soft tissues in the world, works with the community in a number of ways. For example, in the spring of 1990 Scott launched an ongoing community-based initiative of education and information about the environment. It is called 'Be concerned, show concern: make each day Earth Day'. The programme is designed to raise public awareness about complex contemporary environmental issues. It has two goals:

- To provide information to help people better understand complex environmental issues through education.

- To help people and their communities identify and find solutions to environmental problems.

The programme is long term and focused on local communities, especially those where Scott has facilities. In these communities Scott employees are working to tailor programmes to meet local needs. The programme includes the following:

- 'The Environmental Scholars' Program'. In Scott communities scholarships of $2,500 will be awarded to select high-school seniors who plan to pursue environment-related studies.

- 'It's Your World'. This is a US programme in which participating schools have saved the symbols on Scott consumer products in order to redeem them for personal computers, VCRs and other teaching aids and equipment. Schools expressing interest in participating in the promotion receive a special 'It's Your World' teaching programme, which is designed to educate and motivate students about important issues regarding the environment.

- 'The Environmental Ambassadors Program'. Scott environmental experts are available to speak on a variety of environmental subjects at local schools, community organizations and other community gatherings. In addition to a presentation on a specific topic, they can provide brochures and other educational material. Scott in Canada has had a programme of this type for many years.

Scott environmental experts also work with community groups on issues of common interest. For example, in Nova Scotia, Canada, Scott Maritimes is participating in the Saint Mary's River Forestry/Wildlife Project, begun in 1984, as part of public discussion on the role of the forest industry in Nova Scotia's future. This is a co-operative programme with government, industry, public interest groups and the Canadian Institute of Forestry.

In the UK, Scott sponsored a joint-venture promotion with the Woodland Trust, a British conservation charity concerned with saving many of the country's woods through acquisition and reclamation. Working with the trust, Scott sponsored a promotion called Woodland Re-leaf for the purpose of saving ten woodland areas in Britain, and raised over £260,000 for the trust.

In Nova Scotia the tree nursery staff have created a unique 'Grow Your Own Tree' kit, complete with seeds and soil. The kit is given free of charge to young and old on request. Some 11,000 kits were distributed in 1989 alone.

14

Financing and funding environmental investment

◆   ◆   ◆

Governmental financial assistance

The increasing density of government regulations exerts a considerable pressure on businesses to invest. According to the 'polluter pays' principle, the cost of fulfilling these laws in terms of investment and actual industrial implementation is borne by the company. However, it is in the public interest to provide financial support or incentives to assist in the execution of these regulations.

Financial assistance is mostly directed to the small and medium-sized sector where the greatest need lies. The number and range of packages, conditions and possible combinations present a veritable jungle of complexity, while intense advertising on the part of credit institutions offering environmental financing packages shows that there is clearly a growing need for consultancy.

Building up a coherent financing concept draws on company capital, bank facilities and public funding, and in this context it is increasingly recognized that the role of banking must extend beyond the traditional competence of financial institutions to include the consultancy required.

Public financial assistance[*] is only ever provided as a partial support to existing environmental investment: in other words, company or outside finance must be available as well. The flaw inherent in these programmes is that they limit the development of preventive environmental policies by focusing on the additive, curative area of environmental technology; they are directed predominantly at fulfilling government environmental protection regulations.

---

[*] In Germany there are at present more than 50 assistance programmes available.

A move away from these original goals and recognition of the need for innovative, integrated procedures is obviously required. However, it should not be forgotten that incentives to encourage private environmental investment will be effective only if companies are helped to achieve business advantages, e.g. by energy savings or re-exploitation schemes.

The conditions attached to funding in general exhibit many national peculiarities, and even within one package there are too many variations to summarize in any detail.

In Germany, there are around 50 different Federal programmes, sponsored by the Kreditanstalt für Wiederaufbau (KFW), or the Deutsche Ausgleichsbank, as well as schemes within individual states.

In Britain, Environmental Protection Technology (EPT) grants from the Department of the Environment are primarily for research and development purposes.

Federal and State Construction Grants in the USA provide regional and local aid.

At the European level, the main source of funding is the European Investment Bank (EIB). Almost 15 per cent of EIB financial support (ECU1.2 billion) is granted for the protection or improvement of the environment.

Financial credit

Since government funding only ever provides partial support to private investment, credit facilities from private banks are often useful. However, finding the correct, tailor-made financial package can be extremely complicated.

In financing environmental protection investments, banks should aim to develop packages which incorporate a combination of private funding with national or EC support. Banks in Germany have been particularly active in this respect, especially by pointing out the environmental approach in their advertisements. The reorganization of the World Bank to include central and regional environment departments shows the importance of this area of finance, and should encourage private banks to respond to the demands of environmental development.

The large banks in Germany are currently publicizing computer-aided consultancy supported by in-house databanks, which can provide individually designed financial assistance. The Deutsche Bank has developed 'db-select', and the Dresdner Bank uses 'Drefin'. These financial services are usually combined with comprehensive environmental consultancy. A survey carried out by the Chamber of Commerce in Nürnberg showed that medium-sized businesses suffered from a significant lack of information on environmental funding plans. At present, banks are offering favourable credit facilities for the finance of environmental investment, either in the form of independent packages or as part of a plan combined with public funding.

ACORN
Ethical Unit Trust

An opportunity to do good with a good investment

The Acorn Ethical Unit Trust offers you an excellent opportunity to invest your capital and see it grow, while doing good as well.

This is a unit trust which aims to take advantage of every sound development in the search for a greener world and a safer environment.

For example, waste management and recycling is now an increasingly specialised and profitable business.

Similarly, medical technology is becoming a major force, both in the economy and on the stock markets.

Plant biochemistry is another area where, in our view, research and development will lead to significant private investment opportunities. Others include solar power and the increasing greening of the High Street.

On the other side of the coin, investments we don't touch – and won't – include arms, tobacco, alcohol and South Africa.

Overall, our objective is to provide capital growth from sound investments in all parts of the world excluding non-ethical activities.

Of course, the value of the units and the income from them can go down as well as up, and past performance is not necessarily a guide to the future.

In the nine months between the close of the initial offer in December 1988 and 22nd September 1989, the offer price of the accumulation units of Acorn Ethical Unit Trust rose from 100p to 112.8p.

Acorn Unit Trust Managers is a Member of IMRO and LAUTRO and a subsidiary of Acorn Investment Trust Plc, whose Chairman is R. C. Vickers.

To find out more about Acorn Ethical Unit Trust, and for an Application Form, simply complete and return the coupon below.

**To: Acorn Unit Trust Managers Limited
1 White Hart Yard, London Bridge
London, SE1 1NX**

I'd like to know more about Acorn Ethical Unit Trust. Please send me your booklet and an Application Form.

Name _____

Address _____

_____

_____ Postcode _____

ACORN
Ethical Unit Trust

Ethical investments

◊ Commerzbank

Since 1987 the Commerzbank has been offering a combined package including public funding and the bank's own special environmental credit facility for small and medium-sized companies. This designated credit can be given as an annuity, an instalment plan or a lump sum with a period of up to 18 years to repay, a maximum of two years' exemption and interest due periods of up to ten years. The difference between government loans and the total amount needed for investment is financed on special terms, with possible interest discounts dependent on the discretion of the individual bank manager.

According to *Time* magazine, several mutual funds have been set up to buy shares exclusively in corporations judged to follow the Valdez Principles (see Chapter 7).

Artus Ethical Capital Administration has been operating with modest sums in Germany since 1988, and because the company lacks a German title it is compelled to channel investments into British or American funds, such as the Stewardship Unit Trust, Fellowship Trust, Merlin Jupiter Ecology Fund, Select Environmental Services Fund and Merrill Lynch Environmental Technology Fund.

In the USA, $7 billion are invested in ethical shares, and a total of $500 billion are tied up in ethical portfolios: that is, around 10 per cent of the yearly turnover on Wall Street. In Britain around £80 million are invested in green funds; Denmark too has its own eco-funds.

Finance and consultancy under one roof

The exigencies of environmental protection have placed a great responsibility upon banks to develop new forms of credit management, to reconsider risk evaluation and to show imagination in the quest for innovative financial solutions. The traditional banking role of financing business investment is supplemented by a new field of activity in the form of information and consultancy services.

◊ Deutsche Bank

As an environmental protection initiative the Deutsche Bank, Germany's largest bank, presented an environment databank at the 1990 CeBit. The knowledge required for solving environmental problems has previously been scattered among many disparate sources, and the purpose of this new service is to offer small and medium-sized companies a pool of information and consultancy under one roof. The availability of this type of environment information system provides customers with opportunities to realize their environmental aims and to open up new areas of their market; it improves efficiency and stimulates innovation.

As Figure 38 shows, the quick and inexpensive search encompasses a variety of areas:

■ Possible providers of solutions to a given problem can be located.

■ Competent consultants, partners and manufacturers can be found.

■ The system is designed to deal with products and services appropriate to the target group of its users.

This databank service is used in conjunction with two further systems which were presented at CeBit 1989:

■ db-data, which provides business information and contacts on technology, market, trade and customers.

■ db-select, which contains information on over 590 Federal, regional and EC funding schemes, including details of conditions, objectives, application requirements and contacts. Data-processing facilities can be used to search for tailor-made financing combinations including interest repayment plans. This databank is currently being upgraded to 'Euroselect', which will be able to provide this information for all EC member countries.

The case of a company affected by environmental charges will serve to demonstrate how the system is used to solve problems and sound out new markets.

A textile dyeing firm in Berlin is ordered by the Berlin authorities to undertake improvements in the treatment of heavy metals and chlorinated hydrocarbons in waste water, to have ground tests conducted on the site and to instal a plant in the bleaching department for treating fumes containing chloroform.

The company uses the environment data system to search for technologies and suppliers to solve its pollution problems, and an appropriate Berlin engineering

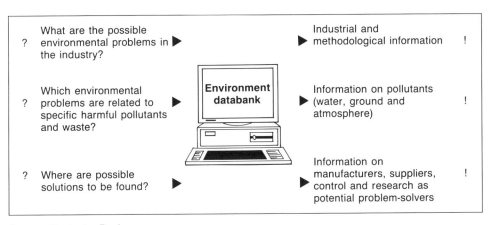

Source: Deutsche Bank

Figure 38 Environment information databank at the Deutsche Bank

office for the ground investigation. These searches can be carried out on db-data.

After making contact with the engineering office and looking through the technical possibilities for waste treatment, the company makes a decision on the pollution treatment plant and once again uses the data base to find a suitable engineering company.

The firm has at its disposal a wide range of information on which to base its choices, and has acquired through the searching process the skills needed for meaningful dialogue with the engineer.

Finally, the dyeing company turns to db-select for information on public funding to finance the investment in waste water treatment technology.

15

Risk management and environmental liability

◆

Business is important, mankind and nature are more important. (Altner)

◆   ◆   ◆

National and European regulations

Many western industrial states are now striving to halt the destruction of nature by means of an ever more complex network of legislation. That is not to say, however, that environmental protection laws are a new idea, for they have existed since the Middle Ages and have accompanied the whole process of industrialization.

Industrial states have applied various legal instruments in an attempt to minimize the damage at source. They include regulations on production processes, pollution regulations, restrictions and licences. In spite of the flood of environmental regulations, however, some of which have been partially successful, the overall effect is still negative. Destruction is still a threat which cannot be assuaged. Although the problems themselves are only too familiar, scientists and politicians are still faced with the question of why the laws fail to work.

A brief look at the structure of environmental laws will shed some light on the current problems. In the eyes of the law, protection is always confined to one medium such as air or water. This has led to fragmentary, unconnected laws. Although environmental protection so obviously cuts across many different areas there is no unified set of laws. Early attempts at inter-medium legislation such as the European Environmental Impact Assessment have been watered down, and problems are generally merely shunted from one medium to another. For example, hardly any atmospheric pollution now escapes from our power stations; instead, the legally imposed desulphuration filter just finishes up as special waste on the dump. The same applies to the sludge from purification plants and so on. At best, technical measures transfer the problem, concentrate it or dilute it; holes are plugged, time is gained, but satisfactory long-term solutions are simply not forthcoming.

A second feature is the actual administration of environmental stipulations, which no doubt accounts for the enormous difficulties encountered by the legal authorities. The need for continual expansion and intensification of laws reveals the limitations of supervision only too clearly.

> Technology is not the solution to our environmental problems. It is tempting to place our hope in these measures, but we should not be blinded by hope. Technology can concentrate or dilute problems locally or regionally, but it cannot provide real, lasting solutions to the basic problems.
>
> Perhaps this insight also explains why so little progress has been made in changing the medium-specific protection laws in most industrial countries into a coherent legal framework. The water technologist still has his sludge to pass on to the incineration technologist. The atmospheric pollution expert has his powders, plasters and slags to dispose of. The ground protection officer tries to ward off excessive dumping and is sometimes even assisted by the water technologist in his fear of toxins trickling into the ground-water. The hot potato is passed on as quickly as possible. If you are playing it by the book you can have a clear conscience at having lived by the law, but if you look honestly at Nature as a whole you cannot help being aware of the absolute folly of these measures. (Bieber)

Numerous environmental protection laws of varying intensity have been passed in all western industrial countries over the last two decades. However, in Europe limitations imposed on industry by national legislation are increasingly being overlaid by European Community laws. Since pollution does not recognize national frontiers it is becoming evident to everyone that we live in a global risk community.

The European Commission, with the introduction of the Single Europe Act in 1988, has defined some basic environmental principles, such as the following:

● Prevention, as the best solution, has highest priority.

● The 'polluter pays' principle.

● Problems should be corrected at their source.

The 'polluter pays' principle is similar to the notion of hazard liability in the new environmental liability law which came into force in Germany on 1 January 1991.

BRITISH GAS GETS THE GREEN LIGHT TO FUEL ELECTRICITY FOR THE FUTURE.

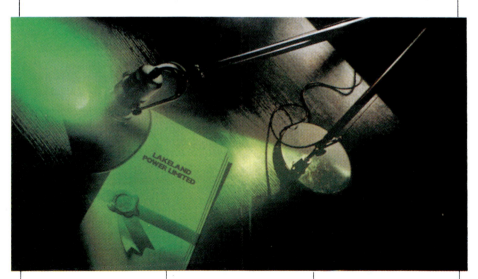

It will come as no surprise that British Gas has been chosen to supply the fuel for Lakeland Power Ltd's combined cycle power generation station in Cumbria, producing electricity for Norweb. It is our first contract of this type to provide natural gas to an independent power generation company.

British Gas, of course, can be counted on to ensure reliable and long-term supplies.

The new combined cycle generating system will produce electricity with remarkable efficiency.

This high efficiency, together with the lower carbon content of natural gas, means that considerably less carbon dioxide is emitted than by a conventional power station. Taking into account the low levels of sulphur and other pollutants, natural gas stands out as a fuel most friendly to the environment.

British Gas continues to make a substantial contribution towards achieving an even more efficient and profitable future for Britain's Industry and Commerce.

After all, energy is our business.

British Gas
ENERGY IS OUR BUSINESS

A
Washing
For Clea

People don't buy AEG just to care for their clothes.

Our Lavamat automatic washing machines are also designed to look after something far more delicate. The environment.

By fitting a unique valve called an ECO Lock into the sump, we can prevent undissolved detergent being pumped out of the wastepipe.

Which means nothin nasty gets flushed into ou ponds, rivers and streams.

These natural habitats a

G
Machines
er Fish.

You probably buy Procter & Gamble products because they deliver the high standards of cleanliness and hygiene you want. You probably don't regard them as particularly "green".

Where we stand

Our policy is to ensure that our products and all our business activities meet the highest standards of safety to people and the environment. We will continually pursue changes which will bring <u>real</u> environmental advantages.

◀ Energy Saving

We have introduced products which perform well at low temperatures, saving in the heating of the wash water. Boiling used to be the necessary norm. Now only 5% of wash loads are boiled and 75% are done at 50 degrees centigrade or below.

Biodegradability

To safeguard the environment, since 1963 we have used only biodegradable surface active agents in all our products. These are broken down into harmless materials by sewage treatment and natural processes.

Made with care for the ▶ environment

We switched to a new kind of pulp for Pampers, made by a process which generates less waste, recycles process chemicals and is self-sufficient in energy. Pampers packaging incorporates recycled plastic. We are now working on projects to compost and recycle disposable nappies.

◀ Doing more with less

We have developed more effective formulations which give better or equal results with less use of resources, saving materials, packaging and energy. One example is Ariel Ultra which uses 30% less materials and packaging per wash than conventional powders. Other examples are Fairy Liquid and Lenor Concentrate which last much longer than normal formulations, saving packaging materials.

PROCTER & GAMBLE LIMITED BRAND RANGES INCLUDE: ARIEL · BOLD · BOUNCE

REVOLUTION

We don't market them on that basis. But we have been steadily improving the environmental friendliness of our products for over 25 years now. Here are some examples.

◀ Right to the heart of the wash

We introduced the 'dosing ball' concept which avoids waste by ensuring that all the detergent gets to work on the wash and saves energy by eliminating the pre-wash step. (The dosing balls are re-usable and are available in 'starter' packs.)

◀ Specialised products

Washing powders used to be the work-horses, used for all kinds of cleaning – with consequent waste of ingredients needed for clothes-washing but not for, say, washing up. Specialist products, tailored for particular jobs, help avoid this.

Saving on packaging ▶

Our usage of packaging materials is being steadily reduced and we are actively seeking to increase use of recycled materials. Our cartons are already made of over 80% recycled paper. We are starting to use recycled plastic in Lenor bottles and Pampers packaging. We are actively encouraging recycling collection schemes. Until such schemes are commonplace we are at least ensuring that the types of plastic we use can be disposed of safely in waste treatment.

◀ Responsibility begins at home

We operate stringent environmental control procedures at our plants and have programmes to conserve resources. For example, over the last ten years we have reduced our energy usage per unit of output by 38%.

Continued improvement ▶

We are continuing to use the best available knowledge and technology to create changes which will represent real environmental improvements. Some will come along soon, others will take a little longer. But they will keep coming.

WATCH
THIS SPACE

CAMAY · DAZ · DREFT · FAIRY · FLASH · LENOR · PAMPERS · TIDE · VORTEX · ZEST

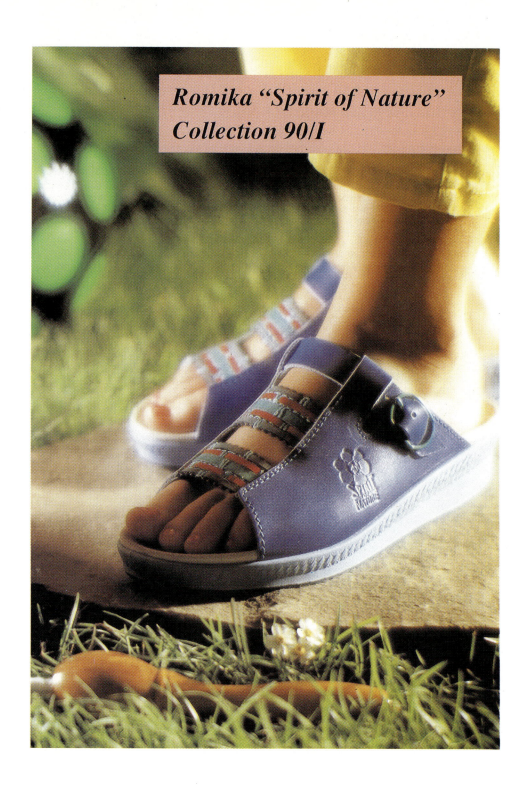

Romika "Spirit of Nature"
Collection 90/I

The operator of plant takes responsibility for any damage caused by that plant regardless of intent; liability applies not only to the effects of accidents but also to damage caused by normal operation of the plant. Cause of damage is presumed when the plant in question is capable of causing the damage; the operator has to prove his innocence. In future, companies will have to produce flawless evidence of their compliance with legal restrictions, in the form of documentation on processes, materials and so on. Comprehensive risk management must ensure observance of all emission thresholds and internal control regulations.

Similar legal principles are in force in Japan too, such as the use of statistical evidence of cause, the disregard of intentional or negligent damage, recognition of the role of all polluters in cases of compound cause and the transfer of the burden of proof away from the victim.

The EC, which has been planning an environmental agency for years, but has been unable to agree on where to locate its headquarters, has produced more than 200 directives and regulations on the environment. These directives apply to areas such as drinking water standards, beaches and sewage pollution, waste disposal (strict civil liability for damage from waste disposal), vehicle emissions, industrial air pollution, environmental impact assessments (EIAs) and freedom of access to environmental information. One of the main problems is that the regulations, which already incorporate the inevitable political compromises and dilutions, are taken up as national laws only after considerable delays. (The laws usually come into force after two years.) Even Germany has procrastinated over a total of 24 regulations.

The EC authorities in Brussels are working on directives to control the free movement of waste across frontiers – so-called 'waste tourism' – and to remove any excess packaging. The directives cover plastic waste, heavy vehicle emissions, ozone-depleting substances, landfill waste and environmental audits. In addition, a unified eco-labelling system is being worked out, based on the successful Blue Angel introduced in Germany many years ago.

Global agreements and international councils exist under the auspices of organizations such as the United Nations Environment Programme (UNEP), the Inter-Governmental Panel on Climate Change (IPCC), the United Nations Economic Commission for Europe (UNECE) and the North Sea Conferences. The International Chamber of Commerce (ICC) also has a significant impact. (See also Chapter 7.)

At a national level, laws of differing intensity have been passed. Over 250 environmental laws and regulations have been instigated in Germany between the early 1970s and the present day. They form an impenetrable thicket which, in spite of computer databanks, still allows an inescapable degree of non-compliance.

Although Germany and Japan have introduced some of the world's toughest environmental regulations, many of their companies have subsumed these legal restrictions under the aegis of their corporate policy structures. Environmental protection is seen as a key factor in business success for the

1990s, not merely as an expense to be met. If green awareness among consumers in other countries develops more quickly than in their industries, this will be a great opportunity for German companies to export. Exports in the German environmental technology industry are already as high as 17 per cent. The strong eco-friendly reputation of German cars and refrigerators in the UK is clear proof of this potential.

In Britain the Environmental Protection Bill (1990) has brought about important changes, and in September 1990 a Government White Paper on the environment was published. On 16 March 1990 the *Financial Times* noted an awareness of change: 'Until recently, environmental law was largely an academic subject considered to have little impact in the commercial world.' The situation has changed not just because of new public awareness of green issues, but because of a massive increase in regulations both in the UK and in the European Community. The new Environmental Protection Bill, which is concerned with all industrial emissions and effluents (including waste) envisages far-reaching changes in the area of responsibility for disposal.

In contrast to Germany where the traditional single-medium approach is still largely predominant, integrated pollution control (IPC) measures regard the environment as a whole. Responsibility extends along the whole disposal chain: from the first producer to the final disposer. Private disposal companies are now beginning to supplement and even replace local council provision.

The Bush administration in the USA was more aware of the environment than was the Reagan government, even though several recent legal initiatives in various states have been postponed because of more topical concerns.

In general, then, 'Cleaning up waste is seen as an increasingly important business issue. The environment was ranked as the biggest challenge facing business at this year's World Economics Forum. It is estimated that the cost of cleaning up past pollution is £150 billion' (*Financial Times*, 26.9.90). Moreover, since legislative regulations cannot seriously be considered as the harbingers of true environmental change, solutions must be sought in preventive technology:

> It is always the same when the penal structure is modernized. No evil is undone by retrospective punishment. The environment and our collective need to maintain it, in all its diversity, demands, however, that future harmful effects are kept to an absolute minimum. Therefore we should not waste too much time on the inevitably vain search for the culprits of past crimes. We would be wiser to direct government energies into the prevention of further evil. At least then, we would be able to do without criminalization and personal recriminations. (Bieber, 1989)

From anthropocentric to ecocentric law

The concept of protecting private property falls short of the demands made by environmental protection. It is a question not of individual rights, but of universal rights, the rights of nature. Rivers, forests or, to take a simple example, seals cannot complain, because they have no inalienable rights.

Nature, the home of mankind, 'has no value in itself, but only as a supplier of raw materials, as a field of action for our freedom and an object for our spiritual edification. That is how it works in practice, and legal and political thought corresponds to this view' (Bosselmann, 1987). He continues elsewhere that, for reasons of ethical survival, a new relationship between mankind and nature must be defined. A move is needed away from a purely anthropocentric image of the world, towards a holistic, ecological view.

Under present circumstances, environmental protection safeguards nature only inasmuch as it serves as the basis for mankind's existence, not for its own sake. Human needs also determine the degree of interference with nature which is acceptable.

> Legal restrictions on noise, unbearable smells or dangerous waste have done some good for nature, but they were instigated for the protection of mankind or human possessions. This anthropocentric conception of protective legislation has persisted until the present. Even the word 'environment' betrays this fact. It implies the world around man, not the totality of nature. (Bieber, 1989)

The 'degree of interference', in terms of an explicitly formulated emission value, is laid down by law. The exact content is controlled by experts using the highest technology available. In all the most sensitive areas of legislative environmental protection, it is technology which prescribes the limits which the law may place on technology. The law, then, is subordinate to the object of its control.

> And here, at the level of establishing and limiting legislative environmental protection on the basis of extra-legal evaluations, is the cause of its downfall. One does not need to be an expert to recognize the alarming arbitrariness with which 'scientifically acceptable risks' are stated, revoked and then restated. Scientific knowledge oscillates on which toxins are tolerable, not just from time to time, but from country to country; in the case of sulphur dioxide by about 300%. In the literature a very pertinent question is raised as to whether there are, in fact, relatively pollution-resistant countries. The litanies of fiction, presumption and absurdity which could be appended to this are endless. One thing is clear though. The undefined legal 'limits', 'risks', 'current state of technology' or 'evaluation of interests' are based not on objective scientific knowledge, but rather on the legally sanctioned decisions of a technocratic élite. *Environment Expert, 1987* makes the sanguine claim that 'the present pollution limits reflect the seriousness with which society pursues the goals of hazard prevention and the reduction of risks'. Very true. 600,000 cubic metres of waste water, to take one minuscule example, flow legally each hour into the Rhine, purified by nothing more

than a few conceptual filters and empty formulas; sixteen million tonnes of chemicals per year. In the name of technology the experts legislate that this is adequate protection for the environment. If anything goes wrong, they will be responsible, but at least they will have had the law on their side.

This should not be misunderstood as a reproach against the legislature, against jurisprudence or against science. Effective, legal alternatives are just not discernible within the horizon of our urbane and technified rapaciousness. The answer to the question, Who, other than technology, could take the blame for the consequences of technology? is: Nobody. However, the naïve, legalistic optimism which permeates society right through to the Greens ought gradually to be seen as the honourable, but antiquated illusion that it is. (Merkel, 1989)

Current discussion on whether or not nature should be granted rights reaches back to Stone in the USA in the 1970s. The structural flaw of equating environmental rights with administrative rights could be removed by introducing a basic right of natural protection, rather like freedom from bodily harm. In Germany various suggestions have been worked out by the political parties. The original ideas within the framework of Article 20 of the German Basic Law have been replaced by the intention of creating a 'state aim' worded roughly as follows: 'The natural basis of human life stands under the protection of the state.'

This has already taken place within some of the state constitutions of the Federal Republic, notably in Baden Württemberg in 1976. By comparison with a basic right a state aim would be less legally binding:

This kind of 'state aim' has less normative force, which implies that it is less legally binding. To put it bluntly, it is not binding at all. The structural error inherent in legislative environmental protection is not removed in any sense. It is just a diversionary tactic, with the advantage that people can now say they are behaving within the law. Maybe environmentalists could win a few cases on the strength of it, for a state aim cannot be entirely without meaning before the courts. Deep down, though, it is eyewash. (Wesel, 1988)

Another possible way of removing the structural error of environmental protection is the type of organization claim for damages which has been practised for many years in the USA by environmental organizations. This has been attempted in Germany not at a general level, but in connection with specific nature reserves. Even the proponents of this instrument are aware that a general lawsuit of this size would bring about the collapse of administrative law.

Market economic means are another form of extra-legal solution based on the introduction of eco-taxes. There is an urgent need for action in the fields of fossil fuel consumption and waste disposal, and obligatory environmental liability insurance has also been mooted.

There are obvious limitations to the present forms of legal thought and the strategic instruments developed around them. According to Bosselmann (1987) environmental law has completely ignored the conflict between economy and ecology, opting pragmatically in favour of the economy. Stock (1990) levels a similar criticism against the outcome of the North Sea Conferences: 'Nothing has changed, because now, as before, environment protection is a function of industrial needs not of the tolerance limits of nature.'

> The attempt to force ecological forms on to our anthropocentric legality by means of 'inalienable rights' for nature is founded on an illusion. There should be no suspicion of a sentimental, harmonious nature. This idea was laconically dismissed long ago by Spinoza when he remarked that it is the 'inalienable right' of small fish to swim, and the 'inalienable right' of large fish to eat them. It is logically inescapable that human beings are going to decide what the rights of nature are to be, and how to act when these rights come into conflict with human rights; how to apportion rights to the seal or the AIDS virus. The rights of the victims of environmental destruction would always be falsified by the perpetrators. The philosopher Kant realized that responsibility towards nature is human responsibility with respect to nature, and therefore ultimately with regard to ourselves ... A society which complains about the destruction of the environment and yet rewards its very causes, human greed and obsession with progress, is bound to come up against the brick wall of its own values: the technocratic laws of an essentially lazy compromise.
>
> Who can change the rules? The law will not do it. Different laws made by different life-forms would be required. Our legal principle of ascribing causality and guilt only to individuals becomes useless in the face of the multifarious, anonymous mass participation of us all. Classical legal analysis, we are reminded by Niklas Luhmann, 'will only lead to the inference that society itself is to blame, and we know that already'. (Merkel, 1989)

Environmental risk management

The role of the law in environmental protection has obvious limitations. Environmental penalties, for example, come into effect only after the damage has been done. Since currently available legal structures do not offer solutions which will be useful in the future, new answers to old questions will have to be found.

The hazard liability law, which was introduced in Germany on 1 January 1991, is independent of intention or neglect. This has important consequences. A more integrated conception of environmental protection can be expected, as well as the avoidance of compensation demands by establishing clean technologies. A situation should be created where the avoidance of dangers or waste is cheaper than any retrospective charges or impositions. The goal of risk reduction gains a new qualitative meaning.

Gasser (1989) maintains that it is impossible to conceive of an industry which is free from risks for the following reasons:

- There is always the possibility of technical failure of certain installations.
- It is impossible to predict the toxicity of certain substances.
- Human error is always possible.

To analyze the total likelihood of risk in a business, collaboration between a wide range of experts is needed, including technologists, economists, insurance experts, lawyers, chemists and geologists. Comprehensive risk management embraces:

- The recognition of all potential risks in processes, products and disposal, in the framework of risk analysis or analysis of weaknesses.
- The integration of effective risk prevention across all functions and as an integrated component of company policy.

To control all the possible dangers resulting from complex technology, risk potential ought to be seen in terms of the relationship between man, machine and environment. Early recognition of dangers should be sought using error analysis, flow charts and hazard and operability studies. In the process of this systematic investigation the effects of breakdown of structural components, regulating mechanisms, power cuts, human error or any combination of these can be assessed (Kuhlmann, 1990). In this way, the optimum operating conditions for industrial plant can be determined, taking into account as much of the unexpected as possible. The results should be extended to an analysis of safety which includes the human factor in terms of behaviour and training.

Various checklists are available for identifying hidden environmental dangers. The initial stage is a type of stocktaking of the current situation. Gasser (1989) suggests the following points:

- Factors specific to site, e.g. surroundings, neighbourhood, geology.
- Industrial buildings, e.g. fire prevention measures, relevant history of the use of the site.
- Products and production processes, e.g. emissions from normal running and in emergencies, relevant safety measures.
- Storage and internal transport of hazardous substances, e.g. warehouse stock checks, supply and maintenance of machines and vehicles.
- Disposal of old lubricants and other waste, e.g. waste water systems.
- Transport of hazardous substances, e.g. stability of packaging, labelling, control of loading.

- Organization and staff, e.g. availability of an environmental officer.
- Induction and in-service training, up-to-date literature and information on risks.
- Legal consequences, especially civil and penal questions.

The knowledge gained from this process leads to an evaluation of the factory based on the following criteria:

- Investigation of the degree of danger from relevant risks in the factory. Supposedly insignificant risks should be checked here.
- Appraisal of already existing preventive measures in the form of a diagram.
- Based on the two preceding results, investigation of the need for further action.

It could be argued that risk prevention measures should consist of several complex components:

- Industrial: appointment of an environment officer, establishment of responsibilities, catalogue of measures, plans for supervision, internal regulations, environmental audits.
- Personnel: continual instruction to refresh awareness of safety.
- Insurance: covering the risks.

The company's most important organizational responsibilities are to limit the occurrence of pollution as much as possible and to ensure safe disposal, for in no sense can liability insurance replace environmental protection.

Reform of environmental cover is, however, associated with the recent introduction of risk liability legislation in Germany. Insurance companies see the danger of risks which even in normal industrial operation appear to be no longer insurable. For companies affected in this way there would be an undesirable rift between liability and insurance cover. This might place insurance companies in the unfortunate position of having to decide on safety and emission standards.

The intention of the new law is to induce businesses to adopt preventive measures out of economic self-interest. It provides new motivation to seek optimum damage prevention. The risk of legal repercussions compels individual managers to serve this purpose out of personal responsibility by initiating planning, control and organizational measures. Merkisch (1990) sees a danger in setting normal running and breakdowns on the same footing because companies may hold back from installing environment-friendly technology, using the money to build up liability reserves.

A company can only govern risks arising from product and environment responsibility through damage prevention. Such measures are not confined to technical environmental protection but imply preventive adaptation of all working processes, production methods and product design. Comprehensive hazard prevention management is also implied by the new product liability law which will compel management to adopt systematic, holistic company policies.

For both laws the solution must be to build up testable 'Total Quality Control' systems.

The future preparation of liability insurance will depend on:

● Efficient risk management by the company itself.

● New forms of collaboration with insurance companies.

In this context, the insurance companies will have to undertake more detailed investigations of risk in order to identify the essential sources of danger. This wider risk analysis might involve the use of detailed questionnaires, works inspections, information on available risk management (registers, environment officers, etc.), insight into notices of approval, or the appointment of experts.

◇ **Colonia**

Colonia Insurance offers a new kind of consultancy and insurance policy on liability risks to the environment. Environmental problems raise completely new legal, technical, scientific and economic questions which necessitate new forms of collaboration between businesses and their insurers.

A number of initial measures have to be tested to ensure that environmental risks are minimized:

■ Organizational processes in the factory.

■ Renovation of outdated plant.

■ Installation of the latest technology.

■ Regular internal assessments and audits.

In the framework of industrial liability insurance there is provision for cover against environmental damage, but only when this can be traced back to breakdowns or accidents.

The new environmental liability law necessitates considerably more open communication. Insurers will have to carry out much more detailed investigations in order to acquire all the information they need. The intention is to recognize and analyze the problems, and to present the customer with feasible solutions.

Colonia environmental consultancy offers much more than just an insurance policy. The team consists of geologists, engineers, chemists and lawyers. The free consultancy assesses:

■ How hazardous substances can be controlled to prevent damage.

■ Which building measures are needed to improve safety.

■ How technical safety can be optimized.

■ How working procedures and production processes can be structured to create a safer working environment.

The paramount goal is damage prevention. The reduction of environmental risks requires a company philosophy based on the following principles:

- Better oversight of risks through central purchasing of substances used.

- Systematic control of all hazardous substances through the use of safety data sheets.

- Reduction of liability risks in cases of damage through careful documentation of all relevant production procedures.

- Creation of optimum safety conditions through, for example, collection tanking or automatic warning devices.

- Central storage of production materials, residue, waste and empty containers.

- Minimization of risks in internal transport through standardized safety procedures.

- Reduction or substitution of extremely dangerous substances.

Since industry and trades will be increasingly confronted with liability claims, Colonia sees the need for close partnership. Only in this way can rationally calculated insurance cover be provided. Preventive measures must be worked out by means of collaborative consultancy.

◇ The Gerling World Institute for Risk Consultancy and Safety Management

This subsidiary company of the Gerling concern, sometimes known as 'Grips', has been offering a comprehensive environmental risk analysis since 1988. On the basis of company documentation and factory inspections, a register of sources of danger is made available to firms which lack the necessary expertise. A certificate is then issued with suggested measures to be undertaken in order of priority. Since Grips is attempting to provide holistic consultancy, an entire concept for environmental safety can be derived from the certificate.

16

The retailer as gatekeeper: pusher or blocker?

Eco goes mainstream. (Grefe/Sontheimer)

Environmental strategies in the retail trade

For a long time now, the importance of the retail trade in environmental protection has been underestimated. However, thanks to the activities of firms like Migros, Tengelmann, Otto Versand, Sainsbury, Tesco and the Co-op, the role of large trading companies as ecological 'gatekeepers' is becoming more evident.

The gatekeeper concept goes back to Lewin, and serves to explain the selectional function of the retail trade between products and the consumer. Retailing can keep market channels for products and information 'open' or 'closed' by means of its own decision criteria. In this sense, it determines the extent to which ecological ideas are disseminated. This mediating role can be seen clearly in an extract from the environmental principles published by Otto Versand.

◇ **Otto Versand**

'We play a significant mediating role between production and consumer, and it is our intention to use this function in the service of environmental protection.

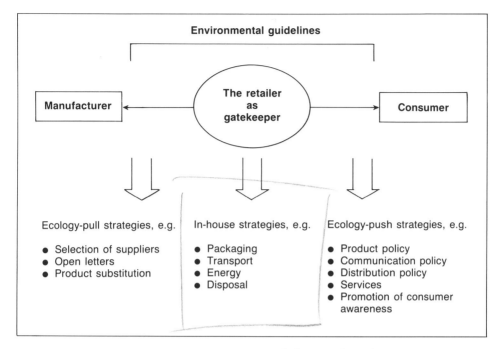

Figure 39 Eco-strategies of the retail trade

'Eco-friendliness is an important criterion in purchasing the products we offer. Our customers are reminded of this in the catalogue, because we feel that only when demand for eco-friendly products rises will manufacturers be able to respond effectively. Environmental protection should not be seen as an added extra. It is a basic purchasing principle.

'It is our goal to bring about changes in manufacturers' behaviour, but also in that of our many millions of customers. Nobody can achieve this alone. Competence and authority are called for, but above all credibility.'

In many countries, powerful effects from trading companies are making themselves felt:

- Green products are offered as part of the range by Migros in Switzerland, almost all the larger firms in Germany, ICA in Sweden and many other companies abroad.

- Green own-brand products are brought in as an addition by, for example, Loblaws in Canada and Sainsbury in Britain.

- Enormous pressure is placed on suppliers to use eco-packaging methods. In the USA, the trading giant Metro International threatened its suppliers that it would strike from the purchasing list products which were not packed in recyclable materials.

In the case studies which follow, companies with an extraordinarily large market and clientele have been selected, because of the efficiency with which they disseminate environmental ideas. They are all firms which have documented environmental protection as an explicit corporate goal. One can generally distinguish between ecology-push and ecology-pull strategies. In ecology-pull strategies the retailer influences ecological demands on the manufacturer. The retailer represents a purchase agent for consumers, and, as a result, gains acquisition potential within certain target groups. Acquisition policy consists in:

- Consciously selecting suppliers on ecological criteria.
- Directly influencing product design, through the use of materials lists, component specifications, etc.

◇ Tengelmann

In 1989 Tengelmann wrote to all its suppliers with an urgent request to 'Abolish the use of chlorine in all products' because chlorine bleaches are particularly detrimental to the waterways. Since, from the manufacturer's point of view, this cannot be achieved overnight, transitional solutions are still acceptable.

The success of this strategy is largely dependent on the compliance of manufacturers and on the market power of the retailer. In the case of detergents and sprays, the reaction from industry was initially very reluctant. Tengelmann has already resorted several times to publishing 'open letters' in the printed media directed at suppliers.

Every day we receive letters from our customers congratulating us on our environmental activities.

Unfortunately we also receive criticism, for example, about the flood of packaging which issues from our 3,5000 branches, and which is causing serious concern.

Good packaging is obviously indispensable for the transport and preservation of products, but it has become traditional to over-indulge in packing materials, causing a waste of resources and using up large volumes of disposal space.

Out of responsibility to the environment I appeal to you to apply all your energies to solving these problems by

– using packing materials only where absolutely necessary for the protection of goods;
– replacing ecologically dubious materials, especially with recyclable materials;
– encouraging the development of collection systems and re-exploitation systems.

Tengelmann offers you support in this vital task, for love of the environment …

■ In 1984 Tengelmann put detergent manufacturers under pressure to produce phosphate-free products. Because at that time there was still great uncertainty about the ecological effects of phosphates, Tengelmann sent questionnaires to the manufacturers. When this failed to produce enlightenment, an open letter addressing all manufacturers of detergents was published in the press.

■ In 1989/90 an appeal was made to all partners in industry, asking for their assistance in stemming the flood of packaging materials. Eco-purchasing policies could lead to mutually beneficial purchasing contracts with suppliers, if they are initiated by large retailers.

In ecology-push strategy retailers can:

● Structure their range in an eco-friendly way, e.g. consciously promoting eco-products and suppressing unfriendly products.

● Provide customers with relevant information.

● Incorporate environment friendliness into the company image, through communication policy.

● Set up recycling points and redistribution channels.

In all the following examples the most powerful influence is the conscious modification of product range. It can consist in taking up and labelling eco-friendly products and in eliminating less desirable products.

◇ Loblaws

Loblaws, one of Canada's biggest retailers, launched its own-label green brand in June 1989 with about 100 different items (President's Choice,Green Products). Since a growth potential of 25 per cent is foreseen for green products, the company intends to increase the proportion of these items. Previously, green-line products constituted only about 0.5 per cent of the total 20,000 articles normally on sale through Loblaws supermarkets. The introduction of the range was supported by environmental groups such as Friends of the Earth and Pollution Probe, but the environmentalists have subsequently adopted a cooler stance.

◇ Wal-Mart

Wal-Mart, number three retailer in the United States, has demonstrated great environmental commitment over recent years:

■ The vice-president has recommended sales outlets to 'look for ways to improve products and packaging so that they are better for the environment'.

- The company is setting up recycling centres in the parking lots of its 1,511 stores, and by 1992 it will print all advertisements, free-standing inserts and circulars on recycled paper.

- A new system of 'green tags' for special products has been awarded to over 300 products so far.

In the Gallup survey of 1,514 consumers, conducted in December 1990, Wal-Mart was the clear winner in its class. Nineteen per cent of respondents ranked the retail chain as 'very concerned' about the environment, far ahead of second place K-Mart Corporation and Sears, Roebuck and Co. (*Advertising Age,* 29.1.91).

◇ Hertie

In 1989 alone, Hertie withdrew, introduced or exchanged 2,000 items on environmental grounds. Early in 1989 an internal working party on purchasing was set up and a purchasing director was nominated 'environment officer'. The members of the purchasing department were instructed, and green views were taken up in all negotiations with suppliers. The primary target was a reduction of 'over-packaging'. Abandoning individual plastic bags for T-shirts brought about a saving of 2.7 million plastic bags.

Limitations to this policy can be found at many levels:

- To what extent is it still possible to avoid eco-damaging products? Is there a strong brand preference in some cases?

- For many products, immediate substitution is not possible. For example, transferring to organic produce might take years.

- Measures can only be taken up selectively because of the size of the range. For example, Otto Versand, the mail-order company, sells over 100,000 items.

- The complexity of evaluation often leads to contrary results, even in science.

- Evaluation of individual components in the whole ecological product life-cycle is partly subjective.

- Difficulties can be experienced in acquiring information from manufacturers.

- Possible negative effects can be felt because of a green image.

◇ Migros

The Migros Co-operative Society takes its obligation to provide ecological information and advice very seriously. A 'green hot-line' telephone number is printed on all Mifa products, enabling customers to contact the advisory service from anywhere in Switzerland at local rates. In 1988 around 1,500 calls were received.

Migros has its own customer enquiry service, which receives, according to the 1988 company report, fewer and fewer actual complaints about products. Customers tend to express their worries about holistic problems such as environmental protection (recycling and packing), product-range policies (ethics and function) and healthy eating (additives and long-term effects). Frequently, appeals are made to Migros to take up modern business approaches. These customer expectations have evoked a new sense of responsibility which is expressed through the company's marketing interest in consumer friendliness and a concern for environmental protection. The customer enquiry desk is gradually acquiring a superordinate role as an outlet for the company's consumer and business policies. 'Customer services can no longer be separated from caring for the environment.'

Migros has a free hand in introducing environmental concepts into its own brands, for the Migros Society has its own associated production works: for example, the Mibelle Company, which contributed to Migros' pioneering success with material savings in toothpaste (tubes without cartons); or, the Mifa Company, which launched propellant-free sprays and eco-friendly detergents and cleaning products.

examples of how it has worked for other co's

One advantage for large retail stores is that they can build up a company image and company loyalty; in contrast to producers, for instance, who are tied to specific products. The broad range of products offered in stores allows for easy compensatory manoeuvres, a high degree of flexibility and rapid response to changes in consumer requirements.

Individual measures and their presentation through advertising, public relations, product promotions or sponsoring contribute to a 'green' corporate image. The case studies show how a basis for trust can be built up, so that customers can feel, 'I buy from Company X because that way I'm making a personal contribution to environment protection.' The more scandalized customers are about damage to the environment, the more effective corporate competence in green matters will be.

The importance of redistribution systems will be strengthened in the near future by the acutely visible evidence of the refuse crisis. Collection points can be set up in the store itself or in centres shared with neighbouring companies. The parlous state of waste disposal demands new forms of customer service from the retail trade.

The contribution of the retailers is to collect and sort returned packaging, containers and goods, which opens up the following possibilities:

- Reuse, e.g. returnable bottles.
- Recycling, e.g. disposable bottles, cardboard packing.
- Controlled, safe disposal, e.g. batteries, used oil.

The importance of the retail trade, however, extends beyond its role as a mediator. All economic activity causes a burden on natural systems, and retailers ought to be aware of their own potential contribution. In-store measures might include using paper and packaging which can be recycled, using eco-friendly cleaning materials, ensuring safe disposal of waste, introducing eco-friendly office stationery, saving energy (heating and lighting),

getting staff involved - know onelsed

and using the railway for goods transport or catalytic converters in company vehicles.

y do bother have enviro friendly cars?

The pioneers

◇ Migros

The Migros Co-operative Society, the largest Swiss retail chain, is certainly one of the pioneers. In 1990 it was the first foreign company to be granted the German Retail Trade Environment Award. The grocery shop, founded in 1925 by Gottlieb Duttweiler, has mushroomed into a huge combine employing 64,000 staff, with a turnover of 12 billion Swiss francs in 1988. The Migros Society consists of 527 traditional retail stores, but also includes its own production works, service branches and charitable foundations. The preservation of the environment is one of the major corporate principles. Migros aims to set an example for the promotion of public health, and so no cigarettes or alcohol are sold.

The Migros Guidelines

- We have enshrined environmental protection in our company goals.

- Relevant ecological factors are considered at all decision-making levels. The means necessary to achieve our goals are undertaken on the basis of profitability and competitiveness.

- We support environmental measures which promote general economic development.

- Our training programmes emphasize general and topical environmental themes. We fulfil our obligations to environmental preservation in partnership with the public, science, economics, politics and the consumer. We are striving towards holistic, economically viable solutions.

- We welcome progressive legislation.

- We keep our colleagues and staff, our customers and the public at large up to date on our activities with comprehensive information.

The realization of these ideals is pursued with the assistance of a four-stage model. During the period 1984–7 environmental protection measures from every area of business were systematically evaluated on the basis of ecological theory. Key examples from each of the four phases are given below.

Stage 1
Saving (economical use of resources), and above all the abandonment of packaging:

- By abandoning toothpaste packaging 40 tonnes per year of cardboard were saved.

- Switching to light-weight glass for spice jars enabled a saving of 160 tonnes/year of glass.

- By reducing the thickness of yoghurt container tops by 20 per cent a saving of 33,000 kg of aluminium per year was possible. This corresponds to the power from 1.4 million litres of fuel oil.

- Reducing the weight of yoghurt containers by 10 per cent saved 112 tonnes of polystyrene per year.

- Halving the mercury content of alkaline batteries brought about an annual reduction of 1,000 kg of mercury used.

- 42,000 litres of solvents were saved through the promotion of solvent-free paints and varnishes.

- 1.2 million litres of fuel oil were saved by improved insulation and heat exchange methods in the Optigal poultry houses.

- In the production works absolute energy consumption has slightly increased, but relative energy consumption, calculated per tonne produced in industrial production and per million of turnover in commercial centres, has fallen.

Stage 2
Substitution (introduction of environment-friendly problem solving):

- Reusable plastic containers, instead of cardboard cartons, are used for the transport of goods from manufacturer to branch. The five million containers currently in use replace 60,000 tonnes per year of cardboard packaging.

- The most modern forms of returnable container have been phased in after successful trials in 1989.

- Increasing use of rail transport (e.g. also for freezer transportation using own containers). The proportion of rail haulage in 1986 was 36 per cent.

- Replacement of plastic carrier bags with artistically designed paper carriers.

- Replacement of aluminium tops with polystyrene lids on 500 g yoghurt containers.

- Introduction of chlorine-free plastics or non-plastics instead of PVC. In the new Mibelle plastic shrinkage plant, polypropylene is used for multi-packs, replacing PVC. In 1988 nine different substitution measures were introduced, replacing 196 tonnes of PVC. Conserves Estavayer represents the largest of these with the 0.7-litre polyethylene salad-dressing bottles causing savings of 103 tonnes.

- Replacement of fuels, e.g. using gas or radiated heat instead of heating oil.

- The proportion of turnover taken up by recycled products is increasing steadily. For toilet paper it is 18 per cent, for kitchen rolls, 30 per cent. In stationery, the proportion has remained stagnant since 1987, in spite of new articles such as wrapping paper.

- In 1986 Migros began commissioning Swiss artists to design carrier bags. The cultural aim is to acquaint a wider public with the work of contemporary artists. From a print run of one million bags, 150 are signed by the artists and sold at 100 Swiss francs. The normal bags are sold at 20 Rappen.

The new freezer wagons will encourage greater use of the railways for transport *Photo: Migros*

Stage 3
Reduction of pollution in the form of noise, emissions and waste:

- An exhaust-gas cleaning plant in Migros' own incineration plant in Bern absorbs 5,000 kg of hydrochloric acid vapour and 3.1 tonnes of dust, among other things.

- Smells from the jam and preserves factory are kept to a minimum with the help of thermal after-burning.

- Only 2 per cent of spray-cans contain CFCs. The previous annual consumption of 450 tonnes of CFCs has been completely replaced by Mibelle with propane/butane; in the Migros branches only one type of spray still contains CFCs.

- Only vehicles with catalytic converters are purchased.

Stage 4
Harmless disposal of all non-reusable products:

- Around 320 tonnes of used batteries are returned per year.

- Refuse incineration plant (and exploitation of heat produced).

Replacing plastic carrier bags with paper carrier bags

- Pre-emptive replacement of condensers containing PCB.
- Light bulbs are now treated as special waste.

◇ Tengelmann

Tengelmann provides an excellent example of a successful eco-corporate policy. The highly positive green image this company has built up in Germany is unprecedented. The company is one of the largest department store chains in the country with around DM17 billion (almost £6 billion) annual turnover and in the region of 900 million customers per year. The worldwide turnover is DM42 billion and the firm has almost 5,500 branches. The stores Plus, Kaiser's Drugstore, Grosso and in the USA A & P also belong to the group.

Profitability and ecological aspects are combined in a consistent business approach, with environmental protection taking the highest priority in business decision making. This company philosophy includes the commitment to use natural raw materials and re-exploited materials, to offer environmentally harmless consumer goods and to replace harmful products.

Even before environmental protection had acquired a high media profile, Tengelmann's 3,300 branches (at that time) were already beginning to promote eco-awareness. A chronological table of the various activities, many of which were ahead of their time, gives a good idea of how committed the family behind this business has been over the last two decades.

1968: Karl Schmitz Scholl Fund, for the preservation of the plant and animal kingdoms and the conservation of waterways and air.
1982: Elisabeth Haub Foundation, for the promotion of efficient environmental policies (e.g. sensitive use of resources from the developing countries).
1984: Conversion to lead-free petrol.
1984: Abandonment of turtle produce, in order to counter the annihilation of this species. Large-scale publicity drive with window posters, notices on shelves, handbills and 250,000 colourful car stickers with the slogan, 'I don't buy turtle soup'.
1984: Frog and Turtle combined, as a registered trade mark.
1984: Returnable bottles introduced as alternative packaging for drinks.
1987: Exclusively phosphate-free washing powders sold, to relieve the waterways. First introduction 1984.
1988: Banning of CFCs to protect the ozone layer. Alternatives available since 1984.
1988: Presentation of a new 'low-noise' lorry.
1989: Presentation of 'whispering freezer-van' at the International Motor Show in Frankfurt.
1989: Abandonment of Icelandic fish produce, as a contribution to saving the whales.
1989: Abandonment of all alkali-manganese batteries containing mercury. Installation of collection points for old batteries in all stores.
1989: Exclusive sale of chlorine-free products (with transition periods for manufacturers). Coffee filter papers made by chlorine-free production methods.
1989: Testing of a new lorry, modified for road safety.

'Steel cow' milk dispensing machine, used by customers to fill returnable
glass jars

In 60 stores a 'steel cow' milk-dispensing machine has been set up. The 500-litre self-service system helps reduce packaging waste. Plastic carrier bags in all Tengelmann stores are made of 'eco-friendly' polyethylene and are illustrated with the frog and turtle logo. Under the title 'For the love of nature' detailed information is available to customers on all of these activities. Excellent PR work helps to build up credibility, competence and trust.

For many years now Tengelmann has been seeking a holistic solution to the problem of refuse. Direct return of packing materials to the stores is rejected for economic as well as for hygiene reasons. The company's own packing expert is working in close collaboration with suppliers on possible solutions.

Tengelmann has received numerous awards for its pioneering activities in environmental protection.

◇ Otto

Otto, the largest mail-order company in the world, is strongly committed to active environmental protection. The initial reason for taking up this goal was that every organization has an obligation to do something for the environment. However, the company is well aware that achieving a completely eco-friendly mail-order business is not going to happen overnight.

Otto wishes to do justice to the environment as far as the present state of science and technology will allow. The basic principle is to evaluate the eco-balance between production, consumption and disposal. Every stage of production and material input is checked to see if it is being carried out in the least harmful way.

The company's long tradition of environmental protection can be seen in the design of the administrative buildings constructed in the 1970s. The very latest techniques were used to ensure that, for example, 60 per cent of traditional energy costs could be saved. In 1973 all cardboard packaging was exchanged for recycled materials, using a particularly thin, resource-saving type of card for most purposes.

In the 1980s a qualitative change in the corporate philosophy took place, when the company began to aim for a consistent environmental commitment. Environmental protection was placed alongside customer and staff satisfaction, collaboration with suppliers and global expansion as an explicit corporate goal. All internal procedures were tested for their compatibility with this goal, and the entire range was sorted through and modified accordingly. Staff were infected with a real enthusiasm for environmental and collaborative approaches. The chairman of the board of directors, the son of the founder, has expressly made environmental protection into a personal mission and has asked staff to follow his lead.

Because of the size and decentralized organization of the company there are good reasons for not having a specific environmental department. Hierarchical structures are avoided. However, ecological knowledge is collected and disseminated by an environmental co-ordinator. The strengths and weaknesses of processes and the qualities of products or whole product sectors are checked by the Quality Control Department, and careful supervision is conducted in Textile Purchasing, Catalogue Publishing and Technical Purchasing departments.

The Policy and Communications Department is well suited to co-ordinating environmental protection because the director reports to the chairman of the board and is occupied with communicating company objectives internally and externally. A control function connecting theory and practice also comes under the aegis of this section: the Environmental Discussion Group is an inter-departmental forum which meets at irregular intervals. The directors of all the relevant departments meet here to exchange information and agree on the group's basic environmental policy strategy. The same organizational principles are applied in the Otto Trading Group's international activities. There are plans to introduce working parties in Trois Suisses, and groups are already operating in the American Mail Order Mirror, Inc. An environment 'task force', closely affiliated to the board, regularly deals with environmental problems, while frequent exchanges of information and experience between national branches provide constant stimulation.

The practical implementation of environmental protection at Otto is directed towards the recognition and removal of weaknesses in the range of goods produced and in working procedures.

The production and sale of eco-friendly products is encouraged by exerting influence on customers and suppliers. Harmful paints, articles made from tropical wood and furs from endangered species have been withdrawn from the catalogue or replaced with eco-friendly goods; a collection service is being organized for returned refrigerators and batteries; packaging has been modified as much as possible; all material, machine and energy input processes are carefully investigated.

In spite of extensive in-house knowledge, Otto still seeks contact with academic research institutes and organizations like the Worldwide Fund for Nature (WWF).

Initially, these institutions are approached for information, but contacts have sometimes led to direct changes. For example, advice from the WWF led to an ecological investigation of all furs on sale.

Eco-friendliness is an important purchasing criterion exerting a positive influence on manufacturers. The seriousness of this is underlined in a letter from the chairman to all suppliers stressing the firm's intention to 'respond to every possibility for improving the environmental impact of its products'.

The catalogue itself provides an ideal vehicle for promoting 'green products'. Customers are presented with simple, clear information about the positive environmental properties of each item. Articles of particular note are marked with a green tree symbol, for easy recognition. In this way, Otto uses its considerable influence over product sales by addressing suppliers and customers directly on green issues.

Environmental aims are also served by the company's financial support of publicly recognized projects. For instance, 'Species Watch', an educational project, was undertaken in April 1989 in collaboration with the WWF.

Experience gained by Otto has shown how difficult it is to take account of all relevant ecological factors. Seemingly simple undertakings have presented unexpected complexity which even experts have failed to disentangle. The company's high hopes of solving all environmental problems have unfortunately not been realized. However, although the goodwill and co-operation of staff have been severely tested, their eventual positive response is one of the most pleasing side-effects. Enthusiasm has swept through all levels of the hierarchy and had a lasting effect on the corporate culture.

All of this has, of course, been unfolding against the background of changing public attitudes. In the 1980s the involvement of a retailer in green issues was seen as a voluntary step. Today, it is not only expected; it is demanded. In the view of Otto, environmental commitment will be a decisive yardstick in judging the success of corporate policies in the 1990s.

◇ Sainsbury

Recognition of Sainsbury's 'green' policy and programme has led to the company being presented with six major environmental awards in the past two years. In March 1990 Sainsbury was presented with the Environmental Management Award in the annual Better Environment Awards for Industry.

Sainsbury's 'Penny Back' initiative was launched early in 1991 in Sainsbury stores. The scheme is simple and straightforward but extremely effective: customers will be given a refund of one penny for every shopping or carrier bag brought back for reuse during a Sainsbury's shopping trip. Sainsbury's customers use ten million plastic carrier bags each week. While many of these are already made from recycled plastic, their manufacture and distribution is expensive in terms of energy usage, and when discarded they add to the waste disposal problem. The 'Penny Back' scheme has been trialled in six of Sainsbury's stores in different areas. Results indicate that the use of new bags will be reduced overall by at least 10 per cent. By encouraging its customers to reuse their own carrier bags or shopping bags, the

company expects to reduce the number of new carrier bags issued by at least 50 million a year. This will save some 1,000 tonnes of plastic, and the energy saved in production and distribution costs is the equivalent of over 1 million gallons of oil.

An additional benefit of the 'Penny Back' scheme is that it is expected to raise some £500,000 per year for charity. Customers will have the choice of whether or not they donate their refunded pennies to charity, and each branch will display collection boxes at the exits. Donations will go to a local or national charity which that store and its staff support.

The scheme forms part of Sainsbury's policy to minimize the use of energy and to conserve resources by encouraging customers to bring their own shopping bags or to reuse carrier bags when visiting Sainsbury stores. Other actions in support of this policy include the following:

- Trolley bags and PVC shopping bags are available in all stores.

- Large, extra-strong reusable carrier bags with loop handles are available. All profits from these go the Worldwide Fund for Nature. Sainsbury also offers its own strong carrier bags. These are reusable too.

- For some time there have been notices at checkouts encouraging customers to conserve energy and resources by reusing carrier bags.

- In September 1990 Sainsbury introduced free carry out-bags made with genuinely recycled plastic. Some of this plastic comes from Sainsbury's own waste packaging.

- Sainsbury's staff are encouraged to prevent unnecessary usage of new carrier bags at checkouts.

◇ Tesco

Tesco is one of Europe's largest retailers and the leading superstore operator in the

UK. Tesco was the first retailer to introduce comprehensive labelling to help customers to identify products which are better for the environment. Through the 'Tesco Cares' initiative, the company is playing an active role in a number of key environmental issues and projects.

Tesco has banned the use of CFCs as the propellant from all its own-label aerosols, and sells only branded aerosol products which are also CFC free. An 'ozone-friendly' logo on own products shows that they are CFC free.

Tesco has carried out extensive research into the subject of what to do with materials used by customers. In common with many other organizations, Tesco has concluded that recycling is preferable to leaving materials to biodegrade. 'Biodegrading material causes its own pollution problem, whereas recycling reuses resources rather than destroying them. Recycling is therefore more beneficial to the environment.'

Tesco operates and is introducing many types of recycling, and in recognition of its leading role, the company is the only retailer represented on the Advisory Council of Waste Watch, the UK agency which promotes recycling.

In response to a government-led drive to have 5,000 bottle banks throughout the UK by the end of 1990, Tesco is making special provision for these units at all its superstore developments. Currently 160 out of a potential 170 stores with adequate space have bottle banks. In 1989 Tesco organized the collection of aluminium cans in connection with the Blue Peter Baby Life Appeal. The original scheme raised more than £600,000 to buy life-saving equipment for babies in intensive care from collecting 40 million cans.

Tesco was the first company in the UK to trial a PET (polyethylene teraphthalate) collection scheme, and has introduced mixed plastics collection in Manchester and Leeds. Fifty stores offer a paper bank facility, but the expansion of paper banks has been halted because there is a glut of low-grade paper on the market at present.

In 1985 Tesco became the first major food retailer to introduce a Healthy Eating Programme. The demand for it from customers is shown by the fact that it is worth over £50 million per year in sales. Today all the company's 3,000 own-brand products provide comprehensive labelling about nutrition (including information on the fat, energy, protein, fibre and, where appropriate, vitamin content of the product). There is also a series of free Healthy Eating guides available to customers, which offer practical advice. Over 100 Tesco stores sell organically grown produce.

The environmental initiatives taken by Tesco have led to a variety of awards and commendations.

17

The need for an environmental controlling system

◆

How much does a tree cost?

Recently Frederic Vester tried to quantify the value of a tree. He arrived at the figure of about ninety pence per annum for a 100-year-old beech tree, in terms of current wood prices. However, if the photosynthesis performed by the tree is taken into account the value increases to around £15. The tree fulfils other functions, though, like bionic regeneration, filtering, storing water, protecting the life-systems in the soil by providing organic matter, and symbiosis. The total balance for the tree in isolation comes out at around £540 each year taking these factors into the calculation. If the tree is standing in a forest it provides a whole range of additional functions such as erosion and landslide prevention. The tree now has an economic value of about £1,800 per year or £180,000 for a 100-year-old tree. That is more than two thousand times its value as wood. How should we reckon the felling of a tree? What is its market value?

(Atteslander, 1989)

Environmental management encompasses planning and control of all operational activities, and it is not possible to fulfil this responsibility without the instruments of an Environmental Controlling System (ECS). Information about all relevant procedures in the company is an indispensable prerequisite. The responsibility of management is to design and control external relationships and internal processes to conform with the company objectives. This requires information on past, present and future processes. Companies can acquire this information by means of an institutionalized information system, in the form of a business accounting system and operational indicators. Control of operational processes can be seen mainly in terms of information problems.

Practical Environment Controlling Systems (ECSs) are effectively still in their infancy. Ideally, they will be based around an Environment Information System (see Chapter 4), and the first stage will be the collection of data for operational evaluation of the environment. This task is now particularly significant in the light of the new hazard liability laws because management instruments, such as environment audits, provide information which can act as evidence.

For some time, there has been a theoretical demand on companies to register 'all' the consequences of their activities, but the actual means of effecting this ecological expansion have seldom passed the pilot phase. The establishment of an Environment Controlling System will require further development of 'indicators' and an 'eco-balance statement' before it can progress.

In business economics it is conventional to treat occurrences of ecological damage as negative, external effects; as social costs and not as goods consumption with a calculable cost. Economic accountancy will have to learn to measure success in terms of new indicators, drawing on comprehensive data of the damage done by the company (costs), as well as the company's achievements (gains). Widenmayer (1981) suggests the following categorization of social costs:

1. In nature, i.e. outside company field of operation:

   (a) damage to the landscape, e.g. refuse dumping;
   (b) damage to the ground, e.g. depletion of resources, karstification;
   (c) damage to the atmosphere, e.g. smoke, gas pollution;
   (d) damage to waterways, e.g. pollution, warming.

2. In human terms, i.e. internally:

   (a) psychological stress, e.g. shiftwork, piecework;
   (b) physical stress, e.g. accidents, industrial illnesses.

Public interest in social costs has increased recently because of their obvious connection with 'quality of life'. The historical tendency to dismiss social costs in evaluating a company or an individual has been replaced by a growing demand for social costs and gains to be paid for, especially in the context of environmental protection. Inordinate difficulties are, however, experienced in trying to categorize these costs:

● Problems of time, e.g. long delays between cause and effect.

- Problems of causality, cf. 'polluter pays' principle.
- Problems of measurement, e.g. level and method.
- Problems of evaluation, e.g. achieving parity between different values.

A counterpart to social costs is provided by social gains, in the form of cultural funding, donations and so on, which represent a positive social effect of industrial activity.

First steps have already been made, on micro and macro levels, towards introducing the following terms to supplement the 'money and goods' of traditional economics:

- An eco-GNP.
- A social or environment report.
- An eco-balance statement.

The ecological effects of business activity should be integrated as components of a comprehensive social account. The economic criteria used in decision making, which may, in fact, lead to correct, rational decisions, can no longer be separated from social costs incurred by economic activity.

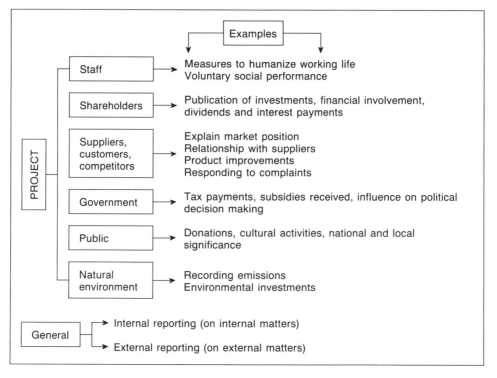

Figure 40 Elements of a social report

The central objective behind this expansion of accountancy is to include social and ecological developments in the structure of operational procedures. This presents practical difficulties because perceptions of social reality are necessarily subjective, and because economic conditions control and determine the field of action.

This new social report should attempt to convey the socio-ecological responsibilities of a company to relevant internal or external bodies, by means of information and documentation. To the outside world, it will serve as a vehicle for stating the company's case and assisting integration. Internally, it will provide management and staff with information and motivation.

Macroeconomic concepts (or, The doubts about GNP)

The development of social accounting should be seen against the background of fundamental changes in individual and public opinion. Changes in values have led to increasing sensitivity among many circles of people towards the negative side-effects of business, particularly in the sense of 'growth at any cost'. Damage to the environment, depletion of resources and job losses can all be seen in this context. These views are no longer confined to 'Greens', 'eco-freaks', ecology groups or consumer organizations.

The key indicator of economic growth is the gross national product, the total value of all final goods and services produced annually by a nation, evaluated in market prices. GNP is also used as an indicator for the standard of living. This has been a cause of growing criticism because an increase in consumption does not automatically mean an increase in welfare, and because many services are either left out of the assessment altogether, such as housework and neighbourly help, or wrongly assessed. The growing financial repercussions from conventional economic activity are breeding grave doubts about the validity of the gross national product as a measure of welfare.

From an ecological point of view this method of evaluation seems particularly inappropriate:

- Damage to health and the environment are ignored because they cannot be given a material value, unless reactive repair measures are actually undertaken.

- If these steps are taken, they do not, as 'repair costs', reduce wealth, but actually increase it in terms of the GNP, when in fact there has been a diminution of capital.

- Rising consumption of energy and raw materials also has the effect of increasing wealth.

Ignoring environmental damage and human encroachment on nature gives false messages to economics and politics, and requires correction. At least 10 per cent of all economic activity can be regarded as a reaction to damage. These costs aimed at preventing a reduction of welfare are interpreted very cautiously.

As was shown in a public hearing in May 1989 in Bonn entitled 'The Development of Ecological and Social Costs in the Federal Republic', there are widespread doubts about the extent of political commitment to these goals, and very few answers to the questions posed. However, suggestions for correcting and completing economic accounts with ecological data have been available for some time. It is assumed that GNP is a good indicator of production, but that it needs to be corrected by the inclusion of certain expenses which raise or lower welfare. All attempts to develop definite categories of damage (to health, capital, production or ecology) have faltered on the common, unsolved problem of evaluation.

The Federal Statistical Office in Germany has announced that it will publish, in an unprecedented move, a corrected version of the GNP. Organizations within the United Nations have also been working on the idea of a modified GNP.

The German research project has come up against enormous difficulties in evaluation. Pollution can be measured only in physical units which it is difficult to convert into financial terms. However, nature can be construed as capital stock whose value is capable of being reduced. It can then be calculated how much money would have to be spent to remove or prevent the relevant damage to the environment.

The first stage, which is currently under way, involves logging annual environmental investments and pollution in a data base. A closely related goal of the Federal Office is to develop 'satellite systems' to supplement GNP. These systems will include information fields on socially important factors which have not yet been expressed in terms of money, but which can be couched in descriptive terms. Klaus and Ebert (1989) give the following examples:

- Aggregation of expenditure on prevention of damage or compensation for damage already done.

- Presentation of environmental burden caused by harmful side-effects of economic activity, including environmental protection measures (register of emissions).

- Description of the qualitative state of the environment and changes to this.

- Evaluation of damage which persists in spite of avoidance and compensatory measures.

In the meantime, however, plans are in motion for combining classical national product statistics in an overall account of environmental economy. These plans will, at least initially, be spread over several years.

As far as technology is concerned, there is a growing demand for qualitative improvements in products and production processes. The ideal form of ecologically orientated economic activity would require as its goal 'qualified growth' or 'sustainable development': that is, growth without adding to the depletion of resources.

Instead of using just one figure, as with GNP, indicator systems are based on several wealth indicators, which will facilitate the inclusion of social factors ignored by traditional economics. Research into social indicators attempts to make relatively vague goals such as job satisfaction and the quality of work and the environment operationally manageable by assigning to them numerical values. Experiments have been conducted by a variety of institutions such as the UN and the EC. The Organization for Economic Co-operation and Development, for example, suggests eight assessment targets, which are subdivided into 24 main indicators. The targets for assessment are as follows:

- Health.
- Personal development and intellectual and cultural growth through learning.
- Work and the quality of working life.
- Time allocation and leisure time.
- Availability of goods and services.
- Physical environment.
- Rights to personal freedom, legal rights.
- Quality of life in the community.

The establishment and selection of indicators can be determined only through soundings of the social consensus. The problems of this type of indicator system are encountered on many levels: for example, unclarified problems of measurement or aggregation, the normative and subjective nature of the system, theoretical difficulties, considerable costs and the lack of criteria for the delimitation of relevant fields.

Microeconomic concepts

At a microeconomic level, internalization of these external effects according to the 'polluter pays' principle is highly differentiated. Possible operational components might be the following:

- Environmental indicators.
- Checklists.
- Product impact matrices.
- Product-line analysis (life-cycle analysis).
- Technology assessments.
- Environmental impact assessments.

- Eco-accounting.
- Eco-balance statements.

The social report

If the social report is to become a feature of modern accounting, some of the less well-defined, qualitative concepts, such as quality of life and welfare, will need to be firmed up. The two main areas are:

- Preservation and improvement of the environment.
- Humanization of work.

Effects in these areas can be measured:

- Either after the fact, as a juxtaposition of a company's social gains and costs.
- Or by means of anticipatory targets, followed by a comparison of the desired and actual outcome after the fact.

The first examples of social accounting were developed in the USA in the 1960s, while the earliest German social balance sheet was published in 1972 by STEAG in Essen. This was followed by companies like Pieroth, Shell (Germany), Rank Xerox, BASF, Rheinbraun, BP (Germany), Wella.

The trade unions gave social accountancy a very cold welcome in the early 1970s, writing it off as a publicity stunt. Towards the end of the decade, however, unions began to develop their own versions, reflecting union requirements for information.

There are no legal regulations governing social reports, and testing or supervision by auditors is not required. One of the chief characteristics of the social report is that it is voluntary. The reports are 'declaratory' in nature. There is a danger that rigid rules in the form of laws or tariff agreements could lead to undesirable control of economic activity. For this reason, the possibility of legal regulations, as for example in France, is neither welcomed in Germany nor to be expected under present political conditions. However, a 17-page suggestion is currently circulating around the EC Commission, in which companies are invited to present detailed plans for environmental protection measures.

The challenge to companies is to optimize economic goals and social responsibility: that is, to integrate economic and social factors in such a way that the needs of as many social groups as possible can be fulfilled with minimum damage to nature. The growth of sensitivity in the business world has been accompanied by the desire for accountability. A business report on profitability alone is no longer adequate, and the demand for a social report has arisen from this shortcoming.

In financial terms the social report is associated with relatively low costs. Problems of measurement and evaluation are not of prime importance because verbal reporting is always possible when difficulties arise. In social reports, company losses and gains are verbalized with the support of indicators and statistics. However, because the scope and content are not prescribed – they are defined at the discretion of the board – the choice of activities included is based on subjective decisions, with the danger that only positive achievements will be reported. For example, the largest manufacturer of CFCs does not mention ozone depletion in its 1988 business report; neither does the electricity company with the highest rate of emissions in Germany give quantitative details of the pollution it causes or the effects of acid rain.

The flourishing of social accountancy in the 1980s has been greeted with contradictory opinions, probably as a result of the wide disparity between the reports. The number of companies in Germany publishing separate social reports varies, depending on the source, between 40 and 200. Dierkes (1984) refers to evidence that 90 per cent of the 500 USA Fortune companies include social achievements in their business reports. Some firms, however, are content to limit their comments to specific activities within the framework of targeted PR campaigns. Unrealistic theoretical complexity has been reproached by business practitioners, who recommend bringing the level of report parameters 'down to earth'. If present achievements are compared with traditional accountancy, it would seem sensible 'not to expect too much, too soon from social reports, but rather to be prepared for steady progress based on practical experiences and continuing theoretical research' (Dierkes, 1984).

The extent to which social reporting may develop into a credible management instrument rather than merely another form of advertising depends ultimately on the conscience of the company and the ability of management to learn.

◇ Migros

The four social reports for 1978, 1980, 1983 and 1986 published by Migros provide excellent examples. The reports cover varying 'burning issues' as well as Migros' activities in relation to customers, staff and the public. Cultural and social obligations are documented, as is environmental protection. Comprehensive guidelines provide an overall framework. Starting from individual concrete objectives, measures adopted to achieve these objectives and the results are described. The extent to which the objectives have been reached is noted, and shortcomings are also included. The report takes the form of text with detailed tables and charts of measures and results in three areas: energy and water consumption; waste and emissions; and product range and packaging. According to Migros the 1986 report was the last; a new social report is not anticipated. Since these reports represent the most extensive examples of their kind, this decision is a serious blow to social reporting.

The environment report

As an analysis by the Berlin Scientific Research Centre of environmental reporting among 20 large businesses shows, the size of eco-reports is growing continually. While most organizations are content to add a few extra pages to their business report, BASF was the first company to publish a separate 35-page environment report. This initiative has subsequently been taken up by other companies.

◇ Norsk Hydro

At Norsk Hydro, Norway's biggest industrial group, management switched, after initially defensive reactions, to a proactive stance. Activists had broken into a chemical factory over a wire fence, and had discovered soil impregnated with mercury. In addition, there were various other environmental problems which caused public criticism. In 1989 Norsk published an environmental investigation of its Norway operations, and in 1990 a UK environmental report. Even if this type of publication makes it easier for outsiders to find points to criticize, such as lack of standardization of information or choice of levels, the report does give details of the first attempts at a rough eco-balance for the company's main products. It also gives data on disposal and recyclability. In the media it was particularly emphasized that Norsk Hydro has both commissioned and published an independent assessment. At the end of the report the results of an investigation of six main factories by Lloyd's Register were given. The comment was made that 'environmental performance is above average'. Five areas were identified in which Norsk failed to fulfil the environmental standards set by Lloyd's Register.

◇ RWE

RWE, the Rhineland-Westfalian Electricity company, which claims to have been the first company to publish an eco-balance statement, wanted to show 'the achievements already made in the field of environmental protection and the tasks still required to make the power stations even more environment friendly'. The 32-page brochure is illustrated with numerous charts and tables of values. The meaning of the term 'balance' is stated as the equilibrium between the goals of safety, profitability and environmental protection.

The idea of social and environmental reporting is generally criticized either on principle or because of features inherent in the reports of specific companies. Critics accuse the reports of 'glossy deception', and see them as nothing more than PR strategies, propaganda brochures and advertising. The concentration on selected pollutants, the lack of comparability and verifiability of data as well as the inadequacy of information all come in for criticism. Research bears out the fact that there is a preponderance of information about annual company investments in environmental protection and company running costs. Timing plans and details on the classic emission, sulphur dioxide, are called for.

Approaches to environmental accountancy

Progress beyond the first stages of eco-controlling systems has not been made yet, although the pioneer work by Müller-Wenk was undertaken almost 20 years ago. Since 1990 efforts have been made to set up new pilot projects in environmental controlling systems. The objective is to keep a running eco-balance statement, in accordance with the standards of financial accounting, with its own binding, procedural forms. The eco-balance statement will be a cornerstone of management information systems.

Knowledge and evaluation of the effects of company activities are a prerequisite for environmental corporate policies. It is important to register relevant information not just quantitatively, in terms of money, but also qualitatively, so that the company is in a position to evaluate its 'ecological relevance'.

The eco-balance statement helps to make environmental criteria of value 'transparent' within the company and publicly. It enables comparison before

Material and energy eco-balance statements	
INPUT	OUTPUT
I. Materials	**I. Products**
1. Raw materials	1. Primary products
2. Subsidiary materials	2. Combined products
3. Fuels	
4. Other materials	**II. Material emissions**
	1. Solid waste
II. Energy	2. Waste water
	3. Atmospheric waste
1. Gaseous	
2. Fluid	**III. Energy emissions**
3. Solid	
	1. Waste heat
	2. Noise

Source: PSI/IÖW

Figure 41 Input–output systems

and after investment; over various intervals; between different companies; and between selected products and production processes.

Environmental accounting encompasses four levels (Pfriem, 1988a,c; future Forum, 1988; future Workshop 1988). Initially, a quantitative register of materials and energy is drawn up on the basis of three types of eco-balance statement. First, the input–output account gives an overview of materials, energy and quantities. Industrial inputs, classified according to material or energy, are entered in the input column, while products and emissions are placed in the output column (see Figure 41). The example in Figure 42 from the pilot project shows the first part of the input entry in the first two stages of filling in the detail.

Input	1986	1987	Input	1986	1987
1.I Materials			**1.I Materials**		
Raw and subsidiary materials:			Raw and subsidiary materials:		
1. Plastic sheeting			1. Plastic sheeting		
2. Synthetic textiles					
3. Paper			Polyethylene sheeting:		
4. Plastic combined with other materials			Polypropylene sheeting:		
5. Ropes			Special sheeting:		
6. Fleeces			• polyethylene sheeting:		
7. Adhesives			PE variants		
8. Solvents			(different thicknesses)		
9. Paints, varnishes			different colourings		
10. Packaging			different additives		
			• polypropylene sheeting:		
Fuels:			• special sheeting		
			variants of Valeron sheeting		
11. Oils			consisting of crosswise overlaid HDPE		
12. Water			(high-density polyethylene) sheeting		
13. Air			partial colouring (pigments)		
			adhesive residues		
Other materials:			various additives		
14. Small items			2. Synthetic textiles:		
Repair materials					
Tools			Polypropylene/polyethylene:		
Replacement parts			Polypropylene:		
			various pigments (dyes)		
			various additives		
1.II Energy			(e.g. brighteners)		
15. Butane					
16. Electricity					
17. Natural gas					

Source: Pfriem (1988).

Figure 42 Levels 1 and 2 of a detailed materials eco-balance statement

Pfriem (1988c) considers this gradual process of completing the details on material and energy consumption as the basis for ecological management:

● Materials can be examined for traces of toxic pollutants and possibly substituted.

● Quantities of water and energy recorded can be used to initiate water and energy management.

Input code	Materials, products, energy, fuels	Quantities	From cost position
In-2	Black plate in slabs	153.5 t	120
	Fine steel in slabs	27.0 t	120
	Hot galvanized plate in slabs	55.5 t	120
	Aluminium plate	6.5 t	120
	Total	242.5 t	
	Copper-plated steel wire for gratings	12.5 t	120
	Welding wire	100 kg	120
In-6	Electromechanical energy	115 MWh	105
	Acetylene 120 Nm	1.7 Gcal	
In-7	Cooling water	150 m^3	105
In-3	Oxygen	14040 Nm^3	120
	Protective gas (argon, nitrogen)	2040 Nm^3	120

Output code	Materials, products, energy, fuels	Quantities	Further to cost position
Out-1	Plate parts	210 t*	141, 146/1
	Gratings	12 t*	146/2
Out-5	Sorted metal waste		
	Black plate and wire	11.5 t	121
	CrNi plate, fine steel plate	7.0 t	
	Copper-plated steel plate	12.0 t	
	Aluminium plate	1.5 t	
Out-6	Metal waste in workshop waste	1.0 t	
Out-7	Cooling water with waste heat, unpolluted	150 m^3	121
	● Material composition:		
	Black plate	142 t	141
	Fine steel plate	20 t	146/1
	Copper plate	43 t	146/1
	Aluminium plate	5 t	146/1

Source: Stahlmann (1988b).

Figure 43 Input–output list from plate processing/wire factory

● The detailed examination of material residues and energies emitted can be regarded as the first stage of systematic emissions management.

Technological input–output analyses of individual production processes have existed for a long time, of course, especially in chemical and biotechnological processes. Stahlmann (1988b) gives an example from the production of refrigerators (see Figure 43).

Several of these product-specific analyses can be merged into input–output tables for the entire factory. 'If all material and energetic inputs and outputs are recorded separately, this will form the framework for real ecological book-keeping, which can allocate the dimensionally different quantities to different accounts' (Strebel, 1980).

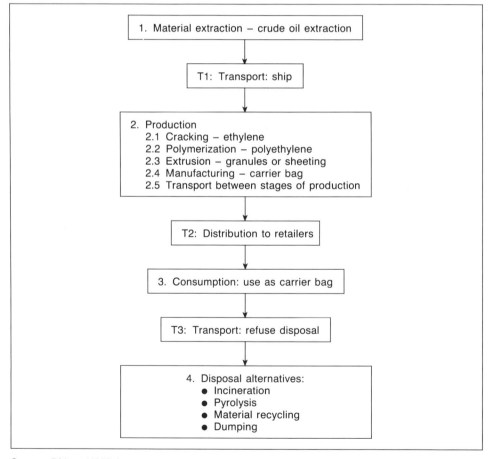

Source: Pfriem (1988c).

Figure 44 The ecological product life-cycle

Four concepts grow out of the above analyses as further developments:

● Materials lists.

● Water and energy input.

● Certificates of product composition.

● Material and energetic emissions (life-cycle).

At the second level, the process balance statement leads on to the next level of environmental accounting: another input–output account.

Here, a detailed analysis is made of operational processes – for example, production plant and transport procedures – which had been treated as a 'black box' in the first level. Finally, product balance statements provide a complete survey of the ecological product life-cycle throughout its five phases (see Figure 44):

● Input of materials and energy.

● Pollutants, waste water and refuse from the production process.

● Product use.

● Product disposal.

● Ecological problems in transport between the above stages.

Product and process balances thus facilitate the testing of existing products and production processes, but also help ecologically to optimize several alternative processes.

An analysis of 'ecological weaknesses' based on the above three eco-balance statements, which contain details of all input materials, can be carried out. Stahlmann (1988b) recommends additional classification of all materials and material groups according to alphabetical coding systems. A catalogue of potential pollutants is drawn up in order of priority, and on the basis of this the quest for alternatives can begin. The left-hand pathway in Figure 45 shows input materials which are relatively simple to reduce or substitute. The right-hand pathway shows a range of problems which have to be investigated further.

The fourth level, a substance balance, constitutes a register of all aspects not hitherto considered. It embraces long-term operational uses, such as use of land, building plans and encroachment on landscape, as well as non-operational processes like decontamination of old waste.

According to Pfriem, an eco-balance statement fulfils two preventive functions within environmental corporate policies: an internal and an external function. The internal function consists of planning and control of operations, and is useful to the following:

● Management: Strategies can be developed on the basis of the analysis of weaknesses; they can lead to improvements in all sections, especially production processes (e.g. introducing circulation systems) and products (e.g. innovations and substitution).

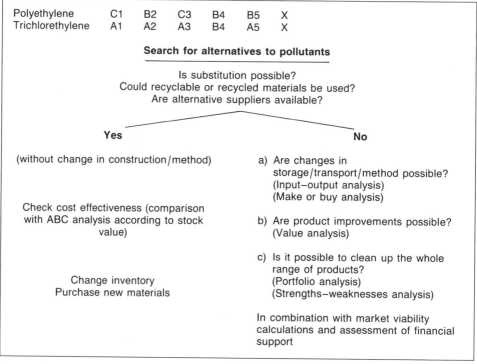

Polyethylene   C1   B2   C3   B4   B5   X
Trichlorethylene   A1   A2   A3   B4   A5   X

Search for alternatives to pollutants

Is substitution possible?
Could recyclable or recycled materials be used?
Are alternative suppliers available?

Yes   **No**

(without change in construction/method)   a) Are changes in
                                                    storage/transport/method possible?
                                                    (Input–output analysis)
                                                    (Make or buy analysis)

Check cost effectiveness (comparison
with ABC analysis according to stock   b) Are product improvements possible?
value)   (Value analysis)

                                                 c) Is it possible to clean up the whole
                                                    range of products?
Change inventory   (Portfolio analysis)
Purchase new materials   (Strengths–weaknesses analysis)

                                                 In combination with market viability
                                                 calculations and assessment of financial
                                                 support

Source: Stahlmann (1988b).

Figure 45 Material eco-controlling

- Departments: For example, it gives marketing departments an indication of which products are eco-friendly in which respects; indications of material savings; and ecological criteria in purchasing.
- Staff: Benefits here include information, motivation and qualifications.

The external function serves communication and dialogue with other companies in the field. It satisfies the increasing demand for environmental information, and is useful to the following:

- Creditors: Mortgaging of land, possibility of existing pollution.
- Suppliers: Adaptation to ecological standards.
- Customers and consumers: Ecological effects as a sales argument, e.g. Blue Angel awards.
- Authorities: Boost in confidence through communication.
- Public: High interest in ecological procedures.
- Institutions and associations: Information for professional discussion.
- Insurance companies: Information on possible liabilities.

There are, however, a number of problems connected with these heuristic eco-balance statements:

- Acquisition of data for product balance statements: Small and medium-sized companies particularly often lack access to the data required. To what extent might a reduction of complexity lead to the neglect of important details? To what extent can the existing system be used for acquiring information?

- Evaluation of data: This question is still largely unsolved. The presence of data does not remove the need to make decisions, although it provides a useful aid.

- Interdisciplinary collaboration: The economists, scientists and technologists involved require an interdisciplinary approach to their individual contributions.

Those working with eco-balance statements ought therefore to be aware of their limitations:

- Eco-control measures have to be embedded in an overall environmental corporate mission.

- Eco-balance statements do not remove the need for traditional evaluation of opposing social requirements and preferences.

In general, it is necessary to develop binding regulations on the form of operational eco-balance statements, so that they do not merely pick out the virtues as a PR exercise.

◇ Unilever

At an environment congress in London in March 1990 Unilever demonstrated the difficulties of establishing the environmental costs of products. It is generally recognized nowadays that in calculating the 'real cost' of an item, its environmental impact has to be assessed over its whole 'ecological life-cycle'. In this context the correct price of a product should represent the traditional price plus the environmental cost. Environmental cost consists of:

- The cost of the product during its use and after its use.

- The cost of its manufacture, including the raw materials used.

Business clearly aims to minimize the overall costs, and Unilever has developed a computer model to help with the calculations for a phosphate-free liquid detergent. The results of this calculation were as follows:

- The main environmental costs appeared in the use of the product. The environmental costs worked out at 0.2 guilders per unit, for a product retailing at about 8 guilders per unit.

- Taking into account recent Dutch legislation affecting the next ten to 15 years, environmental costs are due to rise about fivefold over that period. This would imply 1 guilder per unit instead of 0.2 guilders environmental costs. Unilever does not believe customers will be prepared to pay this, and therefore, 'a lot of work has to be done on reformulating the product to reduce the overall costs and make the product more environmentally friendly at the same time'.

Applying the concept of life-cycle environmental costs enables a number of advantages to be achieved:

- avoiding a shift from one environmental problem to another without overall gain;

- identifying those elements which have the biggest environmental impact;

- directing efforts and money to those areas which are most rewarding environmentally;

- raising the level of debate on environmental issues based on facts and figures. (Unilever, 1990)

◊ Bischof and Klein

The following example shows the development of refillable packaging for fabric softeners over the first year of the project (Future Forum, 1988). Fabric softeners have been sold in 4-litre high-density polyethylene (HDPE) bottles for some time now, but since 1987, concentrates in a free-standing bag have been available as an additional alternative. The 1-litre recyclable containers are made of PET/PE in the ratio 12/180. Since the concentrate corresponds exactly to 4 litres of traditional softener in performance, this constitutes the substitution of a 1-litre packet made of plastic sheeting in place of a 4-litre bottle.

Nowadays eco-friendliness is not enough to establish a product in the market. Packaging has to be fitted into the logistics of sales and transportation, and, in addition, advantages in handling by the consumer have to be assessed.

The following advantages in sales logistics became apparent:

- It was possible to reduce direct product costs by a dramatic 59 per cent with the new packaging. These gains were mainly in central storage, transport and retail.

- The smaller volume takes up less space in the warehouse, during transport and above all on the shelves. (Sales from the same area of shelf space are tripled. Where previously three 4-litre bottles stood, today there is a display carton with ten refillable packs.)

Bischof and Klein provides the following advantages for the consumer:

- Consumers only need to buy one 4-litre bottle, after which the lighter refill bags give a 75 per cent saving in space in the shopping basket.

- The most striking advantage is in disposal. The soft refill pack occupies negligible space in the dustbin.

The ecological advantages of the free-standing bag are determined by various factors:

- The 4-litre bottle weighs around 154 g; the bag, just 17 g. The materials input for the bag is nine times less. Similar reductions in energy consumption and burdens on the environment are achieved.

- A significant reduction in refuse.

The new product represents more than a 70 per cent improvement in the overall ecological balance. Additional, hardly quantifiable advantages are gained from reduced storage space for empty packaging and reduced pollution from heavy goods vehicles.

◇ Deutsche Bank

Experiments with a scoring valuation method for environmental effects have been less far reaching, but more practicable. In 1989 the Deutsche Bank presented a system in which problem fields are drawn up and individual effects are listed and evaluated by means of points (Brochure for Medium-Sized Industries, No. 11).

The first stage is to undertake a rough analysis of weak points, in order to identify the most important risks and classify them. Existing and expected burdens on the environment are assessed at each operational level. At this stage comparative analysis is based only on the sum of burdens on the environment. As a preparation for decision making between several alternatives, the available factors are evaluated with the help of a checklist. If discrepancies occur at this preliminary stage, then it will be worthwhile calculating the alternatives with concrete figures.

In this eco-balance statement, company performance is investigated according to:

- The manufacturing phase, taking account of input materials and production processes.

- The utilization phase: use or consumption.

- The disposal phase.

Company performance is juxtaposed with a more environment-friendly alternative, for comparison. The procedure is as follows:

Step 1 Investigation of the legal context
This involves the assessment of products and their positioning within the framework of existing and foreseeable legislation. The valuation is based on the following scoring system:

- No recognizable restrictions at present or in the future (1).

- No restrictions at present (2).

- Input quantity is restricted (3).

Section of business \ Danger area	I Air	II Water/ ground	III Refuse	IV Noise	Possible consequences	Area
Storage areas					Draw up checklists	
● Raw materials	—	Tanks	Tank cleaning	—	for a control	II
● Part-finished goods	—	Barrels	Empty containers	—	system	III
● Finished goods	—	Canisters	Empty containers	—	Find buyer for	
● Fuels	—	Tanks/barrels	—	—	empty container	
Supply areas	Emissions				Regular	I
● Energy	—	—	—	—	measurement	
● Water	—	—	—	—		
● Heating	Boiler room	Oil tank	—	—	Tank control	II
Production				Noise emission		
● Pre-production	—	—	—	Printing machines	Insulation Noise proofing	IV
● Manufacture	—	Pipe work	Residues	—		
● Packing	—	Leakages	—	Packing	New technology	IV
Transport areas					Solvent-resistant	
● Internal	—	Fuel tanks	—	—	flooring	II
● External	—	—	—	Collection	Relocate parking facilities	IV
Disposal areas						
● Waste water	—	—	—	—		
● Purification plants	—	Function/ capacity	—	—	Instal control system	II

Source: Deutsche Bank (1989).

Figure 46 Example of a field search system for investigating environmental aspects of industrial siting

Evaluation areas \ Aspects under evaluation	Legal bases	Ecological aspects						Total	Remarks
		Emissions	Use of natural resources	Energy consumption	Effect on waste water	Burden on human, animal, plant life	Non-re-exploitable waste		
● Raw materials/ composition									
● Own manufacturing									
● Use/consumption									
● Disposal									
Total									

Source: Deutsche Bank (1989).

Figure 47 Example of an eco-balance statement

- Input is permitted for a limited time (4).
- Fails to meet existing legal requirements (5).

Step 2 Recording ecological aspects

Assessment in each area of the company is made on the following bases:

- Emissions.
- Use of natural resources.
- Energy consumption.
- Risk of damage to humans, animals or plants.
- Quantity of non-exploitable waste.

Valuation is based on a similar scoring system:

- Insignificant (1).
- Very low (2).
- Low (3).
- High (4).
- Very high (5).

If a score of 3 or more is recorded from this qualitative analysis, it is recommended that a quantitative analysis is undertaken in order to obtain exact details. When these two steps have shown where the product or service lies in terms of the legal and ecological context, alternatives to the analyzed performances should be sought. For example:

- Raw materials from renewable resources.
- Production techniques with lower energy consumption.
- Formulations which reduce the environmental burden during use.
- Substitution of ingredients without impairing performance.
- Processing technologies without waste or with the possibility of recycling.
- Creation of closed circulation systems.

Finally, burdens on the environment caused by the 'old' performance can be compared with their alternatives to check the benefits. If these simple calculations show up discrepancies, then there is a need for action. The scoring system can be supplemented with thorough calculations based on the same checklists if necessary. In the brochure published by the Deutsche Bank detergents with and without phosphate are compared.

An environmental performance indicator system

Reference has already been made to the key role occupied by materials management within environmental management. Stahlmann (1988a) recommends the additional setting up of an indicator system. Primarily for use in the control of stock, the system helps with the following functions:

- Increasing capital productivity.

- Promoting economical use of resources through the avoidance of excess stock or rejects.

- Assessing materials required in products and processes.

- Achieving economic and environmentally sound procedures for acquiring and disposing of materials.

In addition to the normal indicators used in this context, such as stock intensity and frequency, terms specifically useful for environmental materials management are given below.

$$\text{Net real product} = \frac{\text{Real turnover}}{\text{Real materials consumption}}$$

$$\text{Recycling quota} = \frac{\text{Proportion of recycled material per year}}{\text{Total materials consumption per year}}$$

Materials include all raw materials, subsidiary materials and fuels.

The recycling quota varies in size according to branch of industry and type of material conversion. Therefore Stahlmann recommends additional indicators to ensure correct interpretation:

- Proceeds from scrap per year.

- Waste water production per year.

'If the proceeds from scrap are low, but the cost of refuse removal and waste water production are high, then the possibility of recycling should be examined with the help of ecologically expanded accounting methods.'

The following terms can be used to express material exploitation:

$$\text{Production scrap quota} = \frac{\text{Value of production scrap per year X 100}}{\text{Materials consumption}}$$

Energy indicators can be calculated in a similar way:

$$\text{Specific final energy consumption (net production)} = \frac{\text{Final energy consumption}}{\text{Net production}}$$

$$\text{Specific final energy consumption (employees)} = \frac{\text{Final energy consumption}}{\text{Number of employees}}$$

$$\text{Specific energy costs (total costs)} = \frac{\text{Energy costs}}{\text{Total costs}}$$

Energy consumption can also be expressed in absolute terms, differentiated according to type of fuel (renewable/non-renewable). In addition, material and non-material emissions can be expressed in terms of volume and structure.

Internal environmental audits

Management is not just a question of setting goals and providing the means for fulfilling them; it also implies control over the way these goals are achieved. Environmental protection is an important aspect of corporate strategy and it therefore requires efficient management methods. Hitherto, supervision of environmental factors has been limited to ensuring compliance with legal restrictions and has been delegated to the environment officer. The purpose of an audit is not simply to provide information on the efficient functioning of relevant plant and other facilities, but to make sure that management and the entire organizational structure of the company are serving the goals of environmental protection. This control system, therefore, assists in business decisions at all levels.

The long-term ideal to be pursued in this context is the implementation of voluntary internal audits, which involve the systematic, regular assessment of internal environmental measures at all levels, culminating in a summary evaluation. This should ensure that environmental protection receives the same amount of attention as other operational areas, that a company's activities and products can be evaluated in terms of ecology, and that potential risks are nipped in the bud.

Construed in this sense, environmental audits are a very important element of management. In content, the audits show great affinity with environmental impact assessments (EIAs). However, they are different in this respect:

- EIAs are anticipatory. They are used before setting up a new plant, changing a process, introducing a new product, etc.

- Environmental audits are carried out during or after an operational phase. They are often described as a review, appraisal, survey or surveillance.

The execution of an audit involves:

- Gathering information on the current state.

- Evaluation of information.

- Deciding on measures.

Several different types of audit can be adopted (*Financial Times*, 6.3.90):

- Compliance audit, to ensure that a company is conforming to legislative regulations.

- Site audits: spot checks of sites.

- Issue audits: for example, audits of distribution activities.
- Full environmental audits of the whole company.

For the president of the Confederation of British Industry the potential benefits of environmental audits are as follows:

- Providing an early warning system.
- Increasing employee awareness.
- Facilitating insurance cover.
- Providing an information base against which environmental performance can be tested.

◇ International Chamber of Commerce

The ICC considers the following conditions necessary for environmental audits:

- Full commitment from management.
- Objectivity of auditors.
- Specialist competence.
- Clearly defined, systematic methodology.
- Written reports.
- Quality assurance.
- Follow-up.

In 1989 the ICC issued a paper on environmental audits in which the first international response is given to this matter. The fundamental steps of an audit – assessment, site investigation and post-assessment – are outlined in the flow chart (Figure 48).

◇ Ciba-Geigy

Ciba-Geigy was one of the first European companies to carry out an environmental audit in all companies within the combine, with the exception of those in the USA. It facilitates a review of environmental performance within each unit, the identification of problems and the initiation of corrective measures to ensure the achievement of the objectives of the unit in question. These objectives can be pitched at the level of compliance with legal norms, or they can be set higher, if internal standards exceed those laid down by the law. The auditing teams are always independent, in that they do not belong to the company being appraised, but the audits are always supervised by the local, company environment officer. Discussion is carried out directly with local managers and production and laboratory staff. The teams usually consist of two persons and spend roughly two weeks auditing each unit.

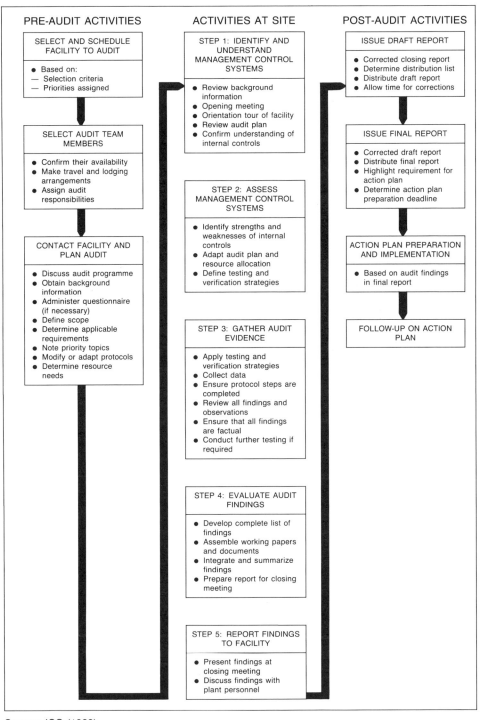

PRE-AUDIT ACTIVITIES

SELECT AND SCHEDULE FACILITY TO AUDIT

- Based on:
  - Selection criteria
  - Priorities assigned

SELECT AUDIT TEAM MEMBERS

- Confirm their availability
- Make travel and lodging arrangements
- Assign audit responsibilities

CONTACT FACILITY AND PLAN AUDIT

- Discuss audit programme
- Obtain background information
- Administer questionnaire (if necessary)
- Define scope
- Determine applicable requirements
- Note priority topics
- Modify or adapt protocols
- Determine resource needs

ACTIVITIES AT SITE

STEP 1: IDENTIFY AND UNDERSTAND MANAGEMENT CONTROL SYSTEMS

- Review background information
- Opening meeting
- Orientation tour of facility
- Review audit plan
- Confirm understanding of internal controls

STEP 2: ASSESS MANAGEMENT CONTROL SYSTEMS

- Identify strengths and weaknesses of internal controls
- Adapt audit plan and resource allocation
- Define testing and verification strategies

STEP 3: GATHER AUDIT EVIDENCE

- Apply testing and verification strategies
- Collect data
- Ensure protocol steps are completed
- Review all findings and observations
- Ensure that all findings are factual
- Conduct further testing if required

STEP 4: EVALUATE AUDIT FINDINGS

- Develop complete list of findings
- Assemble working papers and documents
- Integrate and summarize findings
- Prepare report for closing meeting

STEP 5: REPORT FINDINGS TO FACILITY

- Present findings at closing meeting
- Discuss findings with plant personnel

POST-AUDIT ACTIVITIES

ISSUE DRAFT REPORT

- Corrected closing report
- Determine distribution list
- Distribute draft report
- Allow time for corrections

ISSUE FINAL REPORT

- Corrected draft report
- Distribute final report
- Highlight requirement for action plan
- Determine action plan preparation deadline

ACTION PLAN PREPARATION AND IMPLEMENTATION

- Based on audit findings in final report

FOLLOW-UP ON ACTION PLAN

Source: ICC (1989).

Figure 48 Basic steps of an environmental audit

The environmental audit encompasses more than just the legal dimension. The main points are as follows:

- Legal compliance.
- Compliance with Ciba-Geigy internal norms.
- Proper environmental management.
- Inclusion of environmental matters in the planning procedures.
- Adequate data bases on environmental aspects.
- Efficiency of pollution control measures.

The audit normally begins with the collection of information and ends with a meeting between the team and company management. The results of the audit are discussed at this meeting; agreement on counter-measures is sought and deadlines are fixed. The final report contains all results (actual and desired), along with a prioritization of any major discrepancies, and it is passed on to senior management as a basis for planning corrective measures. A follow-up system has also been installed to help maintain continuity.

Evaluation of environment impact assessments is seen in two ways:

- As a routine function of the local environment officer, reporting to local management.
- As a function of central environmental auditing, carried out by audit teams, reporting to top management.

Motto: The auditor's role is not that of an environmental policeman.

The advantages of environmental audits are seen as:

- Ensuring compliance with the law.
- Ensuring efficient technology.
- Avoidance of long- and short-term problems.
- Problem solving through information transfer.

Motto: An environmentally acceptable operation is an important long-term management objective.

◇ Royal Dutch/Shell Group

Environmental auditing is finding increasing application with Shell, as an aid to management and the board in recognizing that an operation is complying with the management guidelines, that staff are following policies and that relevant legal restrictions are being complied with. Audits are carried out on a yearly basis, and the team consists of three to five persons who are not from the same operating company. Larger-scale audits, undertaken every three to five years, involve personnel from the companies themselves. As a matter of principle the audits are strictly confidential.

A pre-acquisition assessment is conducted when firms are bought up. Contractors and subsidiary companies must apply the same standards as Shell. A safety and environment manager informs the board and provides advice.

◇ Coopers and Lybrand Deloitte

The importance of environmental audits was stressed by numerous speakers at a conference, 'Business and the Environment' (London, March 1990), organized by Coopers and Lybrand Deloitte, the largest firm of management consultants and chartered accountants in the UK. One of this management consulting firm's Environmental Business Units which deals with the implementation of such audits sees the pressure for the audits coming from three sides:

- Compliance with regulations (UK: Environment Protection Bill and EC directives).

- Growing public awareness.

- Business imperatives (regulatory requirements, voluntary codes, own policies).

From a consultant's point of view there are naturally advantages in having audits carried out by an independent auditor rather than by management. 'An independent report adds credibility, enhances reliability and increases the public relations value of any report. It also complements the views of management by providing a new and fresh outlook.' There is no need to make audit reports available externally, but the inclusion of a statement in the annual directors' report is recommended. Three categories of environmental concerns should be addressed: the direct impact of the business's own processes, the indirect impact of the company's activities and final disposal of the business's products. The scope of management actions which are subject to audit are defined as follows:

1. Top management awareness (formulation and implementation of environmental policies and procedures).

2. To ensure that management has appropriate information regarding standards required and the actual performance achieved (responsibilities, objectives, plans, deadlines, timetables). This assessment needs expertise in both environmental and managerial needs, including:

   (a) organization and training;

   (b) proper setting down of responsibilities;

   (c) appropriate action in response to technical reports;

   (d) establishing priorities for further technical analysis;

   (e) procedures to ensure that suppliers take account of environmental concerns.

3. The actual measurement of emissions.

◇ 3M

3M operates in 52 countries and has manufacturing facilities in 42 of them, producing over 60,000 different products in over 40 market sectors. As 3M produces solid wastes at all of its locations and substantial quantities of special wastes at many, environmental auditing is an essential feature. A number of different types of audit have been conducted. Auditing is usually carried out by:

- Checklist – against a set of written questions.

- Interview and observation – with a set of audit criteria.

Before leaving site an international audit team should discuss its main findings with local management. This avoids misunderstandings. The audit report will then contain no hidden surprises, even though it may have some unpopular conclusions.
The positive aspects of the report are as follows:

- It provides opportunities for improvement.

- The importance of environmental issues will be heightened for a time at the location and progress will be stimulated.

- The audit team will learn something.

- The report will provide a valuable positional statement.

Audits are generally associated with negatives, although they need not be:

- The audit report should highlight opportunities and not seek to allocate blame. Successful higher managements appreciate this and use the process for the benefit of the company.

- There is always a fear that an auditor's comment may be used as evidence of negligence in the future.

Example: waste audit
Before the audit starts, the local management will have been made aware of:

- The aims of the audit.

- How it will be conducted.

- The names of the audit team.

- Requests for information on waste types, quantities, costs, etc., although these are centrally available.

The audit team will then seek answers to the following questions:

- Is there a single manager responsible for solid waste despatched from site? (3M calls this manager the 'responsible person'.)

- If there are divisions of responsibility, are these clearly understood by relevant people?

- Has the responsible person received adequate training in new aspects of legislation and waste disposal practice?

- Are there waste disposal procedures in existence, and are they updated regularly? This requirement is to be assisted by the issue of a corporate manual.

- Are there files, easily to hand, which contain details of disposal notifications, in-transit incidents, liaison with contractors, disposal of wastes such as PCBs, radioactive materials and asbestos?

- Are there reports on visits to disposal sites, and local authority liaison?

- Is the storage area licensed or are there limitations on its use?

There is usually much work to be completed in the office before proceeding to look at facilities outside. Once in the factory it is necessary to establish how wastes are collected in the workplace and how they get to the waste storage area.

- Are containers suitable for the waste for which they are intended? Lidded drums should not be used for solvent wastes unless there are sludges which obviate the use of bunghole drums. Are they inspected before use and labelled, and is a lid provided?

- Is waste discipline maintained or does everything end up in the dustbin? There are clearly savings to be made by eliminating the disposal of non-hazardous materials with special waste. Mixing of solvent wastes may discourage recovery and increase disposal costs.

- Are old containers being drained or punctured and labels removed or obliterated?

- Does the waste present an industrial hygiene problem?

On moving to the vast storage area the following aspects would be questioned:

- Are special wastes and general wastes stored in well-separated areas?

- Are special waste types clearly segregated? Are the areas labelled to ensure there is no confusion?

- Is the area bonded? If not, what would be the result of a spillage?

- Are spillage kits and procedures understood by staff? Are the staff trained?

- Are staff aware of hazards and the need for protective clothing?

- What fire precautions are in force? Is the flammable waste well separated from permanent buildings? No-smoking rules?

- Is the waste site secure from outsiders and other employees?

- Is the waste inventory minimized? Are there accumulation problems with certain types of waste?

The policy on recoverable waste should also be examined:

- What happens to old drums? Clean drums may be sold for reuse. How are residues removed? How clean are the old drums sold to laundering firms? How are drums selected for use as waste containers? Are they inspected? Drums which have been laundered by firing will often leak. These must not be used for liquids.

- What happens to contaminated scrap? Old pallets?

On return to the waste collection site, the filled container will need to be:

- Labelled with a generic label, e.g. 'Pumpable Waste', 'Chlorinated Solvent Waste', etc.

- Securely lidded or bunged and checked for leakage.

- Stored in the area reserved for the class of materials.

The labelling of drums is one aspect where we can expect increased attention from the authorities. Good practice dictates that waste containers should be fully labelled before they are issued as waste receptacles, and that old labels are removed or obliterated. If this is not done, the container may be used for any waste by passers-by and there is a potential problem with health and safety obligations. This is one area where there is room for progress.

When ready for despatch from site a waste container will probably have the original label obliterated and the following labels added:

- Particular waste stream within the factory, e.g. 'No. 3 Washout Liquor'.

- Generic title, e.g. 'Pumpable Waste'.

- Transit packaging label. This will contain hazard and risk phrases together with a contact address and telephone number.

Documentation and transport systems should also be physically checked:

- Are the special waste notifications appropriate for the load carried?

- Does the driver carry a Tremcard? 3M has found that contractors' drivers sometimes carry a whole collection of Tremcards and may or may not produce the correct one in an emergency. At present 3M relies on disposal contractors to produce these, but the company is considering generating its own to control this abuse.

- Are Hazchem placards displayed?

- Is the driver going to the site you would expect?

- Does he have a spillage kit, and is he trained to use it? The answer to this question is undoubtedly negative for many contractors. It is possible that a well-trained and -equipped driver could prevent a minor leak from turning into a major motorway catastrophe.

When dealing with disposals of asbestos (after removal by a specialist contractor) or of defective products which could be sold, 3M has followed waste lorries to the ultimate disposal site. This approach has uncovered some malpractices. As a final point, landfill sites and disposal contractors' premises are visited by a local 3M representative and possibly the local disposal contractor. 3M then has some assurance that the deposit is licensed for the waste the company is supplying (in one instance it was not). Also it develops a helpful working relationship with the contractor and the disposal site.

Environment assessment

An evaluation of consequences should be carried out on the basis of eco-assessments. From the ecological point of view, the advantage of assessments is that they precede operational decisions.

Technology assessment

An interesting attempt at institutionalizing the interpretation of technological consequences is to be found in the USA. The Office of Technology Assessment is trying to record and prognosticate all consequences of certain technological applications in all possible areas of society and the environment. Social innovations are also being taken into account. The identification of priorities and their evaluation assist political decision-makers by providing information and knowledge.

The proposal to set up a similar institution in Germany has either been rejected outright or subjected to lengthy discussion according to the prevailing political climate.

Environmental impact assessment

An EC guideline from 1985 recommending the institutionalization of environmental impact assessments has recently been codified as a national law in Germany. This interpretation of environmental effects should enable the relevant authorities to investigate and evaluate potential industrial encroachments on the environment in a scientific, formalized way. The definition of these assessments shows their proximity to technological assessments – in content, at least. The criterion of ecological compatibility thus joins the criteria of profitability and legality on an equal footing. The result should be an effective form of preventive environmental protection. EIAs should assist in the avoidance of future damage. In contrast to previous partial measures, the EIAs provide an overview of the wide range of possible primary effects and side-effects of any given project, including effects on:

● Mankind, animals, plants, ground, water, air, climate and landscape.

● Cultural heritage and material goods.

The process of investigating environmental effects is sketched in Figure 49.

There are a great many projects obliged under German law to use EIAs, ranging from power stations to refuse dumps. The list is given in the appendix to the environmental impact assessment law.

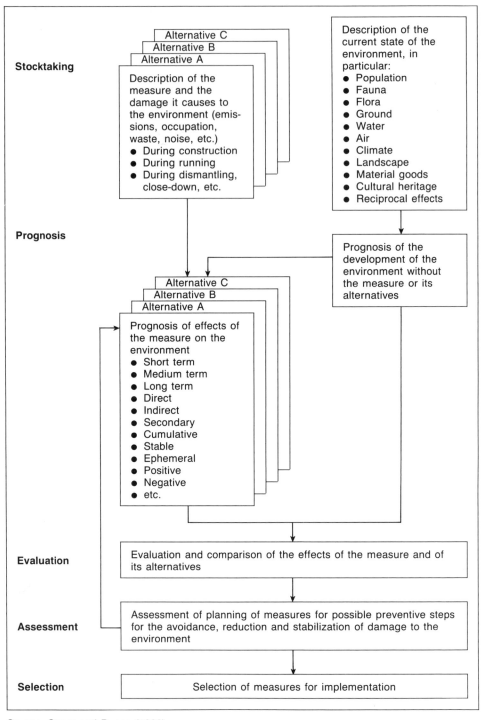

Source: Strom and Bunge (1988).

Figure 49 The process of investigating environmental effects

It's the first tea garden where everything's organic. Even the insecticide.

Of course it would be nice if all tea was organically grown. But sadly, a lot of it these days owes as much to the hand of man as it does to Nature. Helped along as it is by all the latest insecticides and fertilisers.

That's why you may like to try Natureland, Britain's first organic tea. It comes from a plantation in Tanzania where they still practise traditional methods of cultivation.

Chemical fertilisers, for example, are outlawed. Water comes directly from the tropical rainclouds. And like the chameleon on the right, the only insecticides are the ones which hop over the fence.

The result is the world's purest cup of tea. A drink with a fresh, clean taste that does things for you. But not to you.

As you'd expect, it's a little bit more expensive than ordinary tea. But not much when you consider where it's going.

You can find Natureland tea at all good health food stores and selected supermarkets.

Pick some up next time you're shopping. And get a better future in the leaves.

Natureland. The world's purest cup of tea.

HOW THE WORLD'S LEAST EXPENSIVE LIGHT BULB

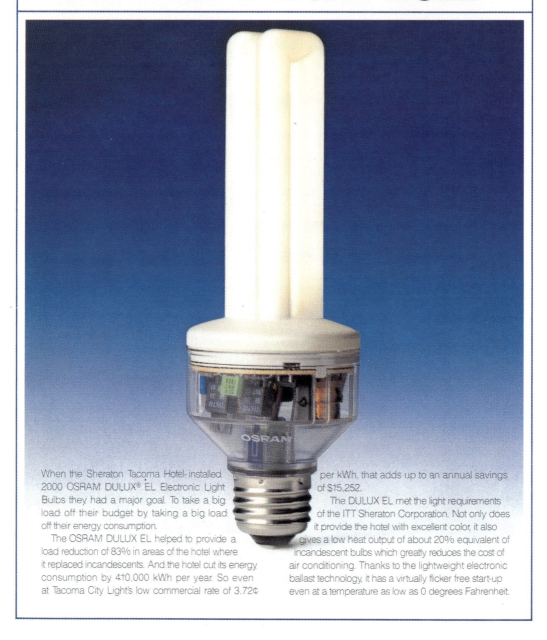

When the Sheraton Tacoma Hotel installed 2000 OSRAM DULUX® EL Electronic Light Bulbs they had a major goal. To take a big load off their budget by taking a big load off their energy consumption.

The OSRAM DULUX EL helped to provide a load reduction of 83% in areas of the hotel where it replaced incandescents. And the hotel cut its energy consumption by 410,000 kWh per year. So even at Tacoma City Light's low commercial rate of 3.72¢ per kWh, that adds up to an annual savings of $15,252.

The DULUX EL met the light requirements of the ITT Sheraton Corporation. Not only does it provide the hotel with excellent color, it also gives a low heat output of about 20% equivalent of incandescent bulbs which greatly reduces the cost of air conditioning. Thanks to the lightweight electronic ballast technology, it has a virtually flicker free start-up even at a temperature as low as 0 degrees Fahrenheit.

TOOK A BIG LOAD OFF THE SHERATON TACOMA.

The world's least expensive light bulb lasts 13 times longer than comparable incandescents. It consumes up to 75% less energy than incandescents. On top of that, the DULUX EL is designed to use in all medium screw base fixtures and no changes are required to your power supply.

Here is what Bruce Jarrard, Chief Engineer of the Sheraton Tacoma, had to say about the DULUX EL. "We have much greater confidence that the hotel will not have lamp outages. We put these lamps in the ceiling of the lobby and won't have to worry about them for one to two years. Which means our staff will have more time for other jobs because we won't have to be concerned about changing light bulbs every day.

And, keep in mind that today most utilities subsidize your replacements of incandescents."

The OSRAM DULUX EL. The world's least expensive light bulb. Designed to take a big load off your budget.

For further information call **1-800-338-2542.**

OSRAM

TECHNOLOGY BROUGHT TO LIGHT

Just how green are you about nuclear power?

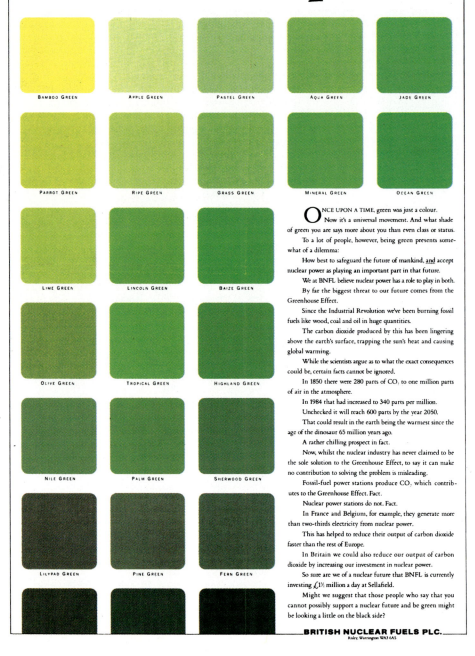

BAMBOO GREEN · APPLE GREEN · PASTEL GREEN · AQUA GREEN · JADE GREEN

PARROT GREEN · RIPE GREEN · GRASS GREEN · MINERAL GREEN · OCEAN GREEN

LIME GREEN · LINCOLN GREEN · BAIZE GREEN

OLIVE GREEN · TROPICAL GREEN · HIGHLAND GREEN

NILE GREEN · PALM GREEN · SHERWOOD GREEN

LILYPAD GREEN · PINE GREEN · FERN GREEN

ONCE UPON A TIME, green was just a colour.

Now it's a universal movement. And what shade of green you are says more about you than even class or status.

To a lot of people, however, being green presents somewhat of a dilemma:

How best to safeguard the future of mankind, and accept nuclear power as playing an important part in that future.

We at BNFL believe nuclear power has a role to play in both.

By far the biggest threat to our future comes from the Greenhouse Effect.

Since the Industrial Revolution we've been burning fossil fuels like wood, coal and oil in huge quantities.

The carbon dioxide produced by this has been lingering above the earth's surface, trapping the sun's heat and causing global warming.

While the scientists argue as to what the exact consequences could be, certain facts cannot be ignored.

In 1850 there were 280 parts of CO_2 to one million parts of air in the atmosphere.

In 1984 that had increased to 340 parts per million.

Unchecked it will reach 600 parts by the year 2050.

That could result in the earth being the warmest since the age of the dinosaur 65 million years ago.

A rather chilling prospect in fact.

Now, whilst the nuclear industry has never claimed to be the sole solution to the Greenhouse Effect, to say it can make no contribution to solving the problem is misleading.

Fossil-fuel power stations produce CO_2 which contributes to the Greenhouse Effect. Fact.

Nuclear power stations do not. Fact.

In France and Belgium, for example, they generate more than two-thirds electricity from nuclear power.

This has helped to reduce their output of carbon dioxide faster than the rest of Europe.

In Britain we could also reduce our output of carbon dioxide by increasing our investment in nuclear power.

So sure are we of a nuclear future that BNFL is currently investing £1½ million a day at Sellafield.

Might we suggest that those people who say that you cannot possibly support a nuclear future and be green might be looking a little on the black side?

BRITISH NUCLEAR FUELS PLC.
Risley, Warrington WA3 6AS

Surveys of consulting agencies have shown great uncertainty regarding the content and duties implied by EIAs, mainly because there is so little experience of them. They recommend using the EIAs in easy stages, as follows:

- For seeking new industrial sites and designing plant.

- For developing optimum eco-friendly production technology.

- For introducing environmentally compatible materials or dealing with disposal problems.

Product impact assessment

The evaluation of product impact is a variation of the EIA, and is generally seen as a first step towards conversion to environmental methods.

As a simple aid Müller-Witt has developed the product impact matrix, which aims to 'help to alert manufacturers to the impact of their activities; to prevent some products coming on to the market; to prevent others from being designed to be harmful, even though they may be profitable ... and to help secure jobs' (Müller-Witt, 1985).

The matrix (see Figure 50) divides the life-cycle of a product into five subordinate cycles in order to evaluate the ecological and social effects in each stage. Two evaluation methods are possible:

- Numerical methods, e.g. with a scale from − 5 to + 5 and weighting criteria.

- Descriptive methods, e.g. verbal description of results.

Müller-Witt, who is well aware of the problems in evaluation, points out that it is a question not of trying to develop a 100 per cent eco-friendly product as quickly as possible, but rather of raising staff awareness through long-term discussion of products, so that holistic, ecological thinking becomes the norm.

This matrix has recently been further developed by the German Eco-Institute in Freiburg ('product line analysis').

A veritable 'nappy war' has flared up recently, especially in the USA. It is centred on the refuse problems caused by throw-away nappies. Around 16 billion tonnes of disposable nappies are used per year in the United States; 2.5 billion tonnes in California alone. In Germany the figure is 6 million per day (2.2 billion per year). The total cost for a mother with one child works out at approximately DM2,739, (around £900) based on five nappies per day for 24–30 months. An ecological comparison with reusable nappies would require investigation of environmental influences throughout the entire life-cycle of the product.

Traditional chlorine bleaching has been abolished by all manufacturers of nappies and replaced with peroxide bleaches. In addition, a large amount of energy is used in the manufacturing stages. In the disposal phase throw-away

Social and ecological effects ╲ Product life-cycle	Materials procurement	Production/ processing	Transport/ distribution	Use/ application	Consumption/ disposal/ removal	Σ
Questions of resource intensity and quality: • Regenerative raw materials • Non-regenerative raw materials • Recycled raw materials • Damage caused by pre-product • Capital intensity • Energy intensity • Side-effects, consequences or distant effects of any other kind						

Questions of ecological damage:
• Ground pollution
• Occupation and use of ground
• Air pollution
• Noise pollution
• Water pollution
• Consumption of water
• Damage to plants
          animals
          people
• Waste heat pollution
• Side-effects, consequences or distant effects of any other kind						

Questions of social impact: • Labour intensity • Damage to health in the workplace • Monotony in the workplace • Error-friendliness • Repair-friendliness • Intensity of use • Side-effects, consequences or distant effects of any other kind						
Σ						

Source: Müller-Witt (1985).

Figure 50 Product impact matrix

nappies represent around 2.8 per cent of domestic waste in Germany (around 2 per cent in the USA). This does not mean an unequivocal return to cloth nappies, though. In February 1990 the Federal German Environment Office in Berlin published a product analysis which showed that 'neither of the two types of nappy shows clear advantages in terms of overall effect on the environment'.

Many towns have special laundry collection services, which cut down the washing load of individual households. Dy-Dee Diaper Service in South California has around 20,000 customers per week. There are similar 'convenience services' in London.

18

Environmental ethics: a management gimmick?

Economic activity must surely be understood in terms of ecological responsibility. One can only really speak of responsibility when people are aware of an alternative form of acting and are free to choose it. With our high standard of living, we experience few material hardships and have plenty of room for free choice. I would conclude from this that we have never had such scope for acting responsibly in ecology and therefore also in the economy.

We have to ask ourselves how irreversible damage to the environment can be prevented; how avoidable stress and risks can be minimized, for there is no doubt that nowadays we produce risks faster than we can deal with them. This is probably a retarded consequence of the highly efficient division of labour in modern societies. It can be characterized by the increasing disequilibrium between the insatiable urge to know 'how', and the lack of answers to the question 'why'. In future, economic activity will consist in avoiding the dangerous chasm between our skill at rational, efficient production and the obvious lack of any discernible sense behind human actions. Perhaps we are too concerned with sums and not enough with values.   (Atteslander, 1989)

Semantic transfiguration
(or, Reality veiled behind words)

Our relationship with nature, the spirit of our time, is given clear expression through language. Especially in official pronouncements on environmental pollution, many realities are disguised behind euphemisms, in an attempt to make them seem less problematic.

A word is a mysterious, oracle-like, ambivalent, treacherous phenomenon. It can be a ray of light in the darkness; it can also be a death-bringing arrow. The worst thing, however, is that one moment it can mean this and another moment it can mean that, or it can even mean both at the same time …

No word conveys only the meaning ascribed to it in the etymological dictionary. Every word contains something of the person who pronounces it; something of the situation in which it was spoken; something of the reason behind uttering it …

Sometimes a word can speak the truth and, at the same time, tell a lie. (President Václav Havel, speech given at the Peace Prize award of the German book trade)

A few topical examples of euphemisms current in Germany show how they can be used to disguise the truth.

- *Entsorgung = Disposal (literally: removal of care).* Does this also imply that we dispose of our responsibility for waste for good? In reality we have done no such thing. We have just shunted the problem along to the dump or the incinerator. What about nuclear waste, for which no adequate disposal has yet been devised? Anxieties about the preservation of ground water are well founded when one thinks of the 60,000 disused dumps in Germany alone, and the unacknowledged dangers they harbour. The Berlin Material Testing Office claims that no dump sites are effectively sealed off.

- *Entsorgungspark = Disposal park.* A nice place for a stroll?

- *Vom Aussterben bedroht = Threatened with extinction.* Does this imply that species are evolving this way, or are we annihilating them?

- *Sondermüll = Special waste.* It is only 'special' because it is so dangerous.

- *Umwelt = Environment (literally: the world around).* Mankind as the centre point. Nature as the world around mankind. Would it not be wiser to think of ourselves as part of nature? We, too, are the victims of pollution.

- *Mülltourismus = Waste tourism.* Out of sight, out of mind? A cynical circumlocution for the export of toxic waste to countries in need of foreign currency. With exports of over 2 million tonnes per year, according to statistics from the Federal Environment Office, Germany is the biggest exporter of waste in the world. In spite of 'drug smuggling methods' it has still only been possible to establish partial prohibitions of this practice. In addition, there is the problem of disguising toxic substances as normal waste. There are UN plans to create an Environment Interpol to combat 'waste tourism'. Could it not be that, one day, the cargo might rear its ugly head again at some point in the global material cycle?

- *Altlast = Existing waste (literally: old burden).* Modern German circumlocution for disused dumps, casual rubbish tips and certain former industrial land. In reality they are just chemical time bombs; swords of Damocles held over the heads of local communities which are unsure about who should pay for the immense cost of decontamination. The cost of treating 70,000 'suspect areas' has been estimated at around DM17 billion (£5.7 billion).

- *Eutropie = Eutrophication.* Greek for 'well nourished', or is it just another way of saying, 'The algal bloom is back'?

- *Energierecycling = Energy recycling.* The stage in a material cycle where (at last?) something can be burned. It is not to do with the reclamation of organic matter; it is a way of exploiting the energy released during burning (thermal exploitation) – a kind of ultimate recycling. Not only the raw material, oil, is irretrievably annihilated, but also the added value from labour invested in the product.

It is not the mirror's fault if it shows the virgin she is with child. (Tucholsky)

Morality and responsibility

Stoll (1984) gives a penetrating warning against attributing contemporary environmental problems to a lack of ecologically directed instruments. There are countless instances of more or less eco-friendly production methods, but Stoll sees the main responsibility of a critical but constructive industrial economics in enlightening consumers and producers:

> The future of the natural environment is our future, too. We must change our form of economy and look on environmental problems as an opportunity; as a challenge to find new ways of thinking and acting. We need new economic concepts which are in tune with nature, for only what is right for ecology is right for the economy in the long run.

Meyer-Abich (1985) regards environmental protection as merely an immunization against our own mistakes, rather than an end to them. The question as to the 'correct' way forward belongs properly to politics, ethics or religion, although in a modern democracy participative, public discussion contributes to the rational evaluation of political issues. Economic science has shown a growing interest in ascribing to 'free' natural resources an appropriate price, because of their increasing scarcity.

Steger (1989) places the role of 'arbiter of value' in the hands of the government, assisted by the mechanisms of free enterprise. If 'environmental standards are not determined by the market, and cannot be derived from individual preferences, they must be established by society'.

This extremely complex and difficult political process will have to be prepared and supported by science and the media. 'Politicization means making issues public' (Spaemann). The difficulty of this task results largely from the lack of knowledge and experience in the highly innovative area of ecology. The state will require the active participation of enlightened citizens.

The natural environment has long been recognized as the basis for all economic activity, and the attitude that nature is an object to be mastered and exploited by mankind is clearly not going to be overcome by environmental management alone. So long as nature is perceived as a mere resource, and mankind is placed at the centre of all moral values, the best intentions in the world are not going to prevent the deterioration of the already damaged eco-balance (Meyer-Abich, 1985).

A fundamental change in human expectations of the natural world is the first prerequisite for ecological regeneration. In the words of Koslowski (1989), 'Man and his science will only begin to understand the limitations of nature as a resource, when they perceive nature as an organic whole instead of just a source of raw materials, energy and land.'

A form of 'ecological ethics' must come to predominate, because the 'minimalist ethics' guaranteed by legislative measures falls short, and is often not even brought into play (Raffée). 'Limits of justifiability' (Biedenkopf, 1989) are sought to guide our responsibility and the 'principle of responsibility' (Jonas) requires that the natural bases of life are preserved intact for future generations. This implies placing restrictions on the exploitation of natural resources, to allow nature to regenerate. Our present rate of consumption represents the erosion of natural stock and a reduction in the chances for future survival.

Biedenkopf sees the possibility for 'social restrictions' through the application of a 'principle of sustained yield'. This principle was first postulated in a forestry law of 1833, in Baden. It stated that more trees should not be felled than could grow back in a given time.

> Man is the only creature known to be capable of responsibility, and responsibility grows in parallel with power. However, we can only exercise this growing responsibility if our perception of future consequences grows proportionately. (Jonas, speech given on receipt of the Peace Prize of the German Book Trade, 1987)

Wicke (1990) translates Immanuel Kant's categorical imperative into environmental ethics thus: 'Always act in such a way that the environment does not suffer from your manufacturing processes, and such that the goods you sell do not harm the environment during use, and that in disposal they cause no more burden than is absolutely unavoidable.'

Rupert Lay has also drawn up eco-maxims based on the wording of the categorical imperative:

- Limit your demands on other people in such a way that a general optimum of maintenance and development is possible.

- Always act in such a way that there will be room for people to live on the Earth in a hundred years' time.

- Do not attempt to solve problems arising from intercourse with the environment through rationality and technology alone.

● Always behave in such a way that your work and its consequences are not directed against nature, and that they do not exceed nature's power of regeneration.

Nowadays, there is hardly a concept more overstretched than 'ethics'; hardly an article or a management seminar which does not refer to this watchword. In university economics departments, ethics is being introduced as a compulsory subject, as for instance at Harvard in 1989, with the appearance of a course, 'Industrial Decisions and Ethical Values'. There is perhaps a danger that ethics is becoming the management gimmick of our time.

Be that as it may, this new-wave ethics in Germany is centred on the 'principle of responsibility' formulated by Jonas: 'Always act in such a way that the effects of your actions are compatible with the continuance of human life on Earth.' Jonas has, incidentally, become something of a guru for those interested in eco-ethics.

The question remains, however, as to how the individual can take responsibility on this scale in a society distinguished by extreme division of labour. Individual action plays only an infinitesimal part in this dynamic. Ethics can provide us with values which guide our conscience, but individual morality is hardly likely to stop the undesired effects of entire industries. One is inclined to ask if it is even possible for business to behave in an ethical way. Or is morality perhaps reserved for the individual conscience?

The need for responsibility in business is widely acknowledged, but it is responded to only half-heartedly. If a company wishes to remain in business, it must build up a reliable identity, possibly doing without short-term successes and taking on additional risks. The economic benefits of integrity will be reaped in the end, and a strong company will have better sales opportunities. Business must build up inner strengths which are not always compatible with self-interest.

> Environmental protection demands more of business than just stature; it requires morality. Companies must not just play at environmentalism, they must mean it, however difficult this may be, and however little it may be appreciated or rewarded. The inner norms of a business should correspond to its proud exterior image, although it might sometimes seem cheaper to have flabby, unformulated norms.
>
> The advantages of business integrity, however, will not be immediately enjoyed by the company itself. Direct benefits will be felt by the economy as a whole, provided that the majority conforms to these standards.
>
> Morality is defined as communal action undertaken without guarantee of individual reward; without it the economy can no longer succeed. (Siemens, 1986)

Society will only grant business its freedom if it demonstrates actual solidarity, ensuring that its success is also the success of the community. (Schmidheini, Swiss businessman, 1987)

The scale of values adopted by management in company policies will have to undergo a transformation from rational, economic considerations to fundamental moral positions.

Hesse (1988) believes that the ethical quest for the good and the right in economic life can no longer be pursued without heeding the call of ecology. Contemporary business ethics must embrace environmental ethics. He suggests two preparatory notions essential to the development of a form of social ethics which is responsive to the whole economic system and which supersedes individual ethical positions:

- Interdisciplinary collaboration and dialogue are needed, e.g. between economists, theologians and philosophers.
- Individual or group moralities ought not simply to be converted into social norms and regulations, especially not in a diverse society characterized by division of labour. Social ethics must be contemporary; morality ought to emerge from an evaluation of interests.

Short-term profit-motivated growth must be accounted for in the long term. In the new-age economics there must be room for learning, for new approaches to problem solving. Only such a transfiguration of consciousness can equip our industrial society to face the challenge of ecology, and convert it into economic success.

Concluding remarks

It is a sobering thought that the expensive array of retrospective environmental technology, the purification plants, incinerators and dumping facilities, can do little more than give us time and space to develop real solutions, to convert our methods of production and consumption.

Business and public opinion need to be shaken out of their complacency over two essential taboos:

- There is no alternative to a change in production methods. Preventive, integrated environmental protection cannot be side-stepped. We need production methods and products which are compatible with the natural ability of the environment to regenerate. We should no longer be allowed to encroach on the 'capital stock' of nature, which rightly belongs to future generations.
- Each and every individual is called upon to change consumer and behavioural habits, to adopt more environment-conscious attitudes. Personal responsibility is manifested in what each of us buys or refuses to buy, in how we each participate voluntarily in 'reverse-channel concepts' and in how we strive to find gratification beyond the desire for material wealth.

These demands presuppose the integration of the levels of production, consumption and disposal. Manufacturers must offer the consumer environmentally friendly alternatives; local communities must provide the opportunity for effective refuse collection systems. All three levels must interlock.

All of this will necessarily bring to light new conflicts between labour and capital because the traditionally 'free' production factor, nature, will have to be paid for. Furthermore, our material, consumer values will have to be measured against moral standards which imply a new outlook on the environment.

While new concepts are still needed, pioneers have already paved the way for consumers and for industry. In congratulating the achievements of free enterprise, though, we should not lose sight of the government's unique competence and obligation to establish terms of reference. Since there can be no industrial activity without impact on the environment, this effect ought to be subject to control by democratic consensus. Market forces alone are not adequate. Only government can control the changes needed to facilitate ecological innovation within our market economy.

From the very start of this book, reference has been made to the inexorable dualism between economy and ecology. I have tried to show some positive examples of management solutions to environmental problems because there is no chance of coping with the future without optimism. Nevertheless, the anxiety still remains that the longer we contemplate the problem of environmental destruction, the less time we will have to solve it.

The only real hope of rescuing nature from the threat to which it is exposed is to be found in conscience, abstention and self-control, regardless of whether it is voluntary or enforced. The philosopher and Peace Prize holder, Jonas, wishes people to prepare for the global challenges of the coming decades by imposing voluntary restrictions on their freedom. One must seek pride and virtue in a 'relative poverty', for freedom would be at an end if such a measure were forced on us.

However illusory consumer moderation may seem, we must begin to exercise it. There is no time left for collective displacement activities. The philosopher K. M. Meyer-Abich warns that if we do not alter the model for our industrial society, the way will lie open for 'eco-dictatorship'. We must find a balance between our human needs and those of the environment we inhabit.

It is time for individuals to act. In the opinion of Greffrath (1990), 'Morals are good; politics is better; people who care are best of all.' If one considers democratic government to be the only viable moral constraint on economic activity, then one must take on individual responsibility for changing the status quo. This will involve personal, daily commitment.

An 'enlightened society' needs political debate on the problems facing it, on how it proposes to solve them and on how it might influence the life of generations to come. 'In changing relationships, in constructing institutions, morality becomes political, and to take part in the political debate on the future of mankind is an act of morality' (Greffrath, 1990). This morality is not reserved for 'Sunday best'; it will mean rolling up the sleeves for work.

Publications in German

Adelt, P., and Sauke, C. (1988) 'Zur Eignung des Markenartikel-Konzepts bei der Vermarktung ökologisch relevanter Produkte', *Markenartikel* (7).

Antes, R. (1988) 'Umweltschutzinvestionen als Chancen des aktiven Umweltschutzes für Unternehmen im sozialen Wandel', *Schriftenreihe des IÖW* (16).

Atteslander, P. (1989) 'Ökonomisches Handeln in ökologischer Varantwortung', *IBM Nachrichten* 39 (296).

Bauer, W., and Müller, F.-J. (1988) 'Umweltverträglichkeit: neues Kriterium im Verpackungswesen', *FhG-Berichte* (4).

Beschorner, D. (1980) 'Gesellschaftsbezogene Rechnungslegung als Folge gestiegenen Umweltbewußtseins und sozialer Verpflichtungen', *Personalwirtschaft* (12).

Biedenkopf, K. (1989) 'Konsequenzen begrenzter Ressourcen für die Gesellschaft', in *Verantwortung für die Zukunft: Konsequenzen begrenzter Ressourcen für Wissenschaft, Wirtschaft und Gesellschaft*, ebs/IWG, Bonn.

Blick durch die Wirtschaft (1989) 'Umweltschutz ist Management-Aufgabe', 28.6.1989.

Blom, F. (1988) 'Ökologische Materialwirtschaft', in *Umweltschutz: Gewinn für die Zukunft*, Förderkreis Umwelt future e.V., Lengerich.

Bongaerts, J., and Kraemer, A. (1987) 'Haftung und Versicherung von Umweltschäden', *Schriftenreihe des IÖW* (8).

Brunowsky, R.-D., and Wicke, L. (1984) *Der Öko-Plan, Durch Umweltschutz zum neuen Wirtschaftswunder* (2nd edn), Munich.

Dehnert, J. (1989) 'Die Verbrennung von Abfällen stellt auf Dauer keine befriedigende Lösung dar', *Handelsblatt*, 3-4.11.89.

Demmer, C. (1989) 'Öko-Sponsoring: Der grüne Schein', *Manager Magazin* (6).

Deutsche Bank (1989) 'Umweltschutz: Fakten, Prognosen, Strategien', *Mittelstandsbroschüre* 11, Frankfurt a.M.

Deutsches Institut für Gütesicherung und Kennzeichnung e.V. (1989) *Umweltzeichen: Produktanforderungen, Zeichenanwender und Produkte*, July.

Dierkes, M. (1984) 'Gesellschaftsbezogene Berichterstattung: was lehren uns die Experimente der letzten 10 Jahre?', *ZfB*, 54 (12).

DIHT/IHK (n.d.) *Umweltschutz-Partner IHK*.

Dreyhaupt, F. (1987) 'Umweltrahmenbedingungen sind für einen Industrie- oder Gewerbestandort von entscheidender Bedeutung', *Handelsblatt*, 6.4.1987.

Duch, K. (1985) 'Zauber der Natur – oder Kulturzauber? Unternehmenskultur auf den Prüfstand', *Personalwirtschaft*, 11.

Dyllick, T. (1989a) *Management der Umweltbeziehungen: Öffentliche Auseinandersetzungen als Herausforderungen*, Wiesbaden.

Dyllick, T. (1989b) 'Ökologisch bewußte Unternehmensführung: der Beitrag der Managementlehre', *Schriftenreihe ÖBU/ASIEGE* (1) 1989.

Edelhoff (1988) *Der Abfall*, Iserlohn.

Faltlhauser, K. (1978) 'Unternehmen und Gesellschaft: Theorie und Praxis der Sozialbilanz', *DIB-Schriftenreihe*, 5, Berlin.

Fischer-Winkelmann, W., and Hohl, E. (1982) 'Zum Stand des Human Resource Accounting', *DU*, 36 (2).

Follmann, R. (1989) 'Tapete und Umwelt', *Vortrag IGI-Kongreß*, 20.6.1989.

Förderkreis Umwelt Future e.V. (1987) Future Forum, (1987) Future Workshop, (1988) Future Forum.

Gasser, V. (1989) 'Konsequenzen aus der Umwelthaftung für das betriebliche Risiko-Management', in Kongreßmanuskript *Betriebe und Umwelt*, Nuremberg.

Gierl, H. (1987) 'Ökologische Einstellungen und Kaufverhalten im Widerspruch', *Markenartikel* (1).

Gleich, M. (1989) 'Zahltag', *Natur* (12).

Gomez, P., and Probst, G. (1987) 'Vernetztes Denken im Management', *Die Orientierung*, 89.

Greffrath, M. (1990) 'Das Prinzip Goldmarie', *Die Zeit*, 2.2.1990.

Grub, M. (1990) *Unternehmen Grün: Ideen, Konzepte, Beispiele für mehr Natur in der Arbeitswelt*, Munich.

Grünewald, R. (1983) 'Umweltanalyse als Instrument strategischer Unternehmensführung', *Büro & Verkauf*, 6.

Hamm, R. (1989) 'Im Zweifel für die Natur ... und gegen das Strafrecht im Umweltschutz', *Die Zeit*, 27.10.1989.

Heeg, F. J. (1984) 'Recycling-Management: eine Gesamtaufgabe von der Produktentwicklung bis zur Produktverwertung', *Management-Zeitschrift io*, 53 (11).

Helgerth, R. (1989) 'Neue Entwicklungen im Umweltrecht und erfolgreiches Risiko-Management durch vorbeugende Maßnahmen', in Kongreßmanuskript *Betriebe und Umwelt*, Nuremberg.

Hermanns, A., and Püttmann, M. (1990) 'Die ökologische Herausforderung für die Marketing-Kommunikation', *Werbeforschung & Praxis*, Folge 1.

Hesse, H. (1988) 'Gewinn mit Moral', *Wirtschaftswoche* (3).

Heyder, H. (1989) 'Umweltbewußtsein zur Chance machen: betonen Sie die Öko-Schiene, auf der Sie Ihre Marketing-Aktivitäten vorantreiben', *Marketing Journal* (2).

Heymann, H.H. (1981) *Die Sozialbilanz als Instrument der Unternehmensführung*, Frankfurt.

Heymann, H. H. (1982) 'Sozialbilanzen: Überlegungen zur konzeptionellen und politischen Entwicklung der Sozialbilanz-Bewegung', *WiSt*, 11, pp. 171ff.

Heymann H., and Seiwert, L. (1985) 'Sozialbilanzen', *Harvard-Manager* (1).

Hopfenbeck, W. (1989) *Allgemeine Betriebswirtschafts- und Managementlehre: Das Unternehmen im Spannungsfeld zwischen ökonomischen, sozialen und ökologischen Interessen*, Landsberg a.L.

ICC (1989) *Umweltschutz Audits*, Cologne.

Jorden, W. (1983) 'Recyclinggerechtes Konstruieren als vordringliche Aufgabe zum Einsparen von Rohstoffen', *Maschinenmarkt*, 89.

Kapp, K. W. (1979) *Soziale Kosten der Marktwirtschaft* (original English edn, 1963), Frankfurt.

Kapp, K. W. (1987) *Für eine ökosoziale Ökonomie: Entwürfe und Ideen – ausgewählte Aufsätze*, Frankfurt.

Kiss, M. (1981) 'Der Energiebeauftragte in der Unternehmung', *Management Zeitschrift io*, 50 (9).

Klaus, J., and Ebert, W. (1989) 'Satellitensystem "Umwelt"', *WiSt* (2).

Klingholz, R. (1989) 'Sehenden Auges in die Katastrophe', *Die Zeit*, 1989.

Kommunikation (1989) 'Sozio- und Umwelt-Sponsoring' (12).

Koslowski, P. (1989) 'Konsequenzen begrenzter Ressourcen für die Wirtschaft', *Verantwortung für die Zukunft: Konsequenzen begrenzter Ressourcen für Wissenschaft, Wirtschaft und Gessellschaft*, ebs/IWG, Bonn.

Kreikebaum, H. (1990) *Integrierter Umweltschutz: Eine Herausforderung für das Innovations-management*, Wiesbaden.

Krekeler, M. (1989) 'Ökomarketing: Zielgruppen querbeet', *Kommunikation* (10).

Krupp, H. (1989) 'Innovation der Innovationspolitik: neue Ressourcenökonomie durch neue Rahmenbedingugen', *FhG-Berichte* (3).

Krusche, P.u.a. (1982) *Ökologisches Bauen*, Umweltbundesamt, Wiesbaden/Berlin.

Kruschke, A. (1989) 'Verschärfung des Umweltrechts: Konsequenzen für die Unternehmen', *Juristische Rundschau* (12).

Linke, W. (1988) 'PKW und Umwelt; ein Zielkonflikt – Umweltschutz hat einen hohen Stellenwert', *Verlagsbeilage der Süddeutschen Zeitung* (137), 16–17.6.1988.

Meffert, H. (1988) *Strategische Unternehmensführung und Marketing*, Wiesbaden.

Meffert, H. (1990) 'Produktealterung als Absatzstrategie? Zur Debatte über die "geplante Obsoleszenz"', *Neue Zürcher Zeitung*, 28.2.1990.

Meffert, H., Benkenstein, M., and Schubert, F. (1987) 'Umweltschutz und Unternehmensverhalten', *Harvard-Manager* (2).

Meffert, H., Bruhn, M., Schubert, F., and Walther, T. (1986) 'Marketing und Ökologie: Chancen und Risiken umweltorientierter Absatzsstrategien der Unternehmungen', *DB* (2).

Meffert, H., Ostmeier, H., and Kirchgeorg, M. (1988) 'Ökologisches Marketing: Ansatzpunkte einer umweltorientierten Unternehmensführung', in H. Burkhard (ed.), *Öko-Marketing, Schriftenreihe des IÖW* (18).

Meffert, H., and Wagner, H. (1985) 'Ökologie und Unternehmensführung: Dokumentation des 9. Münsteraner Führungsgesprächs', Arbeitspapier Nr 26, Münster.

Merkel, R. (1989) 'Die Placeboparagraphen', *Die Zeit*, 43, 1989.

Merkisch, D. (1990) 'Haftung für Umweltschäden: Finanzierbarkeit und Versicherbarkeit aus der Sicht der Industrie', *Betriebsberater* (4).

Meyer-Abich, K. M. (1985) 'Wege zum Frieden mit der Natur', in H. Meffert and H. Wagner (eds), *Ökologie und Unternehmensführung*, Münster.

Müllendorff, R. (1981) *Umweltbezogene Unternehmensentscheidung unter besonderer Berücksichtigung der Energiewirtschaft*, Frankfurt.

Müller, M., and Meyer-Abich, K. M. (1990) 'Kommt die Öko-Diktatur? Das Modell der Industriegesellschaft muß geändert werden', *Die Zeit*, 6.4.1990.

Müller-Wenk, R. (1978) *Die ökologische Buchhaltung: Ein Informations- und Steuerungs-instrument für umweltkonforme Unternehmenspolitik*, Frankfurt/New York.

Müller-Wenk, R. (1980) *Konflikt Ökonomie Ökologie: Schritte zur Anpassung von Unternehmensführung und Wirtschaftsordnung*, Karlsruhe.

Müller-Wenk, R. (1986) 'Die ökologische Buchhaltung', in U. E. Simonis (ed.), *Ökonomie und Ökologie: Auswege aus einem Konflikt* (4th edn), Karlsruhe.

Müller-Witt, H. (1985) 'Produktfolgeabschätzung als kollektiver Lernprozeß', in *Arbeiten im Einklang mit der Natur*, Öko-Institut, Freiburg i.B.

Nahrendorf, R. (1989) 'Ohne Ethos verkommt die Wirtschaft', *Handelsblatt*, 15–16.12.1989.

Neuntinger, U. (1988) 'Umweltexpertensysteme am Beispiel industrieller Anwendungen', in *Von der Öko-Bilanz zum Öko-Controlling: Chancen umweltorientierter Unternehmenspolitik*, Future Forum.

Nickel, V. (1990) 'Aktiv oder sprachlos? Ansatzpunkte für umweltorientierte Öffentlichkeitsarbeit', *Markenartikel* (2).

Oberholz, A. (1989) *Umweltorientierte Unternehmensführung: Notwendigkeit, Einführung, Erfolge*, Frankfurt.

Ondratscheck, D. (1988) 'Umweltschutz in der Oberflächentechnik: Situation und Forschungsaktivitäten am Beispiel der Lackiertechnik', *FhG-Berichte* (4).

Pfriem, R. (1986) *Ökologische Unternehmenspolitik*, Frankfurt/New York.

Pfriem, R. (1987) 'Ansatzpunkte für ein ökologisches Rechnungswesen im Unternehmen', in *Umweltschutz: Gewinn für die Zukunft*, Forderkreis Umwelt Future e.V., Lengerich.

Pfriem, R. (1988a) 'Der Nutzen von Ökobilanzen: Thesen aus der Sicht ökologischer Unternehmensfuhrung', in *Umweltschutz: Gewinn für die Zukunft*, Förderkreis Umwelt Future e.V., Lengerich.

Pfriem, R. (1988b) 'Ökologische Unternehmensführung', *Schriftenreihe des IÖW* (13).

Pfriem, R. (1988c) 'Die Ökobilanz: ein betriebliches Informationsinstrument', in *Von der Öko-Bilanz zum Öko-Controlling: Chancen umweltorientierter Unternehmenspolitik*, Future Forum.

Probst, G., and Gomez, P. (eds) (1989) *Vernetztes Denken: Unternehmen ganzheitlich führen*, Wiesbaden.

Pümpin, C., (1980) 'Strategische Führung in der Unternehmungspraxis', *Die Orientierung*, 76.

Raffée, H., and Wiedmann, K.-P. (1983) *Das gesellschaftliche Bewußtsein in der Bundesrepublik und seine Bedeutung für das Marketing*, Hamburg.

Raffée, H., and Wiedmann, K.-P. (1985) 'Die Selbstzerstörung unserer Welt durch unternehmerische Marktpolitik?', *Marketing ZFP* (4).

Römer, G. (1990) 'Umweltschutz und Controlling', *Controller Magazin* (1).

Roth, P. (1989) *Kultur-Sponsoring*, Landsberg a.L.

Schenkel, W. (1981) 'Abfallverwertung aus ökologischer und ökonomischer Sicht', *Rationalisierung* (4).

Schenkel, W. (1987) 'Anspruch und Wirklichkeit in der Bundesrepublik Deutschland', *Handelsblatt* (86), 6.5.1987.

Schmitt, D., Schubert, H., and Ziegahn, K.-F. (1988) 'Grenzgänger zwischen Technik und Ökologie: Umweltsituation und ihre Prinzipien', *FhG-Berichte* (4).

Schneider, M. (1989) 'Planen für den Ernstfall', *Wirtschaftswoche*, 2.6.1989.

Schober, R. (1987) *Systemdarstellung Umweltschutz*, Siemens, Munich.

Schoenheit, I. (1988) 'Ökologie und Marketing im Meinungsstreit: ein Tagungsbericht', *Markenartikel* (2).

Schreiber, R. L. (1983) 'Ökologische Aspekte der Unternehmensführung', *Schimmelpfeng-Review* (31).

Schreiber, R. L. (1985) 'Öko-Marketing: die Managementjahrhundertaufgabe', *Marketing*, 7 (4).

Schreiner, M. (1988a) 'Marketing und Umwelt: Neuorientierung zum Öko-Marketing', *Gablers Magazin* (10).

Schreiner, M. (1988b) *Umweltmanagement in 22 Lektionen*, Wiesbaden.

Schuh, H. (1990a) 'Die Crux mit dem Risiko: über die Schwierigkeit adaquater Einschätzung von Umweltgefahren', *Die Zeit*, 9.3.1990.

Schuh, H. (1990b) 'Zuviel Angst vor Asbest? Eine vergleichende Bewertung von Risiken tut not', *Die Zeit*, 16.2.1990.

Schütze, Ch. (1984) 'Das Grundgesetz vom Niedergang', *Süddeutsche Zeitung*, 9–10.1.1988.

Seidel, E. (1989) '"Wollen" und "Können": auf dem Wege zu einer ökologisch verpflichteten Unternehmensführung', *zfo* (2).

Siemens (1986) *Umweltschutz: Versuch einer Systemdarstellung*, Berlin/Munich.

Siemens (1989) *Unsere Umwelt erhalten: Informations- und Kommunikationstechnik für den Umweltschutz*, Munich.

Sietz, M. and Michahelles, R. (1989) *Umwelt-Checklisten für Manager*, Taunusstein.

Simonis, U. E. (ed.) (1986) *Ökonomie und Ökologie: Auswege aus einem Konflikt* (4th edn), Karlsruhe.

Sprenger, R.-V. (1981) 'Umweltschutz und unternehmerisches Wettbewerbsverhalten', *IfO-Schnelldienst* (1, 2).

Stahel, W. (1990) 'Eine neue Beziehung zu den Dingen: Verkauf von Nutzen statt von Produkten', *Neue Zürcher Zeitung*, 28.2.1990.

Stahlmann, V. (1988a) *Umweltorientierte Materialwirtschaft: Das Optimierungskonzept für Ressourcen, Recycling, Rendite*, Wiesbaden.

Stahlmann, V. (1988b) 'Öko-Controlling in einer integrierten Materialwirtschaft' in *Von der Öko-Bilanz zum Öko-Controlling: Chancen umweltorientierter Unternehmenspolitik*, Future Forum.

Stahlmann, V., and Beschorner, D.u.a. (1989) 'Betriebliche Umweltschutzbeauftragte: Ausbildungsanforderungen – betriebliche Praxis, Perspektiven', *Schriftenreihe des IÖW* (34).

Steger, U. (1988) *Umweltmanagement, Erfahrungen und Fundamente einer umweltorientierten Unternehmensstrategie*, Frankfurt/Wiesbaden.

Steger, U. (1989) 'Konsequenzen begrenzter Ressourcen für die Wirtschaft', in *Verantwortung für die Zukunft: Konsequenzen begrenzter Ressourcen für Wissenschaft, Wirtschaft und Gesellschaft*, ebs/IWG, Bonn.

Steger, U. (1990) 'Nötige Veränderungen der Rahmenbedingungen: Lob des Marktmechanismus', *Neue Zürcher Zeitung*, 28.2.90.

Steinhilper, R. (1988) 'Recycling in der Industrie: technisch und wirtschaftlich erfolgreicher Umweltschutz', *FhG-Berichte* (4).

Stock, U. (1990) 'Das Nordsee-Ritual', *Die Zeit*, 16.3.1990.

Stoll, E. (1984) 'Betriebliche Umweltpolitik: der ökonomische Zwang zur Naturvergessenheit', in W. H. Stahl and E. Stoll (eds), *Betriebswirtschaftslehre und ökonomische Krise: Kontroverse Beiträge zur betriebswirtschaftlichen Krisenbewältigung*, Wiesbaden.

Strebel, H. (1980) *Umwelt und Betriebswirtschaft*, Berlin.

Strebel, H. (1981) 'Umwelteinwirkungen der Produktion', *ZbfG* (6).

Strebel, H. (1984) 'Gründe und Möglichkeiten betriebswirtschaftlicher Umweltpolitik', in W. H. Stahl and E. Stoll (eds), *Betriebswirtschaftslehre und ökonomische Krise: Kontroverse Beiträge zur betriebswirtschaftlichen Krisenbewältigung*, Wiesbaden.

Strebel, H., and Hildebrant, T. (1989) 'Produktlebenszyklen und Rückstandszyklen: Konzept eines erweiterten Lebenszyklusmodells', *zfo* (2).

Strom, P.-C., and Bunge, T. (1988) *Handbuch der Umweltverträglichkeitsprüfung*, Berlin.

Syrbe, M. (1989) 'Forschung und Entwicklung an der Schwelle des dritten Jahrtausends', *FhG-Berichte* (4).

Thexis (1988) 'Uttwil (Schweiz)', *Sonderheft: Öko-Marketing* (3).

Thomas, J. (1988) 'Die Organisation des industriellen Umweltschutzes', *Der Betrieb* (43), 28.10.1988.

Thome, G. (1981) *Produktgestaltung und Ökologie*, Munich.

Töpfer, A. (1985) 'Umwelt- und Benutzerfreundlichkeit von Produkten als strategische Unternehmensziele', *Marketing ZFP*, 7 (4).

Uhlig, C. A. (1978) *Ökologische Krise und Ökonomischer Prozeß*, Diessenhofen.

Ullmann, A. A. (1981) 'Der Betriebsbeauftragte für Umweltschutz aus betriebswirtschaftlicher Perspektive: umweltpolitische Notwendigkeit oder gesetzgeberischer Perfektionismus?', *ZfbF*, (33).

Ulrich, H., and Probst, G. (1988) *Anleitung zum ganzheitlichen Denken und Handeln: Ein Brevier für Führungskräfte*, Bern/Stuttgart.

Vahrenholt, F. (1987) 'Schluß mit der Heimlichtuerei! Ein Plädoyer für mehr Glasnost in der Umweltpolitik', *Die Zeit*, 21, 1987.

Vester, F. (1988) *Leitmotiv vernetztes Denken*, Munich.

Vogl, J., Heigl, A., and Schäfer, R. (1989) *Handbuch des Umweltschutzes*, 8 (12), Landsberg a.L.

Vollherbst, F.-J. (1984) 'Die externe gesellschaftsbezogene Berichterstattung der Unternehmung als Instrument gesellschaftlicher Konfliktregelung', Diss., Pfaffenweiler.

Wesel, U. (1988) 'Kein Recht auf Bäume', *Die Zeit*, 12, 1988.

Wicke, L. (1982) *Umweltökonomie*, Munich.

Wicke, L. (1984) 'Instrumente der Umweltpolitik, von Auflagen zu marktkonformeren Instrumenten', *WiSt* (2).

Wicke, L. (1985) 'Durch Umweltschutz zum neuen Wirtschaftswunder?' in H. Meffert and H. Wagner (eds), *Ökologie und Unternehmensführung*, Munster.

Wicke, L. (1986) *Die ökologischen Milliarden: Das kostet die zerstörte Umwelt – so können wir sie retten*, Munich.

Wicke, L. (1987) 'Offensiver betrieblicher Umweltschutz', *Harvard-Manager* (3).

Wicke, L. (1989 and 1990) 'Chancen und Probleme der Betriebe durch umweltfreundliche Produkte', parts 1 and 2, *Markenartikel* (12 and 1).

Wicke, L., and Schafhausen, F. (1982) 'Instrumente zur Durchsetzung des Umweltschutzes', *WISU*, 11, p. 409.

Wicke, L., Haasis, H.-D., Schafhausen, F. and Schulz, W. (1992) *Betriebliche Umweltökonomie*, Munich.

Widenmayer, M. (1981) 'Soziale Kosten als Bestandteil gesellschaftsbezogener Rechnungslegung', *ZfB*, 51 (2).

Winter, G. (1990) *Das umweltbewußte Unternehmen: Ein Handbuch der Betriebsökologie mit 22 Checklisten für die Praxis* (3rd edn), Munich.

Würtenberger, G. (1989) 'Keine Tricks', *Absatzwirtschaft* (3).

zfo (1989) *Sonderheft: Organisation des betrieblichen Umweltschutzes* (2).

Publications in English

Berle, G. (1991) *The Green Entrepreneur: Business opportunities that can save the Earth and make you money*, Liberty Hall Press.

Berry, S. (1990) *Who's Who in the Environment*, Environment Council.

Burke, T., and Hill, J. (1990) *Ethics, Environment and the Company: A guide to effective action*, Institute of Business Ethics.

Cairncross, F. (1991) *Costing the Earth*, London: Economist Books.

Confederation of British Industry (1989) *Managing Waste: Guidelines for business*, London: CBI.

Council for Environmental Education (1985) *GCSE and Environmental Education*, CEE.

Council on Economic Priorities, *Rating America's Corporate Conscience*, Reading, MA: Addison-Wesley.

Cutrera, A. (1987) *DocTer Environmental Yearbook 1987*, DocTer International.

Davis, J. (1991) *Greening Business: Managing for sustainable development*, Oxford: Basil Blackwell.

Department of Trade and Industry (1987) *Cutting Your Losses: A business guide to waste minimization*, London: DTI.

Elkington, J., and Burke, T. (1987) *The Green Capitalists: In search of environmental excellence*, London: Victor Gollancz.

Elkington, J., and Hailes, J. (1988) *The Green Consumer Guide*, London: Victor Gollancz.

Elkington, J., Burke, T., and Hailes, J. (1988) *Green Pages: The business of saving the world*, London: Routledge.

Elkington, J., Knight, P., and Hailes, J. (1991) *The Green Business Guide*, London: Victor Gollancz.

Elsworth, E., and Hildgard, N. (eds) (1990) *The Earth Report*, London: Mitchell Beazley.

Environmental Data Services, *Eco Labels: Product management in a greener Europe*, London: ENDS.

Environmental Data Services (1990) *Directory of Environmental Consultants*, London: ENDS.

Haigh, N. (1989) *EEC Environmental Policy and Britain* (2nd edn), Harlow, Essex: Longman.

Henstock, M. *Design for Recyclability*, Institute of Metals.

Hughes, D. (1986) *Environmental Law*, London: Butterworths.

International Chamber of Commerce (1989) *Environmental Auditing*, London: ICC.

International Chamber of Commerce (1990) *Environmental Guidelines for World Industry*, London: ICC.

· Leipart, C. (1986) 'Social costs of economic growth', *Journal of Economic Issues*, vol. 20, pp. 109–31.

Leipart, C. (1987) 'A critical appraisal of gross national product: the measurement of net national welfare and environmental accounting', *Journal of Economic Issues*, vol. 21, pp. 357–73.

Lloyd, T. (1990) *The 'Nice' Company*, London: Bloomsbury.

North, R. (1986) *The Real Cost*, London: Chatto and Windus.

Pearce, D., Markandya, A., and Barbier, E. (1989) *Blueprint for a Green Economy*, London: Earthscan.

Porritt, J. (1984) *Seeing Green*, Oxford: Basil Blackwell.

Schumacher, I. F. (1973) *Small is Beautiful: Economics as if people mattered*, London: Blond and Briggs.

Selke, S., Lai, C. and Yam, K. *Recycled Plastics: Development and applications*.

United Nations Environment Programme (1990) *Environmental Auditing*, Technical Report Series No. 2, London: UNEP.

Usitalo, L. (1986) *Environmental Impacts of Consumption Patterns*, Aldershot, Hants: Gower.

Ward, Sue (1986) *Socially Responsible Investment*, Directory of Social Change.

Winter, G. (1988) *Business and the Environment*, New York: McGraw-Hill.

Wolpert, V., *Recycling of Plastics*, Holly Hill, E. Sussex.

Worldwide Fund for Nature (1990) *The Environmental Audit: A green filter for company policies, plants, processes and products*, Godalming, Surrey: WWF.

Case studies: index of companies

Useful addresses

United Kingdom

Advertising Standards Authority (ASA), Brook House, 2–16 Torrington Place, London WC1E 7HN.

Association for Responsible Communication (ARC), Mickleton House, Mickleton, Gloucestershire GL55 6RY.

Association of Environment Conscious Builders (AECB), Windlake House, The Pump Field, Coaley, Gloucestershire GL11 5DX.

Association of Recycled Paper Suppliers (ARPS), Bow Triangle Business Centre, Unit 2, Eleanor Street, London E3 4NP.

Better Environment Awards For Industry (BEAFI), Royal Society of Arts, 8 John Adam Street, London WC2N 6EZ.

British Library, Environmental Information Service, 25 Southampton Buildings, London WC2A 1AW.

Business in the Community (BITC), 227a City Road, London EC1V 1LX.

Business in the Environment (BiE), 41 Threadneedle Street, London EC2A 8AP.

Business Network, 18 Well Walk, London NW3 1LD.

Centre for Economic and Environmental Development (CEED), 12 Upper Belgrave Street, London SW1X 8BA.

Centre for Environmental Education (CEE), School of Education, University of Reading, Reading RG1 5AQ.

Centre for Environmental Interpretation (CEI), Manchester Polytechnic, John Dalton Building, Chester Street, Manchester M1 5GD.

Centre for Environmental Technology, Imperial College of Science and Technology (ICCET), 48 Princes Gardens, London SW7 1LU.

Centre for International Environmental Law (CIEL), Kings College London, Manresa Road, London SW3 6LX.

Chemical Industries Association (CIA), Kings Buildings, Smith Square, London SW1P 3JJ.

Commission of the European Communities (UK), 8 Storey's Gate, London SW1P 3AT.

Confederation of British Industry (CBI), Centrepoint, 103 New Oxford Street, London WC1A 1DU.

Council for Environmental Conservation (CoEnCo), London Ecology Centre, 80 York Way, London N1.

Department of the Environment, Romney House, 43 Marsham Street, London SW1P 3PY.

Department of Trade and Industry, Environmental Enquiry Point, Warren Spring Laboratory, Gunnels Wood Road, Stevenage, Hertfordshire SG1 2BX.

Department of Trade and Industry, Environment Unit, Ashdown House, 123 Victoria Street, London SW1E 6RB.

Dragon International, Blenheim House, 137 Blenheim Crescent, London W11 2EQ.

Ecology Building Society (EBS), 18 Station Road, Crosshills, Nr Keighley, West Yorkshire BD20 7EH.

Ecotec Research and Consulting, Priory House, 18 Steelhouse Lane, Birmingham B4 6BJ.

Environmental Data Services (ENDS), Unit 24, Finsbury Business Centre, 40 Bowling Green Lane, London EC1R 0NE.

Environmental Law Foundation (ELF), Rubinstein/Callingham, Polden and Gale, 2 Raymond Buildings, Gray's Inn, London WC1R 5BZ.

Environmental Transport Association (ETA), 15a George Street, Croydon CRO 1LA.

Environment Foundation, c/o Bain Clarkson Ltd, Ibex House, Minories, London EC3N 1HJ.

Ethical Investment Research Service (EIRS), 504 Bondway Business Centre, Bondway, London SW8 1SQ.

Euroenviron, Business and the Environment Unit, Department of Trade and Industry, Room 1010, Ashdown House, 123 Victoria Street, London SW1E 6RB.

Friends of the Earth (FoE), 26–28 Underwood Street, London N1 7JQ.

Green Alliance (GA), 49 Wellington Street, London WC2E 7BN.

Green Books, Ford House, Hartland, Bideford, Devon EX39 6EE.

Greenpeace UK, Canonbury Villas, London N1 2PN.

Industry Council for Packaging and the Environment (INCPEN), Premier House, 10 Greycoat Place, London SW1P 1SB.

Institute for European Environmental Policy (IEEP), 3 Endsleigh Street, London WC1H 0DD.

Institute of Environmental Health Officers, Chadwick House, 48 Rushworth Street, London SE1 0QT.

Institute of Environment Assessment, The Old Malthouse, Spring Gardens, London Road, Grantham, Lincolnshire NG3 6JP.

Institute of Wastes Management, 3 Albion Place, Northampton NN1 1UD.

International Chamber of Commerce (ICC), 14–15 Belgrave Square, London SW1X 8PS.

International Institute for Environment and Development (IIED), 3 Endsleigh Street, London WC1H 0DD.

London Ecology Centre, 45 Shelton Street, Covent Garden, London WC2H 9HJ.

National Association for Environmental Education, c/o West Midlands College of Higher Education, Gorway, Walsall, West Midlands WS1 3BD.

National Association of Waste Disposal Contractors, 26 Wheatsheaf House, 4 Carmelite Street, London EC4Y 0BH.

Network for Alternative and Technology Assessment (NATTA) c/o Alternative Technology Group, Faculty of Technology, The Open University, Walton Hall, Milton Keynes, Buckinghamshire.

PA Consulting Group, 123 Buckingham Palace Road, London SW1W 9SR.

Recycling Advisory Unit, Warring Spring Laboratory, Gunnels Wood Road, Stevenage, Hertfordshire SG1 2BX.

Royal Commission on Environmental Pollution, Church House, Great Smith Street, London SW1P 3BL.

SustainAbility, The People's Hall, 91–97 Freston Road, London W11 4BD.

Television Trust for the Environment (TVE), 46 Charlotte Street, London W1P 1LX.

The Other Economic Summit (TOES), 4 Stretche Road, Swanage, Dorset BH19 1NF.

Think Green, Midland Business Centre, Temple House, 43–48 New Street, Birmingham B2 4LJ.
UK Centre for Economic and Environmental Development (UK CEED), 3e King's Parade, Cambridge CB2 1SJ.
UK Environmental Law Association (UKELA), Cameron Markby Hewitt, Sceptre Court, 40 Tower Hill, London EC3N 4BB.
University of East Anglia, School of Environmental Studies, Norwich NR4 7TJ.
Warmer Campaign, 83 Mount Ephraim, Tunbridge Wells, Kent TN4 3BS.
Waste Management Information Bureau, Building 7, 12 Harwell Laboratory, Oxfordshire OX11 0RA.
Wastewatch, 26 Bedford Square, London WC1B 3HU.
Watch Trust for Environmental Education, 22 The Green, Nettleham, Lincoln LN2 2NR.
Worldwide Fund for Nature (WWF), Panda House, Wayside Park, Godalming, Surrey GU7 1XR.

USA and others

American Institute of Chemical Engineers (AIChE), 345 East 47 Street, New York, NY 10017, USA.
BAUM, Tinsdaler Kirchenweg 211, 2 Hamburg 56, Germany.
Commission of the European Communities, rue de la Loi 200, B-1049 Brussels, Belgium.
Conseil Européen des Fédérations de l'Industrie Chimique, avenue L. Quise 250/1, B-1050 Brussels, Belgium.
Environmental Defense Fund (EDF), 1616 P Street, Washington, DC 20036, USA.
Environmental Hazards Management Institute (EHMI), 10 Newmarket Road, Durham, NH 03824, USA.
Environmental Protection Agency (EPA), Washington, DC 20460, USA.
Environmental Protection and Management Division of the Council of Europe, BP 431 R6, F-67006 Strasbourg, Cedex, France.
Europäische Investitionsbank, Boulevard Konrad Adenauer 100, L-2950 Luxembourg.
European Centre for Environmental Communication (ECEC), 55 rue de Varenne, F-75341 Paris, Cedex 07, France.
European Conference on Plastics in Packaging, Association of Plastics Manufacturers in Europe, 250 avenue Louise, Box 73, B-1050 Brussels, Belgium.
European Council of Chemical Manufacturer's Federations (CEFIC), 250 avenue Louise, Box 71, B-1050 Brussels, Belgium.
European Environmental Bureau, 29 rue Vautier, B-1040 Brussels, Belgium.
European Green Table (EGT), PO Box 86, Bryn, 0611 Oslo 6, Norway.
European Round Table for Industrialists, AB Volvo, Box 1, N-1411 Kolbotn, Norway.
European Unit of Eurydice, 29 rue de Archimede, Bte 17, B-1040 Brussels, Belgium.
European Venture Capital Association, clos du Parnasse, B-1040 Brussels, Belgium.
Feruzzi Group, Calata Paita, 19100 La Spezia, Milan, Italy.
Future, Kollegienwall 22a, 4500 Osnabrück, Germany.
Gist-Brocades, PO Box 1, NL-2600 MA Delft, Netherlands.

Global Environmental Management Initiative (GEMI), 1828 L Street, NW, Suite 711, Washington, DC 20036, USA.

International Chamber of Commerce (ICC), 38 Cours Albert, 75008 Paris, France.

International Coalition for Development Action, 22 rue des Bollandistes, B-1040 Brussels, Belgium.

International Environmental Bureau (IEB), 61 route de Chene, CH-1208 Geneva, Switzerland.

International Network for Environmental Management (INEM), Hellgrund 92, 2000 Wedel-Holstein, Germany.

National Solid Waste Management Association (NSWMA), 1730 Rhode Ave NW, Washington, DC 20036, USA.

Network for Environmental Technology Transfer (NETT), square de Meeus 25, B-1040 Brussels, Belgium.

Organization for Economic Co-operation and Development (OECD), 2 rue André Pascal, 75775 Paris, Cedex 16, France.

Public Information Centre, Environment Ontario, 135 St Clair Av. West, Toronto/Ontario, Canada M4V1PS.

Scientific Committee on Problems of the Environment (SCOPE), SCOPE Secretariat, 51 boulevard de Montmorency, 75016 Paris, France.

Society of the Plastics Industry, 1275 K Street, NW, Suite 400, Washington, DC 20005, USA.

Sound Resource Management Group Inc., 7220 Ledroit Street, SW, Seattle, Washington, DC 98136, USA.

United Nations Environmental Programme (UNEP), Tour Mirabeau, 39–43 quai André Citroen, 75739 Paris, Cedex 15, France.

US Agency for International Development (US Aid), Whaley, Room 33/21A, 2201 C Street, NW, Washington, DC 20523, USA.

Waste Management, Inc., 3003 Butterfield Road, Oak Brook, Illinois 60521, USA.

World Bank, 1818 H Street, NW, Washington, DC 20433, USA.

World Environment Center, Inc., 419 Park Avenue South, Suite 1403, New York, NY 10016, USA.

World Resources Institute (WRI), 1709 New York Avenue, NW, Washington, DC 20006, USA.

World Tourism Organization (WTO), Capitan Hiya 42, Madrid-20, Spain.

Index